SCHAUM'S OUTLINE OF

THEORY AND PROBLEMS

OF

ACCOUNTING II
Third Edition

•

JAMES A. CASHIN, M.B.A., CPA
Former Professor of Accounting
Hofstra University

and

JOEL J. LERNER, M.S., P.D.
Chairman, Faculty of Business
Sullivan County Community College

SCHAUM'S OUTLINE SERIES
McGRAW-HILL PUBLISHING COMPANY

New York   St. Louis   San Francisco   Auckland   Bogotá   Caracas
Hamburg   Lisbon   London   Madrid   Mexico   Milan   Montreal
New Delhi   Oklahoma City   Paris   San Juan   São Paulo
Singapore   Sydney   Tokyo   Toronto

JAMES A. CASHIN was Emeritus Professor of Accounting at Hofstra University, where he was formerly Chairman of the Accounting Department. His publishing credits included some fifteen titles: he was coauthor of several accounting textbooks, and the Schaum's Outlines of *Accounting I, Cost Accounting, Intermediate Accounting I*, and *Tax Accounting*. He was also Editor-in-Chief of the *Handbook for Auditors*. Professor Cashin was a Certified Public Accountant and a Certified Internal Auditor. He held a B.S. degree in Accounting from the University of Georgia and an M.B.A. from New York University. He had wide experience in business with large industrial companies and taught in the Graduate School of City University of New York and New York University.

JOEL LERNER is Professor and Chairman of the Business Division at Sullivan County Community College, Loch Sheldrake, New York. He received his B.S. from New York University and his M.S. and P.D. from Columbia University. Professor Lerner has published a booklet for *The New York Times* on teaching college business courses and has acted as editor for both *Readings in Business Organization and Management* and *Introduction to Business: A Contemporary Reader*. He has coauthored the Schaum's Outlines of *Accounting I, Business Mathematics*, and *Introduction to Business* and authored *Bookkeeping and Accounting* and *Introduction to Business Organization and Management*. He recently completed "Financial Planning for the Utterly Confused" published by McGraw-Hill and is the editor of "The Middle/Fixed Income Letter," a monthly national financial newsletter.

Schaum's Outline of Theory and Problems of
ACCOUNTING II

2 3 4 5 6 7 8 9 10 11 12 13 14 15 16 17 18 19 20 SHP SHP 8 9 2 1 0 9

ISBN 0-07-010271-6

Sponsoring Editor, John Aliano
Production Supervisor, Leroy Young
Editing Supervisors, Marthe Grice, Meg Tobin

Library of Congress Cataloging-in-Publication Data

Cashin, James A.
  Schaum's outline of theory and problems of
accounting II.–3rd ed.

  (Schaum's outline series)
  Includes index.
  1. Accounting—Problems, exercises, etc. I. Lerner,
Joel J. II. Title. III. Title: Theory and problems of
accounting II.
HF5661.C383 1989   657'.076   88-27262
ISBN 0-07-010271-6

Preface

The third edition of Accounting II covers the second part of the introductory accounting course and includes mention of FASB requirements for "statement of cash flow." As in Accounting II, the solved-problems approach is used and emphasis is on practical application of basic accounting concepts. The student is provided with:

1. concise definitions and explanations, in easily understood terms
2. fully worked-out solutions to a large range of problems (against which the student can check his or her own solutions)
3. review questions
4. sample examinations typical of those used by two-year and four-year colleges

The two books help the student to develop the all-important know-how for solving problems—on the CPA examination and in everyday work.

The subject matter has been carefully coordinated with the leading textbooks so that any topic can easily be found from the Table of Contents or the Index.

Accounting II differs from Accounting I in that specialized areas (Manufacturing Costs, Budgets, Standard Costs, Financial Ratios, etc.) are discussed rather than general practices of a business. This book will greatly assist those students who may have been able to complete Accounting I but are having difficulty with the specialized topics. Careful study of the solved problems will help such students, including those in special programs, to keep abreast of classwork, thereby reducing the number of drop-outs from Accounting II.

The wide range of areas covered will also benefit Liberal Arts majors and those Business Administration students not majoring in Accounting. In addition, this volume can serve as an accompanying text for various Management Accounting texts which need a tie-in to basic accounting.

The authors wish to acknowledge Carl Klein and Joel Siegel for their contributions in helping to design this revised manuscript.

JAMES A. CASHIN
JOEL J. LERNER
Hofstra University
Sullivan County Community College

Contents

CONTENTS

CONTENTS

Chapter 1

Partnerships: Formation

1.1 CHARACTERISTICS OF THE PARTNERSHIP

According to the Uniform Partnership Act, a *partnership* is "an association of two or more persons to carry on as co-owners a business for profit." Generally speaking, partnership accounting is like that for the sole proprietorship, except with regard to owners' equity. The partnership uses a capital account and a drawing account for each partner.

The partnership has the following characteristics:

Articles of partnership. Good business practice calls for a written agreement among the partners, containing provisions on the formation of the partnership, capital contribution of each partner, profit and loss distribution, admission and withdrawal of partners, withdrawal of funds, and dissolution of the business.

Unlimited liability. All partners have unlimited liability and are individually responsible to creditors for debts incurred by the partnership. The debts of the business can be satisfied not only by the assets of the partnership but also by the personal assets of the partners.

Co-ownership of property. All property invested in the business by the partners, as well as that purchased with the partnership's funds, becomes the property of *all* partners jointly. Therefore, each partner has an interest in the partnership in proportion to his or her capital balance, rather than a claim against specific assets.

Participation in profits and losses. Profits and losses are distributed among the partners according to the partnership agreement. If no agreement exists, profits and losses must be shared equally.

Limited life. A partnership may be dissolved by bankruptcy, death of a partner, mutual agreement, or court order.

1.2 FORMATION OF THE PARTNERSHIP

When a partnership is formed, each partner's capital account is credited for his or her initial investment and the appropriate asset account is debited. If noncash assets are invested, these should be recorded at an *agreed* amount.

If liabilities are to be assumed by the partnership, they are credited to the respective liability accounts.

EXAMPLE 1

William Morrison has agreed to go into partnership with Robert Caine.

Morrison's Accounts	Morrison's Ledger Balances	Agreed Valuations
Cash	$10,000	$10,000
Accounts Receivable	5,400	5,400
Merchandise Inventory	21,000	19,000
Equipment	16,000	14,000
Accumulated Depreciation, Equipment	4,000	
Allowance for Doubtful Accounts	400	400
Notes Payable	8,000	8,000

1

The entry to record the initial investment of Morrison in the firm of Morrison and Caine would be:

Cash	10,000	
Accounts Receivable	5,400	
Merchandise Inventory	19,000	
Equipment	14,000	
Allowance for Doubtful Accounts		400
Notes Payable		8,000
Morrison, Capital		40,000

1.3 DIVISION OF NET INCOME AND LOSS

Partnership profits and losses may be divided in any manner that the partners agree upon. In general, partners may be expected to share in proportion to the amount of capital and/or services they contribute. In the absence of a clear agreement, the law provides that all partners share equally, regardless of the differences in time devoted or capital contributed.

Below are outlined the principal methods for profit and loss distribution. For simplicity the examples are limited to two partners.

Fixed or Capital Basis

Profits and losses are generally divided equally, in a fixed ratio, or in a ratio based on the amounts of capital contributed by the partners.

EXAMPLE 2

Perez and Roth have capital balances of $30,000 and $20,000, respectively. The net income for the first year of operations was $15,000. If the partners have decided to share on an equal basis, the journal entry for the allocation of the net income will be:

Expense and Income Summary	15,000	
Perez, Capital		7,500
Roth, Capital		7,500

If, however, capital investment is to be the determining factor, the entry will run as follows:

Expense and Income Summary	15,000	
Perez, Capital		9,000*
Roth, Capital		6,000†

$$* \frac{30,000}{30,000 + 20,000}(15,000)$$

$$† \frac{20,000}{30,000 + 20,000}(15,000)$$

Interest Basis

Under the interest method, each partner is paid interest on his or her capital investment, and the remaining net income is divided in a fixed ratio or on some other basis. Thus, a partner's share depends *partially* on his or her capital investment.

EXAMPLE 3

Instead of the equal split in Example 2, each partner is to receive 6% interest on his or her capital balance, the remaining net income to be shared equally. The entry would be:

Expense and Income Summary	15,000	
Perez, Capital		7,800
Roth, Capital		7,200

the computation being:

	Perez	Roth	Total
Interest on investment	$1,800	$1,200	$ 3,000
Balance	6,000	6,000	12,000
Totals	$7,800	$7,200	$15,000

Salary Basis

The partners may agree to give recognition to contributions in the form of services, while the remaining net income may be divided equally or in a fixed ratio.

EXAMPLE 4

Assume that the partnership of Perez and Roth (Example 2) agree that a yearly salary allowance of $4,000 be given to Perez and $3,000 to Roth, the balance to be divided equally. The entry would be:

Expense and Income Summary	15,000	
Perez, Capital		8,000
Roth, Capital		7,000

the computation being:

	Perez	Roth	Total
Salary	$4,000	$3,000	$ 7,000
Balance	4,000	4,000	8,000
Totals	$8,000	$7,000	$15,000

Salary-plus-Interest Basis

Under the salary-plus-interest basis, services rendered to the business and capital contribution jointly determine the income division. Each partner gets a salary, and, at the same time, interest on capital. If any balance remains, it is divided in an agreed ratio.

EXAMPLE 5

Perez and Roth (Example 2) decide to allow a credit of 6% interest on capital balances, respective salaries of $4,000 and $3,000, and equal division of any remainder. The entry would be:

Expense and Income Summary	15,000	
Perez, Capital		8,300
Roth, Capital		6,700

which is computed as follows:

	Perez	Roth	Total
Interest	$1,800	$1,200	$ 3,000
Salary	4,000	3,000	7,000
	$5,800	$4,200	$10,000
Balance	2,500	2,500	5,000
Totals	$8,300	$6,700	$15,000

In Example 5, as well as in Examples 3 and 4, the income of the business exceeded the total of the allowances to the partners. However, this may not always be the case. If the net income is less than the total of the allowances, the balance remaining is negative and is divided among the partners equally as though it were a loss.

EXAMPLE 6

Perez and Roth (Example 2) decide to allow a credit of 6% interest on capital balances, respective salaries of $8,000 and $6,000, and equal division of the remainder. The entry would be:

Expense and Income Summary	15,000	
Perez, Capital		8,800
Roth, Capital		6,200

which is computed as follows:

	Perez	Roth	Total
Interest	$1,800	$1,200	$ 3,000
Salary	8,000	6,000	14,000
	$9,800	$7,200	$17,000
Balance	−1,000	−1,000	−2,000
Totals	$8,800	$6,200	$15,000

Solved Problems

1.1 F. Hart and P. Frank have decided to form a partnership. Hart invests the following assets at their original evaluations, and also transfers his liabilities to the new partnership.

Hart's Accounts	Hart's Ledger Balances	Agreed Valuations
Cash	$17,200	$17,200
Accounts Receivable	3,700	3,500
Allowance for Doubtful Accounts	500	400
Merchandise Inventory	11,400	9,300
Equipment	14,600	10,000
Accumulated Depreciation	2,000	
Accounts Payable	4,500	4,500
Notes Payable	2,100	2,100
Mortgages Payable	10,000	10,000

Frank agrees to invest $42,000 in cash. Record (*a*) Hart's investment and (*b*) Frank's investment.

(*a*)

(*b*)

SOLUTION

(*a*)			
	Cash	17,200	
	Accounts Receivable	3,500	
	Merchandise Inventory	9,300	
	Equipment	10,000	
	Allowance for Doubtful Accounts		400
	Accounts Payable		4,500
	Notes Payable		2,100
	Mortgage Payable		10,000
	F. Hart, Capital		23,000
(*b*)	Cash	42,000	
	P. Frank, Capital		42,000

1.2 J. Korr and B. Lear have decided to form a partnership. Korr invests the following assets at their agreed valuations, and also transfers his liabilities to the new firm.

Korr's Accounts	Korr's Ledger Balances	Agreed Valuations
Cash	$18,000	$18,000
Accounts Receivable	7,200	7,000
Allowance for Doubtful Accounts	600	500
Merchandise Inventory	12,200	10,000
Equipment	6,000	4,200
Accumulated Depreciation	1,000	
Accounts Payable	3,500	3,500
Notes Payable	3,600	3,600

Lear agrees to invest $26,000 in cash. Record (*a*) Korr's investment and (*b*) Lear's investment.

(a)

(b)

SOLUTION

(a)			
Cash		18,000	
Accounts Receivable		7,000	
Merchandise Inventory		10,000	
Equipment		4,200	
Allowance for Doubtful Accounts			500
Accounts Payable			3,500
Notes Payable			3,600
J. Korr, Capital			31,600
(b) Cash		26,000	
B. Lear, Capital			26,000

1.3 Adams, Bentley, and Carson have capital balances of $30,000, $25,000, and $20,000, respectively. Adams devotes three-fourths time; Bentley, half time; and Carson, one-fourth time. Determine their participation in net income of $37,500 if income is divided (a) in the ratio of capital investments and (b) in the ratio of time worked.

(a)		
Adams		
Bentley		
Carson		
Net Income		$37,500
(b)		
Adams		
Bentley		
Carson		
Net Income		$37,500

SOLUTION

(a) Total capital is $75,000. Hence:

Adams	($30,000/$75,000) × $37,500	= $15,000
Bentley	($25,000/$75,000) × $37,500	= 12,500
Carson	($20,000/$75,000) × $37,500	= 10,000
Net Income		$37,500

(b) The ratio is 3:2:1. Hence:

Adams	$3/6 \times \$37,500 = \$18,750$
Bentley	$2/6 \times \$37,500 = 12,500$
Carson	$1/6 \times \$37,500 = 6,250$
Net Income	$\$37,500$

1.4 The capital accounts of W. Dunn and S. Evans have balances of $35,000 and $25,000, respectively. The articles of co-partnership refer to the distribution of net income in the following manner:

(1) Dunn and Evans are to receive salaries of $9,000 and $6,000, respectively.

(2) Each is to receive 6% on his capital account.

(3) The balance is to be divided equally.

If the net income for the firm is $32,000, (a) determine the division of net income and (b) present the entry to close the expense and income summary account.

(a)

	Dunn	Evans	Total
Salary			
Interest			
Balance			
Share of Net Income			

(b)

SOLUTION

(a)

	Dunn	Evans	Total
Salary	$ 9,000	$ 6,000	$15,000
Interest	2,100	1,500	3,600
	$11,100	$ 7,500	$18,600
Balance	6,700	6,700	13,400
Share of Net Income	$17,800	$14,200	$32,000

(b)

Expense and Income Summary	32,000	
Dunn, Capital		17,800
Evans, Capital		14,200

1.5 Redo Problem 1.4 for a net income of $12,000.

(a)

	Dunn	Evans	Total
Salary			
Interest			
Balance			
Share of Net Income			

(b)

SOLUTION

(a)

	Dunn	Evans	Total
Salary	$ 9,000	$6,000	$15,000
Interest	2,100	1,500	3,600
	$11,100	$7,500	$18,600
Balance	−3,300	−3,300	−6,600
Share of Net Income	$ 7,800	$4,200	$12,000

(b)

Expense and Income Summary	12,000	
Dunn, Capital		7,800
Evans, Capital		4,200

1.6 Baggetta and Cohen have capital accounts of $20,000 and $40,000, respectively. The partners divide net income in the following manner:

(1) Salaries of $10,000 to Baggetta and $12,000 to Cohen.

(2) Each partner receives 5% on his capital investment.

(3) The balance is divided in the ratio of 1:2.

Determine the division of net income if net income is (a) $34,000 and (b) $22,000.

(a)

	Baggetta	Cohen	Total
Salary			
Interest			
Balance			
Total Share			

(b)

	Baggetta	Cohen	Total
Salary			
Interest			
Balance			
Total Share			

SOLUTION

(a)

	Baggetta	Cohen	Total
Salary	$10,000	$12,000	$22,000
Interest	1,000	2,000	3,000
	$11,000	$14,000	$25,000
Balance	3,000	6,000	9,000
Total Share	$14,000	$20,000	$34,000

(b)

	Baggetta	Cohen	Total
Salary	$10,000	$12,000	$22,000
Interest	1,000	2,000	3,000
	$11,000	$14,000	$25,000
Balance	−1,000	−2,000	−3,000
Total Share	$10,000	$12,000	$22,000

1.7 At the end of the first year of business, Burg & Frank had net income of $62,000. What would be the division of income under each of the following methods: (a) to be shared equally; (b) by capital investment (see Problem 1.1 for capital invested by each partner); (c) time spent working (Burg 40%, Frank 60%); (d) salary plus 10% of investment with the remainder shared equally (Burg salary $10,000; Frank salary $15,000). You may round off to the nearest whole number.

(a)

(b)

(c)

(d)

SOLUTION

(a)

Expense and Income Summary	62,000	
Burg, Capital		31,000
Frank, Capital		31,000

(b)

Expense and Income Summary	62,000	
Burg, Capital		21,938*
Frank, Capital		40,062†

$$*\frac{23,000}{23,000 + 42,000} \times 62,000$$

$$†\frac{42,000}{42,000 + 23,000} \times 62,000$$

(c)

Expense and Income Summary	62,000	
Burg, Capital		24,800*
Frank, Capital		37,200†

*62,000×40%

†62,000×60%

(d)	Expense and Income Summary	62,000	
	Burg, Capital		27,550*
	Frank, Capital		34,450†

	*Burg	†Frank	Total
Salary	$10,000	$15,000	$25,000
Interest on Investment, 10%	2,300	4,200	6,500
Balance equal	15,250	15,250	30,500
	$27,550	$34,450	$62,000

1.8 J. Lee and R. Grant have capital balances of $40,000 and $60,000, respectively. Net income for the year was $38,000. The partnership agreement calls for a salary of $16,000 each, 10% interest on capital, and the remaining income or loss is to be divided by the ratio of their capital balances. Present the entry needed to close the Expense and Income Summary account.

SOLUTION

Expense and Income Summary	38,000	
Lee, Capital		18,400*
Grant, Capital		19,600†

	*Lee	†Grant	Total
Salary	$16,000	$16,000	$32,000
Interest on Investment (10%)	4,000	6,000	10,000
Loss in capital balances ratio	(1,600)	(2,400)	(4,000)
	$18,400	$19,600	$38,000

$$*\frac{40,000}{40,000 + 60,000} \times 4,000$$

$$†\frac{60,000}{40,000 + 60,000} \times 4,000$$

1.9 During its first year of operations the partnership Diamond, Ellis, and Frank earned $41,400. Journalize the entries needed to close the Expense and Income Summary account and to allocate the net income to the partners under the following assumptions:

(a) The partners did not agree on any method for sharing earnings.

(b) The partners agreed to share earnings in the ratio of time invested. Diamond worked full-time; Ellis, full-time; Frank, half-time.

(c) The partners agreed to share earnings in the ratio of their capital investments (Diamond, $25,000; Ellis, $20,000; Frank, $15,000).

(a)

(b)

(c)

SOLUTION

(a) If no formal agreement exists, all profits and losses are assumed to be divided equally.

Expense and Income Summary	41,400	
Diamond, Capital		13,800
Ellis, Capital		13,800
Frank, Capital		13,800

(b) The division ratio is $1:1:1/2 = 2:2:1$.

Expense and Income Summary	41,400	
Diamond, Capital (2/5 × $41,400)		16,560
Ellis, Capital (2/5 × $41,400)		16,560
Frank, Capital (1/5 × $41,400)		8,280

(c) The division ratio is $25,000:20,000:15,000 = 5:4:3$.

Expense and Income Summary	41,400	
Diamond, Capital (5/12 × $41,400)		17,250
Ellis, Capital (4/12 × $41,400)		13,800
Frank, Capital (3/12 × $41,400)		10,350

1.10 Clemenko and Bedell have capital balances of $15,000 and $25,000, respectively. The partnership earned $24,000 (net). Present the entries needed to close the Expense and Income Summary account and divide the income under each of the following different assumptions:

(a) In ratio of time invested. Clemenko devotes full time and Bedell devotes half time.

(b) In ratio of original investment.

(c) Salaries of $10,000 to Clemenko, $5,000 to Bedell; the remainder to be shared equally.

(a)

(b)

(c)

SOLUTION

(a) The division ratio is $1:1/2 = 2:1$.

Expense and Income Summary	24,000	
Clemenko, Capital (2/3 $\times$ $24,000)		16,000
Bedell, Capital (1/3 $\times$ $24,000)		8,000

(b) The division ratio is $15,000:$25,000 = 3:5$.

Expense and Income Summary	24,000	
Clemenko, Capital (3/8 $\times$ $24,000)		9,000
Bedell, Capital (5/8 $\times$ $24,000)		15,000

(c)

Expense and Income Summary	24,000	
Clemenko, Capital		14,500*
Bedell, Capital		9,500†

	*Clemenko	+	Bedell†	=	Income
Salary	$10,000		$5,000		$15,000
Balance	4,500		4,500		9,000
Total	$14,500		$9,500		$24,000

1.11 The abbreviated income statement of James and Kelly for December 31, 19X1, appears below:

Sales (net)	$240,000
Less: Cost of Goods Sold	105,000
Gross Profit	$135,000
Less: Expenses	65,000
Net Income	$ 70,000

The profit and loss agreement specifies that:

(1) Interest of 5% is to be allowed on capital balances (James, $25,000; Kelly, $15,000).

(2) Salary allowances to James and Kelly to be $6,000 and $4,000, respectively.

(3) A bonus is to be given to James equal to 20% of net income without regard to interest or salary.

(4) Remaining profits and losses are to be divided in the ratio of capital balances.

(*a*) Present the distribution of net income. (*b*) Present the journal entry required to close the books.

(*a*)

	James	Kelly	Total
Interest			
Salary			
Bonus			
Balance			
Net Income			

(*b*)

SOLUTION

(*a*)

	James	Kelly	Total
Interest	$ 1,250	$ 750	$ 2,000
Salary	6,000	4,000	10,000
Bonus	14,000		14,000
	$21,250	$ 4,750	$26,000
Balance	27,500*	16,500*	44,000
Net Income	$48,750	$21,250	$70,000

```
*$25,000   James      25/40 × $44,000 = $27,500
  15,000   Kelly      15/40 × $44,000 = $16,500
 $40,000   Total
```

(*b*)

Expense and Income Summary	70,000	
James, Capital		48,750
Kelly, Capital		21,250

Chapter 2

Partnerships: Admission and Dissolution

2.1 ADMISSION OF A NEW PARTNER

The Uniform Partnership Act states that partners may dispose of part or all of their interest in the firm without the consent of the remaining partners.

The individual who purchases the interest receives the selling partner's rights to share in income and expense. However she is not a full partner, since she will have no vote or right to participate in partnership activities unless she is admitted to the firm.

Admission by Purchase of Interest

When the incoming partner purchases an interest from another partner, he pays the purchase price directly to the old partner. The only change required in the partnership's books is an entry transferring capital from the old partner's account to the account established for the new partner. Assets and liabilities of the business are not affected.

EXAMPLE 1

Perez and Roth have capital balances of $30,000 and $20,000, respectively. William Stone is admitted to the partnership by purchasing half of Perez's interest for $18,000. The only entry required is the changing of the capital balances of the affected partners.

Perez, Capital		Roth, Capital		Stone, Capital	
15,000	30,000 Bal.		20,000 Bal.		15,000

Stone's admission results in the transfer of half of Perez's capital to Stone, regardless of the amount paid by Stone for his share of the partnership.

Admission by Investment Assets

The new partner may contribute assets to the partnership, thus increasing both the assets and the capital of the firm.

EXAMPLE 2

Assume that Stone is to be admitted to the partnership of Perez and Roth, whose total capital is $50,000 ($30,000 and $20,000, respectively). Stone is to contribute $25,000 for a 1/3 interest in the new partnership. The entry to record his admission is:

Cash	25,000	
Stone, Capital		25,000

In Examples 1 and 2 it was assumed that the assets of Perez and Roth were stated in terms of the current market prices when Stone was admitted. Because of this, no adjustments were necessary in any of the assets prior to his admission. In some cases, when a new partner is admitted, assets may first have to be revalued or goodwill recognized in order to bring the capital accounts into line with current values.

Revaluation of assets. The book values of certain assets of the partnership must be adjusted before they agree with current prices. The net amount of the revaluation is then transferred to the capital accounts of the old partners according to their income-division agreement. If it appears that a number of assets need revaluation, whether to higher or lower figures, the adjustments may be made in a temporary account, Asset Revaluation, which will subsequently be closed to the partners' capital accounts.

14

EXAMPLE 3

Before admitting Stone to the partnership, Perez and Roth decide that merchandise inventory, carried at $21,000, is to be revalued at $25,000.

The entry to record the above revaluations is:

Merchandise Inventory	4,000	
Asset Revaluation		4,000

After the adjustment has been made, Asset Revaluation is closed as follows:

Asset Revaluation	4,000	
Perez, Capital		2,000
Roth, Capital		2,000

Recognition of goodwill. If a firm has the ability to earn more than the normal rate on its investment (because of a favorable location, established reputation, management skills, or better products or services), goodwill may be indicated, and an incoming partner may be charged for it. If so, the goodwill account is debited, while the old partners' accounts are credited in the ratios set up by the articles of partnership. On the other hand, if goodwill is created by the incoming partner, the goodwill account is debited and the new partner's capital account credited.

EXAMPLE 4   Goodwill to the Old Partners

The capital balances of Perez and Roth are $30,000 and $20,000, respectively. The partnership agrees to admit Stone to their firm, who is to contribute cash of $20,000 and is to receive a 1/4 interest in the firm. Though the total capital of the firm before the admission is $50,000, the parties agree that the firm is worth $60,000. This excess of $10,000 indicates the existence of goodwill; it will be allocated to the old partners equally. The entries to record goodwill and the admission of the new partner are:

Goodwill	10,000	
Perez, Capital		5,000
Roth, Capital		5,000
Cash	20,000	
Stone, Capital		20,000

EXAMPLE 5   Goodwill to the New Partner

Perez and Roth, with capital balances of $30,000 and $20,000, respectively, agree to admit Stone into the firm for a $15,000 investment, giving him a 1/3 share in profits and losses and granting him goodwill recognition of $10,000. The entry to record the above information would be:

Cash	15,000	
Goodwill	10,000	
Stone, Capital		25,000

2.2 LIQUIDATION OF A PARTNERSHIP

If the partners of a firm decide to discontinue the operations of the business, several accounting steps are necessary:

1. The accounts are adjusted and closed.
2. All assets are converted to cash.

3. All creditors are paid in full.

4. Any remaining cash is distributed among the partners according to the balances in their capital accounts (and not according to their profit and loss ratios).

EXAMPLE 6 Liquidation at a Gain

After Perez, Roth, and Stone have ceased business operations and adjusted and closed the accounts, the general ledger has the following post-closing trial balance:

Cash	$20,000	
Noncash Assets	65,000	
Liabilities		$10,000
Perez, Capital		15,000
Roth, Capital		25,000
Stone, Capital		35,000
	$85,000	$85,000

Assume for simplicity that all liabilities are paid at one time and that the noncash assets are sold in one transaction. Then, if the sale price is $80,000 and the partners share equally in profits and losses, we have the following liquidation schedule:

		Assets	=	Liabilities	+	Capital		
		Cash + Other		Accounts Payable		Perez +	Roth +	Stone
	Balances of accounts	$ 20,000 $65,000		$10,000		$15,000	$25,000	$35,000
(a)	Sales of assets	+80,000 −65,000				+5,000	+5,000	+5,000
	Balance after sale	$100,000		$10,000		$20,000	$30,000	$40,000
(b)	Payment of liabilities	−10,000		−10,000				
	Balance after payment	$ 90,000				$20,000	$30,000	$40,000
(c)	Distribution to partners	−90,000				−20,000	−30,000	−40,000

The entries to record the liquidation are then:

(a) Sale of Assets

Cash	80,000	
Other Assets		65,000
Gain on Liquidation		15,000
Gain on Liquidation	15,000	
Perez, Capital		5,000
Roth, Capital		5,000
Stone, Capital		5,000

(b) Payment of Liabilities

Liabilities	10,000	
Cash		10,000

(c) Final Distribution to Partners

Perez, Capital	20,000	
Roth, Capital	30,000	
Stone, Capital	40,000	
Cash		90,000

Note: The final distribution of cash ($90,000) is made to the partners based on their *capital* balances.

EXAMPLE 7   Liquidation at a Loss: No Capital Deficit

The data is the same as in Example 6, except that the noncash assets are now sold for $56,000.

	Assets	=	Liabilities	+	Capital		
	Cash + Other		Accounts Payable		Perez +	Roth +	Stone
Balances of accounts	$20,000 $65,000		$10,000		$15,000	$25,000	$35,000
(a) Sales of assets	+56,000 −65,000				−3,000	−3,000	−3,000
Balance after sale	$76,000		$10,000		$12,000	$22,000	$32,000
(b) Payment of liabilities	−10,000		−10,000				
Balance after payment	$66,000				$12,000	$22,000	$32,000
(c) Distribution to partners	−66,000				−12,000	−22,000	−32,000

The entries to record the liquidation are then:

(a)   Sale of Assets

Cash	56,000	
Loss on Liquidation	9,000	
Other Assets		65,000

Perez, Capital	3,000	
Roth, Capital	3,000	
Stone, Capital	3,000	
Loss on Liquidation		9,000

(b)   Payment of Liabilities

Liabilities	10,000	
Cash		10,000

(c)   Final Distribution to Partners

Perez, Capital	12,000	
Roth, Capital	22,000	
Stone, Capital	32,000	
Cash		66,000

Note: The final distribution of cash ($66,000) is made to the partners based on their *capital* balances.

EXAMPLE 8   Liquidation at a Loss: Partner Deficit

The data are as in Example 7, except that the noncash assets are now sold for $11,000.

	Assets	=	Liabilities	+	Capital		
	Cash + Other		Accounts Payable		Perez +	Roth +	Stone
Balances of accounts	$20,000 $65,000		$10,000		$15,000	$25,000	$35,000
(a) Sale of assets	+11,000 −65,000				−18,000	−18,000	−18,000
Balance after sale	$31,000		$10,000		$ (3,000)	$ 7,000	$17,000
(b) Payment of liabilities	−10,000		−10,000				
Balance after payment	$21,000				$ (3,000)	$ 7,000	$17,000
(c) Distribution to partners	−21,000					−5,500	−15,500
					$ (3,000)	$ 1,500	$ 1,500

Notice that in the foregoing liquidation schedule the $54,000 loss on sale of the noncash assets was divided equally among the three partners. However, Perez's capital balance was not sufficient to absorb his share of the loss. This resulted in a debit balance ($3,000) in his capital account and becomes a claim of the partnership against him for that amount. The $3,000 deficit must be borne by the two remaining partners. And thus, in the distribution to partners, Roth and Stone each take an additional loss of $1,500.

The entries to record the liquidation are as follows:

(*a*)   Sale of Assets

Cash	11,000	
Loss on Liquidation	54,000	
Other Assets		65,000
Perez, Capital	18,000	
Roth, Capital	18,000	
Stone, Capital	18,000	
Loss on Liquidation		54,000

(*b*)   Payment of Liabilities

Liabilities	10,000	
Cash		10,000

(*c*)   Distribution to Partners

Roth, Capital	5,500	
Stone, Capital	15,500	
Cash		21,000

Since there is a capital deficiency outstanding, one of three different possibilities will arise in the future: (1) Perez pays the deficiency in full; (2) Perez makes a partial payment; (3) Perez makes no payment. The entries corresponding to these possibilities are:

(1)   Payment in Full

Cash	3,000	
Perez, Capital		3,000
Roth, Capital	1,500	
Stone, Capital	1,500	
Cash		3,000

(2)   Partial Payment of $2,000

Cash	2,000	
Perez, Capital		2,000
Settlement of Perez's deficiency		
Roth, Capital	500	
Stone, Capital	500	
Perez, Capital		1,000
To close out the balance of Perez's account		
Roth, Capital	1,000	
Stone, Capital	1,000	
Cash		2,000
To distribute cash according to capital balances		

(3) No Payment

Roth, Capital	1,500	
Stone, Capital	1,500	
Perez, Capital		3,000

Summary: Chapters 1 and 2

1. Partnership and sole proprietorship accounting are alike except in _____ .

2. Noncash assets are recorded at _____ amounts when the partnership is formed.

3. The book value of the partnership of Acme and Beam is $60,000, with each partner's account showing $30,000. If Caldwell were to purchase Beam's interest for $40,000, the amount credited to Caldwell's equity account would be _____ .

4. In order to reflect higher current prices, certain assets of the partnership will be debited, with the corresponding credit to _____ .

5. A firm's superior earning power is recognized as _____ .

6. If profits and losses are not to be shared equally, the basis of distribution must be stated in the _____ .

7. Salaries and the interest on partners' capital balances are not included on the income statement but are shown on the _____ .

8. When a partnership decides to go out of business, the process of selling the assets, paying the creditors, and distributing the remaining cash to the partners is known as _____ .

9. The final distribution of cash to the partners is based on their _____ .

Answers: (1) owners' equity; (2) agreed; (3) $30,000; (4) Asset Revaluation; (5) goodwill; (6) partnership agreement; (7) capital statement; (8) liquidation; (9) capital balances

Solved Problems

2.1 D. Rice and B. Hayes were partners with capital balances of $24,000 and $36,000, respectively. O. Newman was to purchase 1/2 of Hayes' interest for $20,000. Make the necessary journal entry to admit O. Newman.

SOLUTION

Hayes, Capital	18,000	
Newman, Capital		18,000

2.2 The capital accounts of P. Henry and W. Schneider have balances of $25,000 each. E. Kurlander joins the partnership. What entry is necessary (*a*) if Kurlander purchases half of Henry's investment for $15,000? (*b*) if Kurlander invests $15,000 in the firm?

(*a*)

(*b*)

SOLUTION

(*a*)	P. Henry, Capital	12,500	
	E. Kurlander, Capital		12,500
(*b*)	Cash	15,000	
	E. Kurlander, Capital		15,000

2.3 F. Saltzman and J. Epstein have capital balances of $20,000 and $30,000, respectively. H. Walker and W. Dunn are to be admitted to the partnership—Walker by purchasing half of Epstein's interest for $18,000 and Dunn by investing $10,000, for which he is to receive full equity value ($10,000).

(*a*) What entry is needed to record the above information?

(*b*) On a capital basis, what is Dunn's share of profits and losses?

(*a*)

(*b*)

SOLUTION

(*a*)	Cash	10,000	
	J. Epstein, Capital	15,000	
	H. Walker, Capital		15,000
	W. Dunn, Capital		10,000
(*b*)	F. Saltzman, Capital		$20,000
	H. Walker, Capital		15,000
	J. Epstein, Capital		15,000
	W. Dunn, Capital		10,000
	Total Capital		$60,000

$$\frac{\text{Dunn's investment}}{\text{Total capital}} = \frac{\$10,000}{\$60,000} = \frac{1}{6}, \quad \text{or } 16\tfrac{2}{3}\%$$

2.4   The capital accounts of D. Jaffee and S. Klein are listed below. Wilma Larkin and Ernst Meyer are to be admitted to the partnership under the following agreement:

(1) Larkin is to invest $30,000, for which she is to receive full ownership equity.

(2) Meyer is to purchase one-third of Klein's interest for $25,000.

D. Jaffee, Capital	S. Klein, Capital
30,000	60,000

(*a*) Present the entry to record the above information.

(*b*) Determine, after the admission of Larkin and Meyer, each partner's share of profits and losses.

(*a*)

(*b*)

SOLUTION

(*a*)

Cash	30,000	
S. Klein, Capital	20,000	
W. Larkin, Capital		30,000
E. Meyer, Capital		20,000

(*b*)

D. Jaffee, Capital	$ 30,000
S. Klein, Capital	40,000
W. Larkin, Capital	30,000
E. Meyer, Capital	20,000
Total Capital	$120,000

$$\frac{\text{Jaffee's investment}}{\text{Total capital}} = \frac{\$30,000}{\$120,000} = \frac{1}{4}, \quad \text{or } 25\%$$

$$\frac{\text{Klein's investment}}{\text{Total capital}} = \frac{\$40,000}{\$120,000} = \frac{1}{3}, \quad \text{or } 33\tfrac{1}{3}\%$$

$$\frac{\text{Larkin's investment}}{\text{Total capital}} = \frac{\$30,000}{\$120,000} = \frac{1}{4}, \quad \text{or } 25\%$$

$$\frac{\text{Meyer's investment}}{\text{Total capital}} = \frac{\$20,000}{\$120,000} = \frac{1}{6}, \quad \text{or } 16\tfrac{2}{3}\%$$

2.5   The financial position of the partnership of Davidson and Fellows, who share income in the ratio 3:2, follows.

Davidson-Fellows Company
Balance Sheet
April 30, 19X1

ASSETS		LIABILITIES AND CAPITAL	
Current Assets	$ 65,000	Liabilities	$ 50,000
Equipment (net)	125,000	Davidson, Capital	85,000
		Fellows, Capital	55,000
Total Assets	$190,000	Total Liabilities and Capital	$190,000

Both partners agree to admit a new partner, Evans, into the firm. Prepare the necessary entries corresponding to each of the following separate situations:

(a) Evans purchases half of Fellows' interest for $30,000.

(b) Evans invests $70,000 in the partnership and receives a 1/3 interest in capital and income.

(c) The original partners feel that goodwill should be recorded at a value of $20,000. Evans' investment is to gain him a 1/3 interest in capital and income.

(a)

(b)

(c)

SOLUTION

(a)	Fellows, Capital	27,500	
	Evans, Capital		27,500
(b)	Cash	70,000	
	Evans, Capital		70,000
(c)	Goodwill	20,000	
	Davidson, Capital		12,000
	Fellows, Capital		8,000
	Cash	80,000	
	Evans, Capital		80,000*

*Total worth before admission is $85,000 + $55,000 + $20,000 = $160,000. To produce three equal parts, Evans has to invest half of this, or $80,000.

2.6   An abbreviated balance sheet of Vance and Upton, who share income equally, appears as follows:

ASSETS		LIABILITIES AND CAPITAL	
Current Assets	$ 73,000	Liabilities	$ 45,000
Equipment (net)	97,000	Vance, Capital	60,000
		Upton, Capital	65,000
Total Assets	$170,000	Total Liabilities and Capital	$170,000

The partners agree to admit a new partner, Williams, into the firm. Present the entries to correspond to each of the following separate situations:

(a)   Williams invests $30,000 to receive an interest in the business.

(b)   Williams purchases half of Vance's interest for $35,000.

(c)   Prior to admission, the partners discover that the merchandise inventory account is understated by $5,000. For his investment Williams is to receive a 1/3 interest in capital and income.

(a)

(b)

(c)

SOLUTION

(a)	Cash	30,000	
	Williams, Capital		30,000
(b)	Vance, Capital	30,000	
	Williams, Capital		30,000
(c)	Merchandise Inventory	5,000	
	Asset Revaluation		5,000
	Asset Revaluation	5,000	
	Vance, Capital		2,500
	Upton, Capital		2,500
	Cash	65,000	
	Williams, Capital		65,000*

*Total worth before admission is $65,000 + $60,000 + $5,000 = $130,000. To produce three equal parts, Williams must invest half of this, or $65,000.

2.7 Before admitting Goldsmith to the partnership, Sudol and Babcock, who share profits and losses equally, decide that merchandise inventory, recorded at $26,000, is to be revalued at $29,000. Present journal entries to record the revaluation.

(*a*)

(*b*)

SOLUTION

(*a*)	Merchandise Inventory	3,000	
	Asset Revaluation		3,000
(*b*)	Asset Revaluation	3,000	
	Sudol, Capital		1,500
	Babcock, Capital		1,500

2.8 After the assets of the partnership have been adjusted to reflect current prices, the capital balances of L. Benjamin and R. Hochron are each $25,000. However, both partners agree that the partnership is worth $60,000. They decide to admit R. Berechad as an equal partner into their firm for a $30,000 investment. (*a*) Record the recognition of goodwill. (*b*) Record Berechad's investment. (*c*) What is the total capital of the firm?

(*a*)

(*b*)

(*c*)

SOLUTION

(*a*)	Goodwill	10,000	
	L. Benjamin, Capital		5,000
	R. Hochron, Capital		5,000
(*b*)	Cash	30,000	
	R. Berechad, Capital		30,000

(*c*)	L. Benjamin, Capital	$30,000
	R. Hochron, Capital	30,000
	R. Berechad, Capital	30,000
	Total Capital	$90,000

2.9 If, in Problem 2.8, R. Berechad invested $20,000 for an equal share of equity, what would the entry be to record his admittance into the firm?

SOLUTION

Cash	20,000	
Goodwill	10,000	
R. Berechad, Capital		30,000

Since the total capital prior to Berechad's admittance was $60,000, an equal share would require an investment of $30,000, as in Problem 2.8. Therefore, the owners must have agreed to recognize the new partner's ability and awarded him capital credit (goodwill) of $30,000 − $20,000 = $10,000.

2.10 C. Sark and G. Dickel each have capital balances of $30,000. The assets of the firm are reflected at current prices; however, the partners feel that the firm is worth $75,000. They decide to admit L. Rodriquez as an equal partner for a $35,000 investment.

(a) Record the recognition of goodwill.

(b) Record Rodriquez's admittance into the firm.

(c) Determine the total capital of the firm.

(a)

(b)

(c)

SOLUTION

(a)	Goodwill	15,000	
	Sark, Capital		7,500
	Dickel, Capital		7,500
(b)	Cash	35,000	
	Goodwill	2,500	
	Rodriquez, Capital		37,500*

*The total capital before Rodriquez's admittance is $75,000. An equal share would require an investment of $37,500; therefore the owners must have granted the new partner goodwill.

(c)	Dickel	$ 37,500
	Sark	37,500
	Rodriquez	37,500
	Total	$112,500

2.11 Kapela, Lesser and Morton, with capital balances of $20,000, $30,000, and $25,000, respectively, decide to terminate their partnership. After selling the noncash assets and paying all debts, there is $75,000 in cash remaining. Assuming that the partners share profits and losses equally, how should this remaining cash be split?

Kapela	
Lesser	
Morton	
Total Cash	$75,000

SOLUTION

Kapela	$20,000
Lesser	30,000
Morton	25,000
Total Cash	$75,000

The final distribution of cash is determined by the capital balances and not by the profit and loss ratio.

2.12 The following T accounts show the balances of the partnership of Greenburg and Holand as of June 30, 19X1, prior to dissolution:

Cash		Merchandise Inventory	
35,000		12,600	

Equipment		Accumulated Depreciation	
15,000			12,000

Prepaid Insurance		Accounts Payable	
1,400			16,000

Greenburg, Capital		Holand, Capital	
	18,000		18,000

The partners share profits and losses equally. The terminating transactions are:

(a) Sold the merchandise for its market value, $16,500.

(b) Realized $1,100 from the surrender of the insurance policies.

(c) Sold the equipment for $2,000.

(d) Distributed the gain to the partners' capital accounts.

(e) Paid all liabilities.

(f) Distributed the remaining cash.

Present journal entries to record the information.

(a)

(b)

(c)

(d)

(e)

(f)

SOLUTION

(a)	Cash	16,500	
	Merchandise Inventory		12,600
	Loss or Gain on Realization		3,900
(b)	Cash	1,100	
	Loss or Gain on Realization	300	
	Prepaid Insurance		1,400
(c)	Cash	2,000	
	Accumulated Depreciation	12,000	
	Loss or Gain on Realization	1,000	
	Equipment		15,000
(d)	Loss or Gain on Realization	2,600	
	Greenburg, Capital		1,300
	Holand, Capital		1,300
(e)	Accounts Payable	16,000	
	Cash		16,000
(f)	Greenburg, Capital	19,300	
	Holand, Capital	19,300	
	Cash		38,600

Summary of Transactions

Transaction	Cash	Other Assets	Liabilities	Greenburg, Capital	Holand, Capital
Balance	$35,000	$17,000	$16,000	$18,000	$18,000
(a) − (d)	+19,600	−17,000		+ 1,300	+ 1,300
	$54,600		$16,000	$19,300	$19,300
(e)	−16,000		−16,000		
	$38,600			$19,300	$19,300
(f)	−38,600			−19,300	−19,300

2.13 H. Hogan, J. Little, and R. Roberts have decided to liquidate their partnership. Below is a post-closing trial balance.

Cash	$ 30,000	
Noncash assets	90,000	
Liabilities		$ 20,000
Hogan, Capital		40,000
Little, Capital		40,000
Roberts, Capital		20,000
	$120,000	$120,000

Prepare a liquidation schedule using the following information:

(1) All noncash assets are sold for $100,000.

(2) Profits and losses are shared on their capital interest in the business.

	Cash	Other	Liabilities	Hogan 40%	Little 40%	Roberts 20%

SOLUTION

	Cash	Other	Liabilities	Hogan 40%	Little 40%	Roberts 20%
Balance	$ 30,000	$90,000	$20,000	$40,000	$40,000	$20,000
Sale of Assets	+100,000	−90,000		+ 4,000	+ 4,000	+ 2,000
	$130,000	−0−	$20,000	$44,000	$44,000	$22,000
Payment of Liabilities	−20,000		−20,000			
Balance after Payment	$110,000		−0−	$44,000	$44,000	$22,000
Distribution to Partners	−110,000			−44,000	−44,000	−22,000
	−0−			−0−	−0−	−0−

2.14 Prepare another liquidation schedule using the same facts except that noncash assets are sold for $60,000.

	Cash	Other	Liabilities	Hogan	Little	Roberts

SOLUTION

	Cash	Other	Liabilities	Hogan	Little	Roberts
Balance	$30,000	$90,000	$20,000	$40,000	$40,000	$20,000
Sale of Assets	+60,000	−90,000		−12,000	−12,000	−6,000
	$90,000	−0−	$20,000	$28,000	$28,000	$14,000
Payment of Liabilities	−20,000		−20,000			
	$70,000		−0−	$28,000	$28,000	$14,000
Distribution to Partners	−70,000			−28,000	−28,000	−14,000
Liquidation Complete	−0−			−0−	−0−	−0−

2.15 The accounts of Sully and Todd had the following balances when they decided to discontinue operations:

Accounts Payable	$ 6,700	Lara Todd, Capital	$15,000
Accumulated Depreciation, Equipment	6,150	Merchandise Inventory	19,000
Cash	16,000	Notes Payable	1,500
Equipment	8,800	Supplies	550
Frank Sully, Capital	15,000		

The partners share profits and losses equally. Present the entries to record the following transactions:

(a) Received $400 upon sale of supplies.

(b) Disposed of the merchandise inventory, receiving $22,000.

(c) Sold the equipment for $3,000.

(d) Distributed the loss or gain to the partners.

(e) Paid all liabilities.

(f) Distributed the remaining cash.

(a)

(b)

(c)

(d)

(e)

(f)

SOLUTION

(a)	Cash	400	
	Loss or Gain on Realization	150	
	Supplies		550
(b)	Cash	22,000	
	Merchandise Inventory		19,000
	Loss or Gain on Realization		3,000
(c)	Cash	3,000	
	Accumulated Depreciation	6,150	
	Equipment		8,800
	Loss or Gain on Realization		350
(d)	Loss or Gain on Realization	3,200	
	Sully, Capital		1,600
	Todd, Capital		1,600
(e)	Accounts Payable	6,700	
	Notes Payable	1,500	
	Cash		8,200
(f)	Sully, Capital	16,600	
	Todd, Capital	16,600	
	Cash		33,200

Summary of Transactions

Transaction	Cash	Other Assets	Liabilities	Sully, Capital	Todd, Capital
Balance	$16,000	$22,200	$8,200	$15,000	$15,000
(a) − (d)	+25,400	−22,200		+ 1,600	+ 1,600
	$41,400		$8,200	$16,600	$16,600
(e)	−8,200		−8,200		
	$33,200			$16,600	$16,600
(f)	−33,200			−16,600	−16,600

2.16 Sochet, Karlin, and Stadler, who divide profits and losses equally, have the following ledger balances as of December 31:

Cash	$36,000
Other Assets	18,000
Liabilities	16,000
Sochet, Capital	15,000
Karlin, Capital	10,000
Stadler, Capital	13,000

The partners decide to liquidate, and sell their noncash assets at a loss of $6,000. After meeting their obligations, they divide the remaining cash. Present all necessary entries.

(a) Loss on realization

(b) Division of loss

(c) Payment of liabilities

(d) Division of remaining cash

SOLUTION

(*a*) Loss on realization

Cash	12,000	
Loss on Realization	6,000	
Other Assets		18,000

(*b*) Division of loss

Sochet, Capital	2,000	
Karlin, Capital	2,000	
Stadler, Capital	2,000	
Loss on Realization		6,000

(*c*) Payment of liabilities

Liabilities	16,000	
Cash		16,000

(*d*) Division of remaining cash

Sochet, Capital	13,000	
Karlin, Capital	8,000	
Stadler, Capital	11,000	
Cash		32,000

Summary of Transactions

Transaction	Cash	Other Assets	Liabilities	Sochet, Capital	Karlin, Capital	Stadler, Capital
Balance	$36,000	$18,000	$16,000	$15,000	$10,000	$13,000
(*a*), (*b*)	+12,000	−18,000		− 2,000	− 2,000	− 2,000
	$48,000		$16,000	$13,000	$ 8,000	$11,000
(*c*)	−16,000		−16,000			
	$32,000			$13,000	$ 8,000	$11,000
(*d*)	−32,000			−13,000	−8,000	−11,000

2.17 Eccleston, Kapela, and Harmin, who share income and losses in the ratio 2:1:1, decide to liquidate their business on April 30. As of that date their post-closing trial balance reads:

Cash	$ 38,000	
Other Assets	82,000	
Liabilities		$ 48,000
Eccleston, Capital		30,000
Kapela, Capital		22,000
Harmin, Capital		20,000
	$120,000	$120,000

Present the entries to record the following liquidating transactions:

(*a*) Sold the noncash assets for $12,000.

(*b*) Distributed the loss to the partners.

(c)   Paid the liabilities.

(d)   Allocated the available cash to the partners.

(e)   The partner with the debit balance pays the amount he owes.

(f)   Any additional money is distributed.

(a)

(b)

(c)

(d)

(e)

(f)

SOLUTION

(a)	Cash	12,000	
	Loss on Realization	70,000	
	Other Assets		82,000
(b)	Eccleston, Capital	35,000	
	Kapela, Capital	17,500	
	Harmin, Capital	17,500	
	Loss on Realization		70,000
(c)	Liabilities	48,000	
	Cash		48,000
(d)	Kapela, Capital	2,000	
	Cash		2,000
(e)	Cash	5,000	
	Eccleston, Capital		5,000
(f)	Kapela, Capital	2,500	
	Harmin, Capital	2,500	
	Cash		5,000

Summary of Transactions

Transaction	Cash	Other Assets	Liabilities	Eccleston, Capital	Kapela, Capital	Harmin, Capital
Balance	$38,000	$82,000	$48,000	$30,000	$22,000	$20,000
(a), (b)	+12,000	−82,000		−35,000	−17,500	−17,500
	$50,000		$48,000	($ 5,000)	$ 4,500	$ 2,500
(c)	−48,000		−48,000			
	$ 2,000			($ 5,000)	$ 4,500	$ 2,500
(d)	− 2,000				−2,000	
				($ 5,000)	$ 2,500	$ 2,500
(e)	+ 5,000			+ 5,000		
	$ 5,000				$ 2,500	$ 2,500
(f)	− 5,000				− 2,500	− 2,500

Chapter 3

The Corporation: Organization

3.1 CHARACTERISTICS OF THE CORPORATION

In essence, the corporation is an artificial being, created by law and having a *continuous* existence regardless of its changing membership. The members are the stockholders; they own the corporation but are distinct from it. As a separate legal entity, the corporation has all the rights and responsibilities of a person, such as entering into contracts, suing and being sued in its own name, and buying, selling, or owning property.

Advantages of the Corporate Form

The corporate form of business in the United States, when compared to the sole proprietorship or partnership, has several important advantages:

Limited liability of stockholders. Each stockholder is accountable only for the amount he or she invests in the corporation. If the company should fail, the creditors cannot ordinarily look beyond the assets of the corporation for settlement of their claims.

Ready transfer of ownership. Ownership of a corporation is evidenced by stock certificates; this permits stockholders to buy or sell their interests in a corporation without interfering with the management of the business. Through the medium of organized exchanges, millions of shares of stock change hands each day.

Continued existence. The death or incapacity of a partner may dissolve a partnership, but the corporation's existence is independent of the stockholders.

Legal entity. The corporation can sue and be sued, make contracts, buy and sell in its own name. This is in contrast to the sole proprietorship, which must, by law, use individual names in all legal matters.

Ease of raising capital. The first two advantages above make the corporation an attractive investment for stockholders. Compare this to the partnership, where capital raising is restricted by the number of partners, the amounts of their individual assets, and the prospect of unlimited liability.

Disadvantages of the Corporate Form

Taxation. Federal and state income taxes constitute the greatest disadvantage of the corporate form. Neither these taxes nor the others outlined below are imposed on the sole proprietorship or the partnership.

Tax Rate

Federal income tax:	
$0–$50,000	15%
$50,000–$75,000	25%
Over $75,000	34%

State income tax: Varies among the states.

Right to do business. An annual payment is required by each state for conducting business in that state.

Franchise tax. This tax is another charge by the state for doing business there. The nationwide average rate is about 2%.

These are taxes borne directly by the corporation; besides them there are:

Taxes on dividends. The stockholders must pay income taxes on any distribution of corporate income made to them (dividends). This amounts to a *double taxation* of the dividends, since, as a part of corporate earnings, they are already subject to income taxes as described above.

Organization costs. The corporation comes into existence with the granting of a charter by the state. For this, the state charges a fee. In addition, there is the cost of printing stock certificates, and various legal and promoters' fees. The total amount is charged to Organization Costs and is carried as an intangible asset on the balance sheet.

Other disadvantages. Various departments of the federal and state governments have the right to exercise certain restrictions and to demand financial reports of the corporation—in particular, the annual report. Vital financial data of the corporation may thereby be disclosed to competitors.

The corporation must operate in accordance with its charter, whereas the sole proprietor or partnership is not so limited.

3.2 CORPORATE TERMINOLOGY

The *stockholder*, as an owner of the business, has the right (*a*) to vote (one vote for every share of stock held), (*b*) to share in profits, (*c*) to transfer ownership, (*d*) to share in the distribution of assets in case of liquidation.

The *board of directors* is elected by the stockholders within the framework of the articles of incorporation. Their duties include the appointing of corporate officers, determining company policies, and the distribution of profits.

A *share* of stock represents a unit of the stockholders' interest in the business. The *par value* of a share is an arbitrary amount established in the corporation's charter and printed on the face of each stock certificate. It bears no relation to the *market value*, i.e., the current purchase or selling price. There are several categories of stock shares:

Authorized shares are shares of stock which a corporation is permitted to issue (sell) under its articles of incorporation.

Unissued shares are authorized shares that have not yet been offered for sale.

Subscribed shares are shares that a buyer has contracted to purchase at a specific price on a certain date. The shares will not be issued until full payment has been received.

Treasury stock represents shares that have been issued and later reacquired by the corporation.

Outstanding stock represents shares authorized, issued, and in the hands of stockholders. (Treasury stock is not outstanding, as it belongs to the corporation and not to the stockholders.)

3.3 EQUITY ACCOUNTING FOR THE CORPORATION

Accounting for the corporation is distinguished from accounting for the sole proprietorship or the partnership by the treatment of owners' (stockholders') equity, which, in the corporation, is separated into *paid-in capital* and *retained earnings*. The reason for this separation is that most states prohibit corporations from paying dividends from other than retained earnings. Paid-in capital is further divided, and so we have three major capital accounts:

Capital Stock. This account shows the par value of the stock issued by the corporation.

Additional Paid-in Capital. Amounts paid in beyond the par value of stock.

Retained Earnings. The accumulated earnings arising from profitable operation of the business.

EXAMPLE 1   Operation at a Profit

Assume that on January 1 two separate businesses are formed, a sole proprietorship operated by Ira Sochet and a corporation having four stockholders. Assume further that the single owner invested $20,000, while the four stockholders each bought 500 shares of common stock at $10 per share. The entries to record the investments are:

Sole Proprietorship			Corporation		
Cash	20,000		Cash	20,000	
Ira Sochet, Capital		20,000	Common Stock		20,000

After a year's operations the net income of each enterprise was $5,000. In the sole proprietorship, the Expense and Income Summary balance is transferred to the capital account; in the corporation, the balance is transferred to Retained Earnings. Thus:

Sole Proprietorship			*Corporation*	
Expense and Income Summary	5,000		Expense and Income Summary	5,000
Ira Sochet, Capital		5,000	Retained Earnings	5,000

The balance sheets of the two firms are identical except for the owners' equity sections, which appear as follows:

Sole Proprietorship		*Corporation*	
Ira Sochet, Capital, Jan. 1, 19X1	$20,000	Common Stock, $10 par (2,000 shares authorized and issued)	$20,000
Add: Net Income	5,000	Retained Earnings	5,000
Ira Sochet, Capital, Dec. 31, 19X1	$25,000	Stockholders' Equity	$25,000

EXAMPLE 2 Operation at a Loss

During the second year of operations, both firms in Example 1 lost $7,000, an amount that exceeds the first year's profits. Observe the difference in the two balance sheets:

Sole Proprietorship		*Corporation*	
Ira Sochet, Capital, Jan. 1, 19X2	$25,000	Common Stock, $10 par (2,000 shares authorized and issued)	$20,000
Deduct: Net Loss	(7,000)	Deduct: Deficit	(2,000)*
Ira Sochet, Capital, Dec. 31, 19X2	$18,000	Stockholders' Equity	$18,000

*Retained Earnings	
7,000	5,000

The $7,000 was treated as a net loss in the sole proprietorship; in the corporation, it was reduced by the net profit from the first year and titled "Deficit."

3.4 COMMON AND PREFERRED STOCK

Common Stock

If a corporation issues only one class of stock, it is known as *common stock*, with all shares having the same rights. The ownership of a share of common stock carries with it the right to:

1. Vote in the election of directors and in the making of certain important corporate decisions

2. Participate in the corporation's profits

3. Purchase a proportionate part of future stock issues

4. Share in assets upon liquidation

Preferred Stock

In order to appeal to a broader market, the corporation may also issue *preferred stock*. This class of stock does not ordinarily carry voting rights (although such rights are sometimes conferred by a special provision in the charter); however, as its name implies, this stock does take preference over common stock in several respects.

Prior claim against earnings. The board of directors has the power to declare and distribute dividends to the stockholders. In such distributions, the claims of preferred stock are honored before those of common stock. However, the amount of dividends paid to preferred stock is usually limited to a fixed percentage of par value, while no limit is usually placed on the amount paid to common stock. From an accounting viewpoint, the priority in receiving dividends constitutes the most important benefit of preferred stock.

EXAMPLE 3

Eppy Corporation has outstanding 1,000 shares of $100 par preferred stock with a preference of a $5 dividend (5% of $100 par value), and 3,000 shares of common stock. Net income was $20,000 and $40,000 for the first two years of operations. The board of directors has authorized the distribution of all profits.

	Year 1	Year 2
Net profit	$20,000	$40,000
Dividends on preferred (1,000 shares, $5 per share)	5,000	5,000
Balance to common	$15,000	$35,000
Number of common shares	÷3,000	÷3,000
Common stock dividend per share	$5.00	$11.67

Prior claim to assets. If, upon liquidation of a corporation, the assets that remain after payment of all creditors are not sufficient to return the full amount of the capital contributions of preferred and common stockholders, payment must first be made to preferred stockholders. Any balance would then go to common stockholders.

Preferred stock may also carry the following benefits:

Call privilege. The issuing company has the right to redeem (call) the stock at a later date for a predetermined price. This call price would be in excess of the original issue price, such as 105% of par value.

Conversion privilege. The stockholder, at his option, may convert preferred stock into common stock. This might be done if the corporation's common stock should become more desirable than the preferred stock because of large earnings (see Example 3).

Participation in Earnings

In Example 3 the preferred stock was *nonparticipating*: It did not partake in dividends beyond a certain fixed percentage. *Participating* preferred stock, on the other hand, shares in dividends with common stock, usually as follows:

1. The amount stipulated in the preferred stock agreement is paid to preferred stock.
2. A dividend of the same amount or based on the same percentage rate is paid to common stock.
3. Any additional earnings are divided between preferred and common stock in the manner set forth in the agreement.

If, after step 1, insufficient earnings remain to allow step 2, then the remainder is divided equally among the common shares.

EXAMPLE 4

The data for Eppy Corporation is as in Example 3, except that preferred stock is now fully participating. The distribution of net profit for the first and second year would be as follows:

Net Profit $20,000	Preferred	Common
To Preferred (1,000 shares, $5 per share)	$5,000	—
To Common (3,000 shares, $5 per share)	—	$15,000
	$5,000	$15,000
Amount per Share	$5	$5

Net Profit $40,000	Preferred	Common
To Preferred (1,000 shares, $5 per share)	$ 5,000	—
To Common (3,000 shares, $5 per share)	—	$15,000
	$ 5,000	$15,000
*Balance: 1/4 to Preferred	5,000	—
3/4 to Common	—	15,000
	$10,000	$30,000
Amount per Share	$10	$10

*The balance is divided in the ratio 1:3, which is the ratio of 1,000 shares to 3,000 shares.

Cumulative Preferred Stock

To ensure the continuity of dividends in the event that there is no dividend declared during some period, the corporation may issue a class of preferred stock for which dividends accumulate. Holders of this *cumulative* preferred stock must be paid their back dividends (*arrears*) before common stockholders receive any dividends.

EXAMPLE 5

Eppy Corporation, with 1,000 shares of cumulative preferred stock paying $5 per share and 3,000 shares of common stock, declares no dividends for the first year. In the second year, all net profits are to be distributed. The net profit for the second year is $40,000.

	First Year	Second Year
To Preferred (1,000 shares, $5 dividend)	—	$10,000, or $10 per Share*
To Common (3,000 shares)	—	30,000, or $10 per Share
Net Profit		$40,000

*$5 per share for each of two years.

Suppose now that Eppy Corporation did not declare dividends for two years and that the profit for the *third year* was $40,000.

	First Year	Second Year	Third Year
To Preferred (1,000 shares, $5 dividend)	—	—	$15,000, or $15 per Share*
To Common (3,000 shares)	—	—	25,000, or $8.33 per Share
Net Profit			$40,000

*$5 per share for each of three years.

Most preferred stock is cumulative, and we shall make this assumption in the remaining chapters. We shall also assume the stock to be nonparticipating.

Solved Problems

3.1   Two separate business organizations, a partnership and a corporation, are formed on January 1, 19X1.

(1)   The initial investments of the partners, Blue and Gray, are $25,000 and $20,000, respectively.

(2)   The Green Corporation has five stockholders, each owning 90 shares of $100 par common.

At the end of the calendar year, the net income of each company was $15,000. (*a*) For each organization, show the proper entry to close the Expense and Income Summary account. (*b*) Prepare a capital statement for the partnership and a stockholders' equity statement for the corporation, as of December 31, 19X1.

(*a*)   Partnership entry

Corporation entry

(*b*)

Partnership Capital Statement

Stockholders' Equity Statement

SOLUTION

(*a*)   Partnership entry

Expense and Income Summary	15,000	
Blue, Capital		7,500*
Gray, Capital		7,500*

*Profits and losses are to be divided equally if no other distribution is specified.

Corporation entry

Expense and Income Summary	15,000	
Retained Earnings		15,000

(*b*)

Partnership Capital Statement

	Blue	Gray	Total
Capital, Jan. 1, 19X1	$25,000	$20,000	$45,000
Add: Net Income	7,500	7,500	15,000
Capital, Dec. 31, 19X1	$32,500	$27,500	$60,000

Stockholders' Equity Statement

Common Stock, $100 par	
(450 shares authorized and issued)	$45,000
Retained Earnings	15,000
Stockholders' Equity	$60,000

3.2   Redo Problem 3.1 assuming that each business suffers a loss of $18,000 in the second year of
operations.

(*a*)   Partnership entry

Corporation entry

(*b*)
Partnership Capital Statement

Stockholders' Equity Statement

SOLUTION

(*a*)   Partnership entry

Blue, Capital	9,000	
Gray, Capital	9,000	
Expense and Income Summary		18,000

Corporation entry

Retained Earnings	18,000	
Expense and Income Summary		18,000

(*b*)
Partnership Capital Statement

	Blue	Gray	Total
Capital, Jan. 1, 19X2	$32,500	$27,500	$60,000
Less: Net Loss	9,000	9,000	18,000
Capital, Dec. 31, 19X2	$23,500	$18,500	$42,000

Stockholders' Equity Statement

Common Stock, $100 par	
(450 shares authorized and issued)	$45,000
Less: Deficit*	(3,000)
Stockholders' Equity	$42,000

*Retained Earnings (Jan. 1, 19X2)	$15,000
Less: Net Loss (Dec. 31, 19X2)	18,000
Deficit	($ 3,000)

3.3 The board of directors' policy is to distribute *all* profits earned in a year to preferred and common stockholders. During the first three years of operations, the corporation earned $68,000, $180,000, and $320,000. There are outstanding 10,000 shares of 6%, $100 par preferred stock and 40,000 shares of common stock. Determine the amount per share applicable to common stock for each of the three years.

	Year		
	1	2	3

SOLUTION

	Year		
	1	2	3
Net Profit (after taxes)	$68,000	$180,000	$320,000
Dividend on preferred stock	60,000	60,000	60,000
Balance to common stock	$ 8,000	$120,000	$260,000
Common dividend per share	$0.20	$3.00	$6.50

3.4 The Agin Corporation has outstanding 5,000 shares of 6%, $100 par participating preferred stock and 20,000 shares of common stock. The preferred stock is entitled to equal participation with common *per share* in any dividend distribution that exceeds both the regular preferred dividend and a $6 per share common dividend. Find the dividend per share on preferred stock and common stock if net profit is (*a*) $110,000, (*b*) $200,000.

(*a*)

	Preferred	Common

(*b*)

	Preferred	Common

SOLUTION

(*a*)

	Preferred	Common
Preferred dividend		
($100 par, 6%, 5,000 shares)	$30,000	—
To common stock (20,000 shares)	—	$80,000
	$30,000	$80,000
Dividend per share	$6	$4

Common stock did not receive its full dividend, $6 \times 20,000 = \$120,000$, because there was not sufficient net income after the payment of the regular preferred dividend. In this case preferred stock receives its stated dividend and common stock the balance.

(b)

	Preferred	Common
Preferred dividend		
($100 par, 6%, 5,000 shares)	$30,000	—
Common dividend (20,000 shares at $6)	—	$120,000
	$30,000	$120,000
Balance ($50,000)	10,000*	40,000†
	$40,000	$160,000
Dividend per share	$8	$8

$*\dfrac{5,000}{5,000 + 20,000} \times \$50,000$

$†\dfrac{20,000}{5,000 + 20,000} \times \$50,000$

3.5   The outstanding stock of the Roland Corporation consists of 10,000 shares of 5%, $100 par cumulative preferred stock and 20,000 shares of $50 par common stock. The company pays out as dividends *all* of its net income. Annual earnings for the last four years are $30,000 (first year of operations), $40,000, $90,000 and $210,000. Determine the distribution per share on each class of stock for each of the four years.

Year	Total	Preferred	Common
1			
2			
3			
4			

SOLUTION

Year	Total	Preferred	Common
1	$ 30,000	$3.00	—
2	40,000	4.00	—
3	90,000	8.00*	$0.50
4	210,000	5.00	8.00

*In order to guarantee the continuation of dividends to preferred stock, no distribution may be made to common stockholders if any dividends are in arrears to preferred stockholders. Since there are arrears for Years 1 and 2, the computation for Year 3 is:

Arrears for Year 1	$20,000	($50,000 − $30,000)
Arrears for Year 2	10,000	($50,000 − $40,000)
Regular dividend for Year 3	50,000	
	$80,000	
Distribution per preferred share	$8.00	

3.6   The outstanding stock of ABC Corporation consists of 20,000 shares of 8%, $50 par cumulative preferred stock and 4,000 shares of $25 par common stock. The company pays out as dividends 90% of its net income. Annual earnings for the last four years are $60,000 (first year of operations), $80,000, $180,000, and $440,000, respectively. Determine the distribution per share on each class of stock for each of the four years.

Year	Total Net Income	To Stockholders	Preferred Stock	Common Stock
1				
2				
3				
4				

SOLUTION

Year	Total Net Income	To Stockholders	Preferred Stock	Common Stock
1	$ 60,000	$ 54,000	$2.70	—
2	80,000	72,000	3.60	—
3	180,000	162,000	5.70*	$1.20
4	440,000	396,000	4.00	7.90

*Arrears for Year 1	$ 26,000	($80,000 − $54,000)
Arrears for Year 2	8,000	($80,000 − $72,000)
Regular dividends for Year 3	80,000	
	$114,000	
Distribution per preferred share in Year 3	$ 5.70	

3.7 The Glatt Company has outstanding 5,000 shares of $100 par, 6% preferred stock and 10,000 shares of $50 par common stock. Complete the table below under each of the following assumptions: (*a*) preferred stock is noncumulative and nonparticipating; (*b*) preferred stock is cumulative and nonparticipating; (*c*) preferred stock is noncumulative and participates equally per share after common stock receives $5 per share dividend.

(*a*)

Year	Total Dividends	Paid to Preferred	Total Arrears	Dividend per Share Preferred	Paid to Common	Dividend per Share Common
1	$ 10,000					
2	25,000					
3	40,000					
4	80,000					
5	200,000					

(*b*)

Year	Total Dividends	Paid to Preferred	Total Arrears	Dividend per Share Preferred	Paid to Common	Dividend per Share Common
1	$ 10,000					
2	25,000					
3	40,000					
4	80,000					
5	200,000					

(*c*)

Year	Total to Dividends	Paid Preferred	Total Arrears	Dividend per Share Preferred	Paid to Common	Dividend per Share Common
1	$ 10,000					
2	25,000					
3	40,000					
4	80,000					
5	200,000					

SOLUTION

(a)

Year	Total Dividends	Paid to Preferred	Total Arrears	Dividend per Share Preferred	Paid to Common	Dividend per Share Common
1	$ 10,000	$10,000	—	$2.00	—	—
2	25,000	25,000	—	5.00	—	—
3	40,000	30,000	—	6.00	$ 10,000	$ 1.00
4	80,000	30,000	—	6.00	50,000	5.00
5	200,000	30,000	—	6.00	170,000	17.00

(b)

Year	Total Dividends	Paid to Preferred	Total Arrears	Dividend per Share Preferred	Paid to Common	Dividend per Share Common
1	$ 10,000	$10,000	$20,000	$2.00	—	—
2	25,000	25,000	25,000	5.00	—	—
3	40,000	40,000	15,000	8.00	—	—
4	80,000	45,000	—	9.00	$ 35,000	$ 3.50
5	200,000	30,000	—	6.00	170,000	17.00

(c)

Year	Total Dividends	Paid to Preferred	Total Arrears	Dividend per Share Preferred	Paid to Common	Dividend per Share Common
1	$ 10,000	$10,000	—	$ 2.00	—	—
2	25,000	25,000	—	5.00	—	—
3	40,000	30,000	—	6.00	$ 10,000	$ 1.00
4	80,000	30,000	—	6.00	50,000	5.00
*5	200,000	70,000	—	14.00	130,000	13.00

*In Year 5 preferred stockholders receive a normal dividend of $30,000 and common stockholders a normal dividend of $50,000. The balance, $200,000 − ($30,000 + $50,000) = $120,000, is divided equally among the 15,000 preferred and common shares. Thus, each share gets an additional $8, as shown below.

	Preferred		**Common**		**Total**
Normal dividend	$30,000		$ 50,000		$ 80,000
Participating dividend	40,000	(5,000 × $8)	80,000	(10,000 × $8)	120,000
	$70,000		$130,000		$200,000

Chapter 4

The Corporation:
Stock Issue and Book Value

4.1 ISSUE OF STOCK

Issue at Par

When a corporation is organized, the charter states how many shares of common and preferred stock are authorized. Often more stock is authorized than is intended to be sold immediately. This allows the corporation to expand in the future without applying to the state for permission to issue more shares. When stock is sold for cash and issued immediately, the entry to record the security has the usual form: Cash is debited and the particular security is credited.

EXAMPLE 1

Carey Corporation, organized on January 1 with an authorization of 10,000 shares of common stock ($40 par), issues 8,000 shares at par for cash. The entry to record the stockholders' investment and the receipt of cash is:

Cash	320,000	
Common Stock		320,000

If, in addition, Carey Corporation issues 1,000 shares of preferred 5% stock ($100 par) at par, the combined entry would be:

Cash	420,000	
Preferred Stock		100,000
Common Stock		320,000

A corporation may accept property other than cash in exchange for stock. If this occurs, the assets should be recorded at fair market value, usually as determined by the board of directors of the company.

EXAMPLE 2

In exchange for 1,000 shares of $100-par common stock, Walker Corporation receives, at fair market value, machinery worth $50,000, and land and buildings worth $30,000 and $20,000, respectively. The transaction is recorded as:

Machinery	50,000	
Land	30,000	
Buildings	20,000	
Common Stock		100,000

Issue at a Premium or a Discount

The market price of stock is influenced by many factors, such as potential earning power, general business conditions and other prospects, financial condition and earnings records, and dividend records. Stock will be sold at a price above par if investors are willing to pay the excess, or *premium*. The premium is not profit to the corporation but rather part of the investment of the stockholders.

EXAMPLE 3

Carey Corporation issues 8,000 shares of its authorized 10,000 shares of common stock ($40 par) for $45 a share. The entry to record the transaction is:

Cash	360,000	
Common Stock		320,000
Premium on Common Stock		40,000

If the purchaser will not pay par value, the corporation may issue the stock at a price below par. The difference between par value and the lower price is called the *discount*.

EXAMPLE 4

Carey Corporation issues 1,000 shares of 5% preferred stock ($100 par) at 98.

Cash	98,000	
Discount on Preferred Stock	2,000	
Preferred Stock		100,000

EXAMPLE 5

Based on Examples 3 and 4, the stockholders' equity section of the balance sheet of Carey Corporation is as follows:

Paid-in Capital		
Preferred Stock, 5%, $100 par		
(1,000 shares authorized and		
issued)	$100,000	
Less: Discount on Preferred Stock	2,000	$ 98,000
Common Stock, $40 par		
(10,000 shares authorized, 8,000		
shares issued)	$320,000	
Premium on Common Stock	40,000	360,000
Total Paid-in Capital		$458,000
Retained Earnings		22,000*
Stockholders' Equity		$480,000

*Assumed.

4.2 BOOK VALUE

The *book value*, also known as equity per share, is obtained by dividing the stockholders' equity amount by the number of shares outstanding. It thus represents the amount that would be distributed to each share of stock if the corporation were to be dissolved.

Individual book values for common and preferred stock are defined by separating the stockholders' equity amount into two parts and dividing each part by the corresponding number of shares. All premiums and discounts, as well as retained earnings or deficits, go to common stock only. (See Example 6.)

EXAMPLE 6

For the data in Example 5, the allocation of the total equity between preferred and common stock would be:

Total equity	$480,000
Allocation to preferred stock	100,000
Balance to common stock	$380,000

and the book values would be:

$$\text{Book value of preferred} = \frac{\$100,000}{1,000 \text{ shares}} = \$100 \text{ per share}$$

$$\text{Book value of common} = \frac{\$380,000}{8,000 \text{ shares}} = \$47.50 \text{ per share}$$

Summary: Chapters 3 and 4

1. The right to vote and to share in the profits of the company rests with the _____ .

2. The greatest disadvantage of the corporate form of business is the _____ on income.

3. The value established for stock is called _____ .

4. Shares of stock that a corporation is allowed to sell are called _____ .

5. The profit and loss of the corporation is recorded in the _____ account.

6. If a corporation issues only one class of stock, it is known as _____ .

7. To achieve a broader market and a more attractive issue price, preferred stock may _____ in profits beyond the specified rate.

8. To ensure the right to unbroken dividends, _____ stock may be issued.

9. The amount paid in excess of par by a purchaser of newly issued stock is called a _____ , while the amount paid below par is known as a _____ .

10. Past dividends owed to preferred stockholders are called dividends in _____ .

Answers: (1) stockholders; (2) tax; (3) par value; (4) authorized shares; (5) Retained Earnings; (6) common stock; (7) participate; (8) cumulative preferred; (9) premium, discount; (10) arrears

Solved Problems

4.1   On January 1 the J. Walter's Corporation issued for cash at par 5,000 shares of its authorized 10,000 shares of $10 par common stock. Three months later it was decided to issue another 5,000 shares of common stock at par and also 1,000 shares of 5%, $100 par preferred stock at par. What entries are required to record the January and April transactions?

Jan. 1		
Apr. 1		

SOLUTION

Jan. 1	Cash	50,000	
	Common Stock		50,000
Apr.1	Cash	150,000	
	Common Stock		50,000
	Preferred Stock		100,000

4.2 For Problem 4.1, present the stockholders' equity section (*a*) as of January 31, (*b*) as of April 30.

(*a*)

(*b*)

SOLUTION

(*a*) Paid-in Capital

Common Stock, $10 par		
(10,000 shares authorized, 5,000 shares issued)	$ 50,000	
Stockholders' Equity		$ 50,000

(*b*) Paid-in Capital

Preferred Stock, 5%, $100 par		
(1,000 shares authorized and issued)	$100,000	
Common Stock, $10 par		
(10,000 shares authorized and issued)	100,000	
Stockholders' Equity		$200,000

4.3 Rund Corporation issues 2,000 shares of 6%, $50 par preferred stock at $48 and 5,000 shares of $25 par common stock at $30. (*a*) Present the entry needed to record the above information. (*b*) Present the stockholders' equity section.

(a)

(b)

SOLUTION

(a)

Cash		246,000	
Discount on Preferred Stock		4,000	
Preferred Stock			100,000
Common Stock			125,000
Premium on Common Stock			25,000

(b)

Paid-in Capital			
Preferred Stock, 6%, $50 par	$100,000		
Less: Discount on Preferred Stock	4,000	$ 96,000	
Common Stock, $25 par	$125,000		
Add: Premium on Common Stock	25,000	150,000	
Stockholders' Equity		$246,000	

4.4 Boaches, Inc., receives in exchange for 3,000 shares of $100 par preferred stock and 2,000 shares of $50 par common stock the following fixed assets:

Asset	Cost	Fair Market Value
Building	$200,000	$125,000
Land	100,000	80,000
Machinery	150,000	150,000
Equipment	60,000	45,000

Provide the entry to record the above information.

SOLUTION

Building	125,000	
Land	80,000	
Machinery	150,000	
Equipment	45,000	
Preferred Stock		300,000
Common Stock		100,000

4.5 The Toback Corporation agrees to issue 10,000 shares of common stock in exchange for equipment valued at $250,000. Present the required journal entry if par value of the common stock is (*a*) $25, (*b*) $20, (*c*) $30.

(*a*)

(*b*)

(*c*)

SOLUTION

(*a*)	Equipment	250,000	
	Common Stock		250,000
(*b*)	Equipment	250,000	
	Common Stock		200,000
	Premium on Common Stock		50,000
(*c*)	Equipment	250,000	
	Discount on Common Stock	50,000	
	Common Stock		300,000

4.6 On January 1, J. Cutler, Inc., was organized with an authorization of 5,000 shares of preferred 6% stock, $100 par, and 10,000 shares of $25 par common stock.

(*a*) Record the following transactions:

Jan. 10 Sold half of the common stock at $28 for cash.
Jan. 15 Issued 2,000 shares of preferred and 1,000 shares of common at par in exchange for land and building with fair market values of $140,000 and $85,000, respectively.
Mar. 6 Sold the balance of the preferred stock for cash at $105.

(*b*) Present the stockholders' equity section of the balance sheet as of March 6.

(a)

Jan. 10		
Jan. 15		
Mar. 6		

(b)

SOLUTION

(a)

Jan. 10	Cash	140,000	
	Common Stock		125,000
	Premium on Common Stock		15,000
Jan. 15	Land	140,000	
	Building	85,000	
	Preferred Stock		200,000
	Common Stock		25,000
Mar. 6	Cash	315,000	
	Preferred Stock		300,000
	Premium on Preferred Stock		15,000

(b)

Paid-in Capital		
Preferred Stock, 6%, $100 par		
(5,000 shares authorized and issued)	$500,000	
Add: Premium on Preferred Stock	15,000	$515,000
Common Stock, $25 par		
(10,000 shares authorized, 6,000 shares issued)	$150,000	
Add: Premium on Common Stock	15,000	165,000
Total Paid-in Capital		$680,000

4.7 On March 1, Fawn Corporation was organized with an authorization of 10,000 shares of preferred 8% stock $75 par, and 20,000 shares of $30 par common stock.

(a) Record the following transactions:

Mar. 15 Sold half of the common stock at $32 cash per share.
Mar. 28 Issued 4,000 shares of preferred and 2,000 shares of common at par in exchange for land with a fair market value of $360,000.
Apr. 3 Sold the balance of the preferred and common for par.

(b) Prepare the Paid-in Capital portion of the stockholders' equity section.

(a)

Mar. 15		
Mar. 28		
Apr. 3		

(b) Paid-in Capital:

SOLUTION

(a)

Mar. 15	Cash	320,000	
	Common Stock		300,000
	Premium on Common Stock		20,000
Mar. 28	Land	360,000	
	Preferred Stock		300,000
	Common Stock		60,000
Apr. 3	Cash	690,000	
	Preferred Stock		450,000
	Common Stock		240,000

(b)

Paid-in Capital:			
Preferred Stock, 8%, $75.00 par			
(10,000 shares authorized and issued)		$ 750,000	
Common Stock, $30 par			
(20,000 shares authorized, 20,000 issued)	$600,000		
Premium on Common Stock	20,000	620,000	
Total Paid-in Capital		$1,370,000	

4.8 Corporations A and B each have 10,000 shares of common stock outstanding. Assuming that the two stocks have the same book value, complete the following table:

	Corporation A	Corporation B
Assets	$350,000	?
Liabilities	100,000	$ 70,000
Common Stock	200,000	175,000
Retained Earnings	?	?

SOLUTION

	Corporation A	Corporation B
Assets	$350,000	$320,000†
Liabilities	100,000	70,000
Common Stock	200,000	175,000
Retained Earnings	50,000*	75,000‡

---

*Assets	=	Liabilities	+	Stockholders' Equity
$350,000	=	$100,000	+	($200,000 + ?)

†Assets	=	Liabilities	+	Stockholders' Equity
?	=	$70,000	+	$250,000

‡Because the book values of the common stock in both corporations are identical, Corporation B must have the same total for stockholders' equity: $250,000 ($175,000 + $75,000).

4.9 The corporation's equity accounts appear below:

Preferred Stock, 5%, $100 par (5,000 shares authorized, 3,000 shares issued)	$300,000
Discount on Preferred Stock	30,000
Common Stock, $50 par (10,000 shares authorized, 4,000 shares issued)	200,000
Premium on Common Stock	10,000
Retained Earnings (credit balance)	35,000

In order to secure additional funds, the board of directors approved the following proposals:

(1) To borrow $100,000, with an 8% mortgage
(2) To sell the remaining common stock at par
(3) To issue the balance of the preferred stock in exchange for equipment valued at $185,000

Prepare (a) journal entries for the transactions and (b) the stockholders' equity section.

(a) (1)

(2)

(3)

(b) _____

SOLUTION

(a)

(1)	Cash		100,000	
	Mortgage Payable			100,000
(2)	Cash		300,000	
	Common Stock			300,000
(3)	Equipment		185,000	
	Discount on Preferred Stock		15,000	
	Preferred Stock			200,000

(b)

Paid-in Capital:		
Preferred Stock, 5%, $100 par (5,000 shares authorized and issued)	$500,000	
Less: Discount on Preferred Stock	45,000	$ 455,000
Common Stock, $50 par (10,000 shares authorized and issued)	$500,000	
Add: Premium on Common Stock	10,000	510,000
Total Paid-in Capital		$ 965,000
Retained Earnings		35,000
Total Stockholders' Equity		$1,000,000

4.10 Determine the equity per share of preferred and of common stock, if the balance sheet shows:

(a)

Preferred Stock, $100 par	$200,000
Common Stock, $25 par	100,000
Premium on Common Stock	10,000
Retained Earnings	40,000

(b)

Preferred Stock, $100 par	$200,000
Premium on Preferred Stock	10,000
Common Stock, $25 par	100,000
Retained Earnings (deficit)	(40,000)

(a)   **Preferred Stock**   **Common Stock**

_____

(b)   **Preferred Stock**   **Common Stock**

_____

SOLUTION

(a)

Preferred Stock		Common Stock	
$200,000	To preferred stock	$100,000	Common stock
		10,000	Premium
$100.00	Per share	40,000	Retained earnings
		$150,000	To common share
		$37.50*	Per share

*$150,000 ÷ 4,000 shares. The number of shares outstanding is determined by dividing the value of the stock, $100,000, by its par value, $25.

(b)

Preferred Stock		Common Stock	
$200,000	To preferred stock	$100,000	Common stock
		10,000*	Premium
$100.00	Per share	(40,000)	Deficit
		$ 70,000	To common stock
		$17.50	Per share

*The premium on preferred stock is allocated to common stock when computing equity per share.

4.11 The capital accounts of the Sullivan Corporation are as follows:

Preferred Stock, 7%, $100 par	$1,000,000
Common Stock, $50 par	500,000
Premium on Common Stock	50,000
Retained Earnings	100,000

Dividends are in arrears for the current year and the previous year. Find the equity per share of each class of stock if (a) preferred stock is entitled to par plus unpaid cumulative dividends regardless of the availability of retained earnings; (b) preferred stock is entitled to par plus unpaid cumulative dividends to the extent of retained earnings.

(a)

Preferred Stock	Common Stock

(b)

Preferred Stock	Common Stock

SOLUTION

(a)

Preferred Stock		Common Stock	
$1,000,000	Preferred stock	$500,000	Common stock
140,000*	Dividends in arrears	50,000	Premium
$1,140,000	To preferred stock	100,000	Retained earnings
$114	Per share	(140,000)	Arrears
		$510,000	To common stock
		$51	Per share

*10,000 shares × $7 per share per year × 2 years.

(b)

Preferred Stock		Common Stock	
$1,000,000	Preferred stock	$500,000	Common stock
100,000*	Dividends in arrears	50,000	Premium on common stock
$1,100,000	To preferred stock	100,000	Retained earnings
$110	Per share	(100,000)	Arrears
		$550,000	To common stock
		$55	Per share

*Dividends in arrears amount to $140,000 but can be paid only to the extent of retained earnings ($100,000).

4.12   Below are data from four different corporations, labeled (a) through (d). Determine for each corporation the equity per share of preferred and common stock.

(a)

Preferred Stock, 6%, $100 par	$400,000
Premium on Preferred Stock	40,000
Common Stock, $25 par	250,000
Discount on Common Stock	20,000
Retained earnings	100,000

(b)

Preferred Stock, 6%, $100 par	$500,000
Common Stock, $25 par	100,000
Premium on Common Stock	10,000
Retained Earnings	40,000

The corporation is being dissolved and preferred stock is entitled to receive $110 upon liquidation.

(c)

Preferred Stock, 7%, $100 par	$500,000
Common, Stock, $50 par	500,000
Retained Earnings	50,000

Dividends on preferred stock are in arrears for three years, including the present year. Preferred stock is entitled to par plus payment of dividends in arrears up to the extent of retained earnings.

(d)

Preferred Stock, 7%, $100 par	$500,000
Premium on Preferred Stock	20,000
Common Stock, $50 par	500,000
Discount on Common Stock	10,000
Retained Earnings	70,000

Dividends on preferred stock are in arrears for three years, including the present year. Preferred stock is entitled to par plus payment of dividends in arrears regardless of the availability of retained earnings.

(a)

Preferred Stock	Common Stock

(b)

Preferred Stock	Common Stock

(c)

Preferred Stock	Common Stock

(d)

Preferred Stock	Common Stock

SOLUTION

(a)

Preferred Stock		Common Stock	
$400,000	To preferred stock	$250,000	Common stock
$100	Per share	40,000	Premium on preferred stock
		(20,000)	Discount on common stock
		100,000	Retained earnings
		$370,000	To common stock
		$37	Per share

(b)

Preferred Stock		Common Stock	
$550,000	To preferred stock	$100,000	Common stock
$110	Per share	10,000	Premium
		40,000	Retained earnings
		(50,000)	Preferred liquidation excess
		$100,000	To common stock
		$25	Per share

(c)

Preferred Stock		Common Stock	
$500,000	Preferred stock	$500,000	Common stock
50,000	Dividends in arrears	50,000	Retained earnings
$550,000	To preferred stock	(50,000)	Preferred dividend arrears
$110	Per share	$500,000	To common stock
		$50	Per share

(d)

Preferred Stock		Common Stock	
$500,000	Preferred stock	$500,000	Common stock
105,000	Dividends in arrears	20,000	Premium on preferred
$605,000	To preferred stock	(10,000)	Discount on common
$121	Per share	70,000	Retained earnings
		(105,000)	Preferred dividend arrears
		$475,000	To common stock
		$47.50	Per share

Chapter 5

The Corporation:
Subscriptions and Treasury Stock

5.1 STOCK SUBSCRIPTIONS

In the examples in Chapter 4, it was assumed that capital stock is paid for in full immediately upon issuance. This is indeed the case when the corporation sells the stock in the open market or through an underwriter (who pays the corporation in full and then resells to investors at a higher price). On occasion, however, stock may be purchased on an installment plan (*subscription basis*). The buyer signs a subscription stating the number of shares he or she wishes to purchase and the method of installment payment. The subscription is treated like any other receivable: The account Stock Subscriptions Receivable is debited when the subscription is received and is credited as the subscriber makes payments. Any balance in Stock Subscriptions Receivable at the end of the year is classified on the balance sheet as a current asset.

When the number of subscribers is large, a separate *subscribers' ledger* is established with an account for each subscriber and with Stock Subscriptions Receivable as the control account. This control account operates in the same manner as does Accounts Receivable for the accounts receivable ledger.

Stock bought on subscription is not actually issued by the corporation until final payment has been received. Therefore, a *temporary* account, Capital Stock Subscribed, is used to record the par value of the subscribed stock. This account is credited at the time the subscription is received and debited when final payment is made and the stock is issued. If a balance sheet is prepared prior to the issuance of the stock, Capital Stock Subscribed appears in the stockholders' equity section.

If the subscription is sold for a price above or below par, Stock Subscriptions Receivable is debited for the subscription price rather than for par value. Capital Stock Subscribed is credited at par, while the difference between the subscription price and par is debited to the discount account (if the subscription price is below par) or credited to the premium account (if the subscription price exceeds par).

In case the corporation offers more than one class of stock for subscription, each class has its own subscriptions receivable and stock subscribed accounts.

EXAMPLE 1

The Phillips Corporation received various subscriptions for a total of 5,000 shares of $10-par common stock. The subscription price was $12 per share, with a down payment of 50% of this price. Three months later the balance was paid and the stock issued.

Entry 1	Common Stock Subscriptions Receivable	60,000	
	Common Stock Subscribed		50,000
	Premium on Common Stock		10,000
	To record subscriptions to 5,000 shares of $10-par common stock at $12		
	Cash	30,000	
	Common Stock Subscriptions Receivable		30,000
	To record receipt of 50% down payment on the subscription price		
Entry 2	Cash	30,000	
	Common Stock Subscriptions Receivable		30,000
	To record final payment of the subscription price		

Entry 3   Common Stock Subscribed   50,000

Common Stock   50,000

Issued stock certificates (5,000 shares at $10 par)

The above transactions have the same final effect in the accounts as if the stock has originally been purchased in full for cash:

Cash		Common Stock Subscriptions Receivable	
(1) 30,000		(1) 60,000	30,000 (1)
(2) 30,000			30,000 (2)

Common Stock Subscribed		Premium on Common Stock	
(3) 50,000	50,000 (1)		10,000 (1)

Common Stock	
	50,000 (3)

Trial Balance

Cash	$60,000	
Premium on Common Stock		$10,000
Common Stock		50,000
	$60,000	$60,000

Default on Subscription

There is always the possibility that a subscriber may pay part of the subscription price but not fulfill his or her obligation. No one method for the accounting of this default prevails, as each corporation must act within the laws of the state of its incorporation. In some states the subscriber will forfeit the amount paid, to compensate the corporation for any damages. This income becomes part of capital and must be shown in an account describing the transaction—for example, Capital from Forfeited Subscriptions. In other states, however, the subscriber who defaults is entitled to a refund or to a number of shares based on the amount paid.

5.2 TREASURY STOCK

Shares of a corporation's issued stock that have been reacquired by the corporation are known as *treasury stock*. A corporation may want to reacquire some of its outstanding stock:

1. To have shares available for resale to its employees in stock option or stock purchase plans

2. To have shares available for use in the acquisition of other companies

3. To keep the price of its stock stable

The differences and similarities between treasury stock and unissued stock should be noted. Treasury stock had at one time been owned by stockholders, whereas unissued stock has never been in stockholders' possession. On the other hand:

1. Both types of stock are equity items rather than assets. (Treasury stock cannot be an asset, as a corporation cannot own itself.)

2. To calculate outstanding stock, both are subtracted from authorized stock.

3. There are no voting rights or dividend distributions for either type.

Most states limit the amount of treasury stock that a corporation may acquire. This is done for the protection of the creditors, whose claims might be jeopardized if a great deal of the corporation's assets had been converted into treasury stock.

Donation of Treasury Stock

If a company finds itself in need of cash, it may ask its stockholders to give shares of stock back to the company to be resold. As there is no cost involved when the company reacquires the donated stock, and as assets, liabilities, and equity are unaffected, the only entry needed to record the acquisition is a memorandum indicating the number of shares reacquired. As this reacquired stock (treasury stock) is sold, Cash is debited and Donated Capital is credited for the amount of the proceeds. When the corporation resells its treasury stock to the public, the par value of the stock is not recognized, and any proceeds received are charged directly to Donated Capital.

EXAMPLE 2

Before a donation of stock, the financial position of Sunco Corporation is as follows:

Sunco Corporation
Balance Sheet
October 1, 19X1

ASSETS		STOCKHOLDERS' EQUITY	
Cash	$ 25,000	Paid-in Capital	
Other Assets	235,000	Common Stock, $25 par	
		(10,000 shares authorized	
		and issued)	$250,000
		Retained Earnings	10,000
Total Assets	$260,000	Stockholders' Equity	$260,000

The corporation (1) receives 1,000 shares of donated stock from its stockholders, (2) sells 600 shares of treasury stock at $30 per share, then (3) sells 300 shares at $20 per share.

Entry 1	Memo: Received 1,000 shares common stock, $25 par, as donation		
Entry 2	Cash	18,000	
	Donated Capital		18,000
Entry 3	Cash	6,000	
	Donated Capital		6,000

Summary

Cash			Donated Capital	
Bal.	25,000		18,000	(2)
(2)	18,000		6,000	(3)
(3)	6,000			

The new financial position of Sunco Corporation appears as follows:

Sunco Corporation
Balance Sheet
October 15, 19X1

ASSETS		STOCKHOLDERS' EQUITY		
Cash	$ 49,000	Paid-in Capital		
Other Assets	235,000	Common Stock, $25 par		
		(10,000 shares authorized		
		and issued, less 100 shares		
		donated treasury stock)		$250,000
		Donated Capital		24,000
		Total Paid-in Capital		$274,000
		Retained Earnings		10,000
Total Assets	$284,000	Stockholders' Equity		$284,000

Purchase of Treasury Stock

Subject to certain legal restrictions, a corporation may acquire treasury stock by buying its own shares from stockholders. Under the most common accounting method, the reacquired stock is recorded at cost, with Treasury Stock debited for its purchase price and Cash credited. The price at which the stock was originally bought and its par value are ignored.

When the stock is resold to the public, Treasury Stock is credited for the purchase price paid by the corporation, while the difference between selling and purchase price is recorded in the account Paid-in Capital from Sale of Treasury Stock. When the balance sheet is prepared, any balance in the treasury stock account is subtracted from the total stockholders' equity.

EXAMPLE 3

Before a purchase of treasury stock, the balance sheet reads:

Sunco Corporation
Balance Sheet
October 1, 19X1

ASSETS		STOCKHOLDERS' EQUITY		
Cash	$ 25,000	Paid-in Capital		
Other Assets	235,000	Common Stock, $25 par		
		(10,000 shares authorized		
		and issued)		$250,000
		Retained Earnings		10,000
Total Assets	$260,000	Stockholders' Equity		$260,000

The corporation (1) buys 500 shares of its outstanding stock at 30, (2) sells 200 shares of treasury stock at 40, then (3) sells 200 shares at 25.

Entry 1	Treasury Stock	15,000	
	Cash		15,000

Entry 2   Cash   8,000
                    Treasury Stock   6,000
                    Paid-in Capital from Sale of Treasury Stock   2,000

Entry 3   Cash   5,000
                    Paid-in Capital from Sale of Treasury Stock   1,000
                    Treasury Stock   6,000

Summary

Cash				Treasury Stock				Paid-in Capital from Sale of Treasury Stock			
Bal.	25,000	15,000	(1)	(1)	15,000	6,000	(2)	(3)	1,000	2,000	(2)
(2)	8,000					6,000	(3)				
(3)	5,000										

In the adjustment of the balance sheet, the $1,000 credit balance in Paid-in Capital from Sale of Treasury Stock is treated in the same manner as a premium on a common stock. (A debit balance would be treated as a discount.)

Sunco Corporation
Balance Sheet
December 31, 19X1

ASSETS		STOCKHOLDERS' EQUITY	
Cash	$ 23,000	Paid-in Capital	
Other Assets	235,000	Common Stock, $25 par (10,000 shares authorized and issued)	$250,000
		Paid-in Capital from Sale of Treasury Stock	1,000
		Total Paid-in Capital	$251,000
		Retained Earnings	10,000
		Total	$261,000
		Less: Treasury Stock (100 shares at cost)	3,000
Total Assets	$258,000	Stockholders' Equity	$258,000

The result of the treasury stock transactions was to reduce the number of outstanding common shares by 100 (the number of treasury shares kept by the corporation).

Summary

1. When a person agrees to pay over a period of time for stock purchased, the sale is said to be on _____ .

2. When the number of subscribers is large, a separate _____ is established.

3. The control account used in Question 2 is the _____ account.

4. Stock Subscriptions Receivable is a _____ on the balance sheet, while Capital Stock Subscribed is part of _____ .

5. Whether there is a premium or discount on subscribed stock, Capital Stock Subscribed is credited at _____ .

6. Issued stock later reacquired by the corporation is known as _____ .

7. Treasury stock may be acquired by either _____ or _____ .

8. Treasury stock cannot be considered an asset, because a corporation _____ .

9. In order to calculate outstanding stock, treasury stock is subtracted from _____ .

10. The difference between selling and purchase price of treasury stock is recorded in the account _____ .

Answers: (1) subscription; (2) subscriber's ledger; (3) Stock Subscriptions Receivable; (4) current asset, stockholders' equity; (5) par; (6) treasury stock; (7) purchase, donation; (8) cannot own itself; (9) authorized and issued stock; (10) Paid-in Capital from Sale of Treasury Stock

Solved Problems

5.1 Identify each account in the table below by inserting its balance (debit or credit) in the appropriate column.

Account	Asset	Liability	Equity	Income	Expense
Common Stock					
Common Stock Subscriptions Receivable					
Common Stock Subscribed					
Discount on Preferred Stock					
Donated Capital					
Expense and Income Summary					
Organization Costs					
Paid-in Capital from Sale of Treasury Stock					
Premium on Common Stock					
Retained Earnings					
Treasury Stock					

SOLUTION

Account	Asset	Liability	Equity	Income	Expense
Common Stock			Credit		
Common Stock Subscriptions Receivable	Debit				
Common Stock Subscribed			Credit		
Discount on Preferred Stock			Debit		
Donated Capital			Credit		
Expense and Income Summary				Credit	
Organization Costs	Debit				
Paid-in Capital from Sale of Treasury Stock			Credit		
Premium on Common Stock			Credit		
Retained Earnings			Credit		
Treasury Stock			Debit		

5.2 On May 1 the Bard Corporation received subscription to 42,000 shares of $50 par common stock at $52 per share, collecting 60% of the subscription price. Four months later the balance was received and the stocks were issued. Present the entries to record the transaction.

(a) May 1

(b)

(a) Sept. 1

(b)

SOLUTION

(a)	May 1 Common Stock Subscription Receivable	2,184,000	
	Common Stock Subscribed		2,100,000
	Premium on Common Stock		84,000
(b)	Cash	1,310,400	
	Common Stock Subscriptions Receivable		1,310,400
(a)	Sept. 1 Cash	873,600	
	Common Stock Subscriptions Receivable		873,600
(b)	Common Stock Subscribed	2,100,000	
	Common Stock		2,100,000

5.3   On September 1 the Stevens Corporation received subscriptions at $14 to 50,000 shares of $10-par common stock, collecting one-half of the subscription price immediately. Three months later the remainder was received and the stock issued. Present entries to record the transactions.

Sept. 1		
Dec. 1		

SOLUTION

Sept. 1	Common Stock Subscriptions Receivable	700,000	
	Common Stock Subscribed		500,000
	Premium on Common Stock		200,000
	Cash	350,000	
	Common Stock Subscriptions Receivable		350,000
Dec. 1	Cash	350,000	
	Common Stock Subscriptions Receivable		350,000
	Common Stock Subscribed	500,000	
	Common Stock		500,000

The final effect on the accounts is the same as if the stock had originally been purchased in full for cash:

Cash			
Sept. 1	350,000		
Dec. 1	350,000		

Common Stock Subscribed			
Dec. 1	500,000	500,000	Sept. 1

Common Stock Subscriptions Receivable			
Sept. 1	700,000	350,000	Sept. 1
		350,000	Dec. 1

Common Stock		
	500,000	Dec. 1

Premium on Common Stock		
	200,000	Sept. 1

5.4   Using the information in Problem 5.3, present the asset and equity sections of the balance sheet (*a*) as of September 2 and (*b*) as of December 2.

(a) **ASSETS**   **STOCKHOLDERS' EQUITY**

(b) **ASSETS**   **STOCKHOLDERS' EQUITY**

SOLUTION

(a)

ASSETS		STOCKHOLDERS' EQUITY	
Cash	$350,000	Paid-in Capital	
Common Stock		Common Stock Subscribed	$500,000
Subscriptions Receivable	350,000	Premium on Common Stock	200,000
Total Assets	$700,000	Total Stockholders' Equity	$700,000

(b)

ASSETS		STOCKHOLDERS' EQUITY	
Cash	$700,000	Paid-in Capital	
		Common Stock	$500,000
		Premium on Common Stock	200,000
Total Assets	$700,000	Total Stockholders' Equity	$700,000

5.5 On the first day of operations, the High Tech Corporation completed several transactions that culminated in the following account balances:

High Tech Corporation
Trial Balance
October 31, 19X1

Cash	$120,000	
Common Stock Subscriptions		
Receivable	240,000	
Equipment	160,000	
Land	136,000	
Building	144,000	
Mortgage Payable		$280,000
Preferred Stock, 8%, $100		100,000
Premium on Preferred		20,000
Common Stock, $60 par		160,000
Common Stock Subscribed		200,000
Premium on Common Stock		40,000
	$800,000	$800,000

Prepare all entries to record the results of the above transactions, assuming that (1) land and building were secured by a mortgage; (2) common stock was issued at par in exchange for the equipment; and (3) no cash was received on the common stock subscribed.

SOLUTION

Cash	120,000	
Preferred Stock		100,000
Premium on Preferred Stock		20,000
Common Stock Subscriptions Receivable	240,000	
Common Stock Subscribed		200,000
Premium on Common Stock		40,000
Equipment	160,000	
Common Stock		160,000
Land	136,000	
Building	144,000	
Mortgage Payable		280,000

5.6 Prepare in general journal form the entries required for the transactions listed below.

Apr.   2   Murry Corporation received 10,000 shares of donated common stock from a stockholder (30,000 shares had been issued at par value $45).

July 10   Sold 7,000 shares of treasury stock at $54 per share.

July 28   Sold the remaining shares of treasury stock at $42 per share.

Aug.   4   Purchased 3,000 shares of treasury stock at $40 per share.

Apr. 2		
July 10		
July 28		
Aug. 4		

SOLUTION

Apr. 2	Memo: Receipt of 10,000 shares of donated common stock		
July 10	Cash	378,000	
	Donated Capital		378,000
July 28	Cash	126,000	
	Donated Capital		126,000
Aug. 4	Treasury Stock	120,000	
	Cash		120,000

5.7 Prepare in general journal form the entries required for the transactions below:

Mar. 1 Englefield Corporation received 5,000 shares of donated common stock from its stockholders (15,000 shares had been issued at par value of $20).

May 1 Sold 3,000 shares of treasury stock at $25 per share.

July 1 Sold the remaining shares of treasury stock at $15.

(a) Mar. 1

(b) May 1

(c) July 1

SOLUTION

(a)

Mar. 1	Memo*: Receipt of 5,000 shares of donated common stock		

*There is no entry needed as no cost is involved when the company acquires treasury stock by donation.

(b)

May 1	Cash	75,000	
	Donated Capital		75,000

(c)

July 1	Cash	30,000	
	Donated Capital		30,000

5.8 From the information in Problem 5.7, prepare the stockholders' equity section as of (a) March 31, (b) May 31, and (c) July 31.

(a)

(b)

(c)

SOLUTION

(a) Paid-in Capital:
     Common Stock, $20 par (15,000 shares authorized and issued,
       less 5,000 shares of donated treasury stock) $300,000
     Stockholders' Equity $300,000

(b) Paid-in Capital:
     Common Stock, $20 par (15,000 shares authorized and issued,
       less 2,000 shares of donated treasury stock) $300,000
     Donated Capital 75,000
     Stockholders' Equity $375,000

(c) Paid-in Capital:
     Common Stock, $20 par (15,000 shares authorized and issued) $300,000
     Donated Capital 105,000
     Stockholders' Equity $405,000

5.9 Suppose that in Problems 5.7 and 5.8, the 5,000 shares of treasury stock had been purchased for $120,000 instead of being donated. (a) What entries would be required? (b) Prepare the stockholders' equity section as of March 31, May 31, and July 31.

(a) Mar. 1

     May 1

     July 1

(b) **Mar. 31**

     May 31

July 31
_____
_____
_____
_____
_____
_____
_____
_____

SOLUTION

(a)

Mar. 1	Treasury Stock	120,000	
	Cash		120,000

May 1	Cash	75,000	
	Treasury Stock		72,000*
	Paid-in Capital from Sale of Treasury Stock		3,000

*(3,000/5,000) × $120,000

July 1	Cash	30,000	
	Paid-in Capital from Sale of Treasury Stock	18,000	
	Treasury Stock		48,000*

*(2,000/5,000) × $120,000

(b)

Mar. 31

Paid-in Capital	
Common Stock, $20 par (15,000 shares authorized and issued)	$300,000
Less: Treasury Stock	120,000
Stockholders' Equity	$180,000

May 31

Paid-in Capital	
Common Stock, $20 par (15,000 shares authorized and issued)	$300,000
Paid-in Capital from Sale of Treasury Stock	3,000
Total Paid-in Capital	$303,000
Less: Treasury Stock	48,000
Stockholders' Equity	$255,000

July 31

Paid-in Capital	
Common Stock, $20 par (15,000 shares authorized and issued)	$300,000
Less: Paid-in Capital from Sale of Treasury Stock	15,000
Stockholders' Equity	$285,000

5.10 The board of directors of the Kotin Corporation presented to the stockholders for their approval a plan to expand facilities at a cost of $1,000,000. This sum was to come from:

(a) Issuing 5,000 shares of 7% preferred stock, $50 par, at par.

(b) Borrowing $450,000 from the bank.

(c) A donation of 10% of all common stock outstanding (100,000 shares authorized and issued, par value $20). It is assumed that this treasury stock will be sold for $30 per share.

Prepare entries for the transactions.

(a)

(b)

(c)

SOLUTION

(a)	Cash	250,000	
	Preferred Stock		250,000
(b)	Cash	450,000	
	Notes Payable		450,000
(c)	Memo: Received 10,000 shares common stock as a donation		
	Cash	300,000	
	Donated Capital		300,000

5.11 The stockholders' equity section at December 31 is presented below:

Paid-in Capital:			
Preferred Stock, 7%, $50 par (10,000 shares authorized, 5,000 shares issued)	$ 250,000		
Premium on Preferred Stock	25,000	$ 275,000	
Common Stock $40 par (100,000 shares authorized, 70,000 shares issued)	$2,800,000		
Premium on Common Stock	70,000	2,870,000	
Total Paid-in Capital		$3,145,000	
Retained Earnings		440,000	
Total Stockholders' Equity		$3,585,000	

The selected transactions below took place during the following fiscal year.

Jan. 10 Purchased 8,000 shares of treasury common for $400,000.

Mar. 15 Received subscriptions to 10,000 shares of common stock at $41, collecting half the subscription price.

May 10 Sold 2,000 shares of treasury common for $90,000.

Aug. 31　Sold 5,000 shares of treasury common for $255,000.

Sept. 15　Received the final 50% on common stock subscribed and issued the shares.

Present the entries to record the transactions.

Jan. 10		
Mar. 15		
May 10		
Aug. 31		
Sept. 15		

SOLUTION

Jan. 10	Treasury Stock	400,000	
	Cash		400,000
Mar. 15	Common Stock Subscriptions Receivable	410,000	
	Common Stock Subscribed		400,000
	Premium on Common Stock		10,000
	Cash	205,000	
	Common Stock Subscriptions Receivable		205,000
May 10	Cash	90,000	
	Paid-in Capital from Sale of Treasury Stock	10,000	
	Treasury Stock		100,000
Aug. 31	Cash	255,000	
	Treasury Stock		250,000
	Paid-in Capital from Sale of Treasury Stock		5,000
Sept. 15	Cash	205,000	
	Common Stock Subscriptions Receivable		205,000
	Common Stock Subscribed	400,000	
	Common Stock		400,000

5.12 Below is the stockholders' equity section of the balance sheet as of April 30.

Paid-in Capital		
Preferred Stock, 5%, $100 par (20,000 shares authorized, 15,000 shares issued)	$1,500,000	
Premium on Preferred Stock	40,000	$1,540,000
Common Stock, $50 par (100,000 shares authorized, 60,000 shares issued)	$3,000,000	
Premium on Common Stock	100,000	3,100,000
Total Paid-in Capital		$4,640,000
Retained Earnings		500,000
Stockholders' Equity		$5,140,000

During the next eight months, selected transactions are:

May 10 Received subscriptions to 5,000 shares of preferred stock at $102, collecting half of the subscription price.

July 15 Purchased 10,000 shares of treasury common for $400,000.

Sept. 10 Received 25% of the subscription price on the preferred stock.

Oct. 25 Sold 6,000 shares of treasury common for $300,000.

Dec. 10 Received the balance due on preferred stock subscribed and issued the shares.

Dec. 20 Sold 3,000 shares of treasury common for $100,000.

Prepare all entries necessary to record the above information.

May 10		
July 15		
Sept. 10		
Oct. 25		
Dec. 10		
Dec. 20		

SOLUTION

May 10	Preferred Stock Subscriptions Receivable	510,000	
	Preferred Stock Subscribed		500,000
	Premium on Preferred Stock		10,000
	Cash	255,000	
	Preferred Stock Subscriptions Receivable		255,000
July 15	Treasury Stock	400,000	
	Cash		400,000
Sept. 10	Cash	127,500	
	Preferred Stock Subscriptions Receivable		127,500
Oct. 25	Cash	300,000	
	Treasury Stock [(6,000/10,000)× \$400,000]		240,000
	Paid-in Capital from Sale of Treasury Stock		60,000
Dec. 10	Cash	127,500	
	Preferred Stock Subscriptions Receivable		127,500
	Preferred Stock Subscribed	500,000	
	Preferred Stock		500,000
Dec. 20	Cash	100,000	
	Paid-in Capital from Sale of Treasury Stock	20,000	
	Treasury Stock		120,000

5.13 Based on the information in Problem 5.12, prepare the stockholders' equity section of the balance sheet as of (*a*) July 31 and (*b*) December 31.

(*a*)

(b)

SOLUTION

(a) Paid-in Capital

Preferred Stock, 5%, $100 par (20,000 shares authorized, 15,000 shares issued)	$1,500,000	
Premium on Preferred stock	50,000	$1,550,000
Preferred Stock Subscribed		500,000
Common Stock, $50 par (100,000 shares authorized, 60,000 shares issued)	$3,000,000	
Premium on Common Stock	100,000	3,100,000
Total Paid-in Capital		$5,150,000
Retained Earnings		500,000
Total		$5,650,000
Less: Treasury Stock (10,000 shares at cost)		400,000
Total Stockholders' Equity		$5,250,000

(b) Paid-in Capital

Preferred Stock, 5%, $100 par (20,000 shares authorized and issued)	$2,000,000	
Premium on Preferred Stock	50,000	$2,050,000
Common Stock, $50 par (100,000 shares authorized, 60,000 shares issued)	$3,000,000	
Premium on Common Stock	100,000	3,100,000
Paid-in Capital from Sale of Treasury Stock		40,000*
Total Paid-in Capital		$5,190,000
Retained Earnings		500,000
Total		$5,690,000
Less: Treasury Stock (1,000 shares at cost)		40,000
Total Stockholders' Equity		$5,650,000

*   **Paid-in Capital from Sale of Treasury Stock**

Dec. 20	20,000	60,000	Oct. 25

Chapter 6

The Corporation: Retained Earnings

6.1 THE NATURE OF RETAINED EARNINGS

Retained earnings are the accumulative earnings of a corporation that have not been distributed to stockholders. Normally the Retained Earnings account will have a credit balance, but a debit balance (deficit) results if accumulated losses have exceeded accumulated profits. This deficit would be deducted from the total of the stockholders' equity accounts in the balance sheet.

6.2 APPROPRIATION OF RETAINED EARNINGS

Retained earnings may be specifically reserved (*appropriated*) or may be free (*unappropriated*) for distribution as dividends. When an appropriation account is established, the Retained Earnings account is debited and the appropriation account credited. This has the effect of reducing the balance of unappropriated retained earnings by the amount put into the appropriation account. The following appropriations are frequently made:

Appropriation for contingencies. An account is created to set up a reserve to meet unforeseen happenings—for instance, the event that future earnings might be insufficient to allow the normal payment of dividends.

Appropriation for expansion. The corporation may have plans to expand operations or build more facilities. It might, in the future, sell additional stock to obtain the assets needed, or it might float bonds.

Appropriation for treasury stock. In most states, an amount equal to the cost of the treasury stock held by the corporation must be set aside out of retained earnings. Like the payment of a cash dividend, a purchase of treasury stock reduces both corporate assets and stockholders' equity. Thus, the restriction on retained earnings serves to protect the corporation's creditors and other concerned parties.

Appropriation for bonded indebtedness. A corporation may borrow money by issuing bonds (see Sec. 7.1) and, as an inducement, may agree to protect the loan by restricting dividends.

EXAMPLE 1

The Barker Corporation has retained earnings of $60,000. The board of directors decides to set up a fund of $5,000 annually out of earnings, to meet unforeseen happenings.

Entry 1	Retained Earnings	5,000	
	Appropriation for Contingencies		5,000

The board also decides to set up an appropriation of $20,000 a year for the next 5 years for plant expansion.

Entry 2	Retained Earnings	20,000	
	Appropriation for Expansion		20,000

The corporation buys some of its own stock for $10,000; this calls for a restriction of retained earnings, limiting the distribution of dividends.

Entry 3	Retained Earnings	10,000	
	Appropriation for Treasury Stock		10,000

When, at a later date, the corporation sells $8,000 of its treasury stock, part of the appropriation for treasury stock becomes unnecessary.

Entry 4   Appropriation for Treasury Stock   8,000
                                   Retained Earnings   8,000

The corporation decides to borrow, through an issue of bonds, $75,000 over a 10-year period. Equal annual appropriations of $7,500 would be made over the life of the bonds.

Entry 5   Retained Earnings   7,500
                             Appropriation for Bonded Indebtedness   7,500

Summary

Retained Earnings				Appropriation for Contingencies		Appropriation for Expansion	
(1)	5,000	60,000	Bal.	5,000	(1)	20,000	(2)
(2)	20,000	8,000	(4)				
(3)	10,000						
(5)	7,500						

Appropriation for Treasury Stock				Appropriation for Bonded Indebtedness	
(4)	8,000	10,000	(3)	7,500	(5)

Retained Earnings Statement
Barker Corporation
Year Ended December 31, 19X1

Appropriated:		
For Contingencies	$ 5,000	
For Expansion	20,000	
For Treasury Stock	2,000	
For Bonded Indebtedness	7,500	
Total Appropriated Retained Earnings		$34,500
Unappropriated Retained Earnings		25,500
Total Retained Earnings		$60,000

6.3 DIVIDENDS

A *dividend* is a distribution to stockholders by a corporation's board of directors. Dividends are ordinarily made from retained earnings. (In the event of liquidation, distributions may be made from paid-in capital.) Unless otherwise stated we will be concerned with distributions from retained earnings only. The distribution may be in cash, other assets, promissory notes (scrip), or the corporation's own stock. In this section we confine ourselves to distributions of cash or of stock.

Cash Dividends

The cash dividend is the most common type of dividend; it is normally stated in terms of dollars and cents per share. (Sometimes, if the dividend is on preferred stock, it is stated as a percentage of par.) A cash dividend can be declared only if (1) there is sufficient cash; (2) there is sufficient unappropriated retained earnings; and (3) there has been a positive vote by the board of directors. When a dividend is declared, it becomes a current liability of the corporation.

There are three different dates associated with the declaration of a dividend:

(1) *Date of declaration.* On this date the board of directors votes to declare the dividend.

(2) *Date of record.* Any person listed as a stockholder on this date is legally entitled to receive the dividend.

(3) *Date of payment.* On this date payment is made to stockholders of record [see (2)].

A journal entry is made on the date of declaration, reducing the stockholders' equity and recording the liability. No entry is needed for the date of record. A second entry, on the date of payment, records the payment.

EXAMPLE 2

On December 15, 19X1, the board of directors declares a dividend of $2 per share on 20,000 shares of outstanding common stock, to stockholders of record as of January 2, 19X2. Payment is to be made on January 10, 19X2.

Dec. 15, 19X1	Retained Earnings	40,000	
	Cash Dividend Payable		40,000
Jan. 2, 19X2	Memo: $2 per share dividend on 20,000 shares		
Jan. 10, 19X2	Cash Dividend Payable	40,000	
	Cash		40,000

Stock Dividends

A stock dividend is a pro rata distribution of stock to stockholders; it requires a transfer of retained earnings to paid-in capital. From an accounting viewpoint, the number of shares to be distributed by the corporation must be less than 25% of the number of shares outstanding before the distribution. Anything greater than 25% would be a *stock split*.

To maintain a consistent dividend policy the corporation may issue a stock dividend in place of cash when it is necessary or desirable to conserve cash. Unlike a cash dividend, *a stock dividend provides no income to stockholders and affects neither corporate assets nor owners' equity in the corporation* (see Examples 3 and 4). However, it does sustain the stockholders' confidence in the company.

EXAMPLE 3

The balances in the stockholders' equity accounts of the Nuco Corporation, as of December 1, are:

Paid-in Capital	
Common Stock, $100 par	
(15,000 shares authorized,	
10,000 shares issued)	$1,000,000
Premium on Common Stock	120,000
Total Paid-in Capital	$1,120,000
Retained Earnings	430,000
Stockholders' Equity	$1,550,000

On December 24, 19X1, the board of directors declares a 10% stock dividend distributable to the shareholders of record as of January 2, 19X2, for payment January 18, 19X2. If the market value of the stock on December 24 is $120 per share, the following entries will be made to record the dividend declaration and payment:

Dec. 24, 19X1	Retained Earnings	120,000*	
	Common Stock Dividend Distributable		100,000
	Premium on Common Stock		20,000
	*1,000 shares (10% × 10,000 shares) at $120 per share		
Jan. 2, 19X2	Memo: 1,000 shares stock dividend at $120 per share		
Jan. 18, 19X2	Common Stock Dividend Distributable	100,000	
	Common Stock		100,000

In effect, the above transactions transfer $120,000 from Retained Earnings to Paid-in Capital and increase the number of shares outstanding by 1,000.

If a balance sheet is prepared between the date of declaration (December 24) and the date of payment (January 18), then the amount of the stock dividend distributable is shown in the Paid-in Capital section:

Paid-in Capital	
Common Stock, $100 par	
(15,000 shares authorized,	
10,000 shares issued)	$1,000,000
Premium on Common Stock	140,000
Common Stock Dividend	
Distributable	100,000
Total Paid-in Capital	$1,240,000
Retained Earnings	310,000
Stockholders' Equity	$1,550,000

EXAMPLE 4

Jean Schneider owned 100 shares in the Nuco Corporation. Her holdings before and after the transactions of Example 3 are displayed below.

	Prior to Dividend	After Payment of Dividend
Nuco Corporation		
Common stock	$1,000,000	$1,100,000
Premium on common stock	120,000	140,000
Total	$1,120,000	$1,240,000
Retained earnings	430,000	310,000
Stockholders' equity	$1,550,000	$1,550,000
Number of shares outstanding	÷ 10,000	÷ 11,000
Book value per share	$155	$140.91
Jean Schneider		
Number of shares owned	100	110
Book value of shares	$15,500	$15,500
Percent of corporation owned	1%	1%

Before the stock dividend, Schneider owned 100/10,000, or 1%, of the corporation, with a book value of $15,500. After January 12, when the stock dividend was paid, she owned 110/11,000, or 1%, and her holdings were still valued at $15,500. The stock dividend transactions had no effect on either Schneider's books or the corporation's capital. Though a stock dividend might appear to be beneficial for both the corporation and the individual stockholder, neither benefits, as no shift in equity or assets occurs.

Effect on Retained Earnings

The Retained Earnings account is affected whether a cash or stock dividend is declared.

EXAMPLE 5

The accounts below show changes that affect retained earnings. The retained earnings statement for the end of the period appears directly below these accounts.

Retained Earnings

June 30	Semiannual Dividend	8,000		Jan. 1	Balance	100,000
Dec. 31	Semiannual Dividend	8,000		Dec. 31	Net Income	60,000
Dec. 31	Stock Dividend	12,000		Dec. 31	Appropriation for Contingencies	10,000
Dec. 31	Appropriation for Expansion	20,000				

Appropriation for Expansion		Appropriation for Contingencies	
	Jan. 1 Bal. 35,000	Dec. 31 10,000	Jan. 1 Bal. 25,000
	Dec. 31 20,000		

Statement of Retained Earnings

Appropriated:			
For Expansion			
Balance, Jan. 1	$35,000		
Add: Transfer from Retained Earnings	20,000	$ 55,000	
For Contingencies			
Balance, Jan. 1	$25,000		
Deduct: Transfer to Retained Earnings	10,000	15,000	
Appropriated Retained Earnings			$ 70,000
Unappropriated:			
Balance, Jan. 1		$100,000	
Add: Net Income	$60,000		
Transfer from Appropriation for Contingencies	10,000	70,000	
		$170,000	
Deduct: Cash Dividends Declared	$16,000		
Stock Dividends Declared	12,000		
Transfer to Appropriation for Expansion	20,000	48,000	
Unappropriated Retained Earnings			$122,000
Total Retained Earnings			$192,000

Stock Split

On occasion the board of directors of a corporation may decide on a stock split. This is a decision to reduce the par value of their stock and to issue a proportionate number of shares. The purpose of the stock split generally is to reduce the price per share in order to encourage more investors to purchase the company's shares.

EXAMPLE 6

Sonar Corporation, with 100,000 shares of $5 par stock outstanding, decides to reduce the par value to $1 and increase the number of shares to 500,000.

No entry is required, because the corporation's account balances do not change.

EXAMPLE 7

Based on the above information, William Howard, who owned 50 shares of stock with a par value of $5 before the split, would now own 250 shares of stock with a par value of $1. The total value of his holdings has not changed.

Before Split		After Split
50 shares		250 shares
× $5 par		× $1 par
$250	←――――――→	$250
	same value	

Summary

1. The undistributed accumulated earnings of a corporation are known as _____ .

2. If accumulated losses exceed accumulated profits, the result is a _____ .

3. Retained earnings put in reserve are called _____ ; otherwise, they are called _____ .

4. A distribution to stockholders from retained earnings by a corporation's board of directors is known as a _____ .

5. In the event of a firm's liquidation, distributions could be made from _____ .

6. The date of _____ determines which stockholders receive a dividend.

7. Dividends are most commonly in the form of _____ , but on occasion dividends may be declared in _____ .

8. A pro rata distribution of stock to stockholders is called a _____ .

9. The _____ account is affected whether a cash or stock dividend is declared.

Answers: (1) retained earnings; (2) deficit; (3) appropriated, unappropriated; (4) dividend; (5) paid-in capital; (6) record; (7) cash, stock; (8) stock dividend; (9) Retained Earnings

Solved Problems

6.1 The retained earnings accounts of the Cozy Corporation are as follows:

Appropriation for Bonded Indebtedness	$110,000
Appropriation for Contingencies	130,000
Unappropriated	200,000

During the month of August, the following transactions took place:

(*a*) Declared cash dividend of $60,000.

(*b*) Decreased the appropriation for contingencies to $100,000.

(*c*) Established an Appropriation for Plant Expansion account with annual deposits of $20,000.

(*d*) Increased the appropriation for bonded indebtedness by $20,000.

Record the transactions.

(*a*)

(*b*)

(c)

(d)

SOLUTION

(a)	Retained Earnings	60,000	
	Cash Dividend Payable		60,000
(b)	Appropriation for Contingencies	30,000	
	Retained Earnings		30,000
(c)	Retained Earnings	20,000	
	Appropriation for Plant Expansion		20,000
(d)	Retained Earnings	20,000	
	Appropriation for Bonded Indebtedness		20,000

6.2   The retained earnings accounts of the B.I.C. Corporation are as follows:

Appropriation for Bonded Indebtedness	$140,000
Appropriation for Contingencies	170,000
Unappropriated	260,000

During the month of May the following transactions took place:

(a)   Declared cash dividend of $86,000.

(b)   Decreased the appropriation for contingencies $90,000.

(c)   Established an Appropriation for Land Acquisition account with annual deposits of $12,000.

(d)   Increased the appropriation for bonded indebtedness by $18,000.

Record the transactions.

(a)

(b)

(c)

(d)

SOLUTION

(a)	Retained Earnings	86,000	
	Cash Dividend Payable		86,000
(b)	Appropriation for Contingencies	90,000	
	Retained Earnings		90,000

(c)	Retained Earnings	12,000	
	Appropriation for Land Acquisition		12,000
(d)	Retained Earnings	18,000	
	Appropriation for Bonded Indebtedness		18,000

6.3   The retained earnings accounts of Brandon Company appear below.

Appropriation for Contingencies		Appropriation for Plant Expansions	
	60,000		110,000

Retained Earnings	
	240,000

During the month of December, the board of directors decided to:

(a)   Increase the appropriation for contingencies *by* $20,000

(b)   Decrease the appropriation for plant expansion *to* $60,000

(c)   Establish an appropriation for bonded indebtedness, with an annual deposit of $10,000

(d)   Declare a cash dividend of $70,000

Present entries to record the decisions of the board.

(a)

(b)

(c)

(d)

SOLUTION

(a)	Retained Earnings	20,000	
	Appropriation for Contingencies		20,000
(b)	Appropriation for Plant Expansion	50,000	
	Retained Earnings		50,000
(c)	Retained Earnings	10,000	
	Appropriation for Bonded Indebtedness		10,000
(d)	Retained Earnings	70,000	
	Cash Dividend Payable		70,000

6.4 Prepare a retained earnings statement for Brandon Company (Problem 6.3).

Brandon Company
Statement of Retained Earnings
Year Ended December 31, 19X1

Appropriated Retained Earnings

Unapropriated Retained Earnings

Total Retained Earnings

SOLUTION

Brandon Company
Statement of Retained Earnings
Year Ended December 31, 19X1

Appropriated Retained Earnings			
Appropriation for Contingencies, Balance	$ 60,000		
Add: Appropriation Increase	20,000	$ 80,000	
Appropriation for Plant Expansion, Balance	$110,000		
Less: Appropriation Decrease	50,000	60,000	
Appropriation for Bonded Indebtedness		10,000	
Total Appropriated Retained Earnings			$150,000
Unappropriated Retained Earnings			
Balance	$240,000		
Add: Transfer from Appropriation			
for Plant Expansion	50,000	$290,000	
Less: Transfer to Appropriation			
for Contingencies	$ 20,000		
Transfer to Appropriation			
for Bonded Indebtedness	10,000		
Cash Dividends Declared	70,000	100,000	
Total Unappropriated Retained Earnings			190,000
Total Retained Earnings			$340,000

6.5 A $45,000 cash dividend was declared by the Bowes Corporation. The dates involved in the cash dividend transactions are November 5, 19X1, December 14, 19X1, and January 6, 19X2. (*a*) What is the significance of each date, and what entry is made on it? (*b*) What legal obligation does the declaration of the dividend carry?

(*a*)

Nov. 5, 19X1		
Dec. 14, 19X1		
Jan. 6, 19X2		

SOLUTION

(*a*)

Nov. 5, 19X1. Date of declaration		
Retained Earnings	45,000	
Cash Dividend Payable		45,000
Dec. 14, 19X1. Date of record		
Memo: Stockholders owning shares on this		
date will receive the cash dividend		
Jan. 6, 19X2. Date of payment		
Cash Dividend Payable	45,000	
Cash		45,000

(*b*) The board of directors of a corporation does not legally have to declare a dividend, even though sufficient cash and unappropriated retained earnings exist. However, if a cash dividend is declared, it becomes a current liability of the corporation.

6.6 On June 15 the board of directors declared a cash dividend of $0.80 per share on 70,000 shares of outstanding common stock to stockholders of record as of July 1, payable on July 15.

(*a*) Record the necessary entries.

(*b*) Under what conditions is a dividend declared?

(*a*)

SOLUTION

(a)

Date of declaration			
June 15	Retained Earnings	56,000	
	Cash Dividend Payable		56,000
Date of record			
July 1	Memo: $0.80 per share dividend		
	on 70,000 shares		
Date of payment			
July 15	Cash Dividend Payable	56,000	
	Cash		56,000

(b) Before the board of directors decides to declare a cash dividend they take into consideration such factors as (1) sufficient balance in retained earnings, (2) sufficient cash, and (3) estimated net income.

6.7   On May 10, the board of directors declared a cash dividend of $110.00 per share on 120,000 of outstanding common stock to stockholders of record as of June 1, payable on June 15. Record the necessary entries.

May 10			
June 1			
June 15			

SOLUTION

May 10	Retained Earnings	132,000	
	Cash Dividend Payable		132,000
June 1	Memo: $1.10 per share per dividend		
	on 120,000 shares.		
June 15	Cash Dividend Payable	132,000	
	Cash		132,000

6.8   The stockholders' equity section of the Willard Corporation's balance sheet shows:

Paid-in Capital
   Common Stock, $100 par
     (10,000 shares authorized,
      8,000 shares issued) $800,000
     Premium on Common Stock   40,000 $ 840,000
   Retained Earnings   200,000
   Total Stockholders' Equity $1,040,000

The board of directors declares an annual cash dividend of $7 per share, and, in addition, a 10% stock dividend. At the time of declaration, the fair market value of the common stock to be issued is

$120. Present (*a*) the entry to record the declaration of the cash dividend, (*b*) the entry to record the declaration of the stock dividend, and (*c*) the stockholders' equity section after the completion of the above transactions and the payment of the stock dividend.

(*a*)

(*b*)

(*c*)

SOLUTION

(*a*)	Retained Earnings	56,000	
	Cash Dividend Payable		56,000
(*b*)	Retained Earnings	96,000	
	Stock Dividend Distributable		80,000
	Premium on Common Stock		16,000

(*c*)	Paid-in Capital		
	Common Stock, $100 par (10,000 shares authorized, 8,800 shares issued)	$880,000	
	Premium on Common Stock	56,000	$936,000
	Retained Earnings		48,000
	Total Stockholders' Equity		$984,000

6.9   Redo (*a*) and (*b*) of Problem 6.8 if 1,000 shares of common stock had been reacquired by purchase.

(*a*)

(*b*)

SOLUTION

(*a*)	Retained Earnings	49,000	
	Cash Dividend Payable		49,000*
(*b*)	Retained Earnings	84,000	
	Stock Dividend Distributable		70,000*
	Premium on Common Stock		14,000

*Dividends are neither declared nor paid on treasury stock, whether donated or purchased.

6.10   The accounts below bear on the retained earnings of Ivy Industries during the year.

Appropriation for Plant Expansion				**Appropriation for Contingencies**		
	Jan. 1	Bal. 40,000	Dec. 31	5,000	Jan. 1	Bal. 70,000
	Dec. 31	10,000				

Retained Earnings

Mar. 31	Quarterly Dividend	5,000	Jan. 1	Bal.	205,000
June 30	Quarterly Dividend	5,000	Dec. 31	Appr. for Contingencies	5,000
Sept. 30	Quarterly Dividend	5,000	Dec. 31	Net Income	65,000
Dec. 31	Quarterly Dividend	5,000			
Dec. 31	Appr. for Plant Expansion	10,000			

Prepare a retained earnings statement as of December 31.

Ivy Industries
Statement of Retained Earnings
Year Ended December 31, 19X1

Appropriated Retained Earnings

Unappropriated Retained Earnings

Total Retained Earnings

SOLUTION

Ivy Industries
Statement of Retained Earnings
Year Ended December 31, 19X1

Appropriated Retained Earnings		
Appropriation for Plant Expansion, Jan. 1 Balance	$40,000	
Add: Appropriation, Dec. 31	10,000	$ 50,000

Appropriation for Contingencies, Jan. 1 Balance	$70,000		
Less: Transfer to Retained Earnings	5,000	65,000	
Total Appropriated Retained Earnings			$115,000
Unappropriated Retained Earnings			
Balance, Jan. 1		$205,000	
Add: Transfer from Appropriation for			
Contingencies	$ 5,000		
Net Income	65,000	70,000	
		$275,000	
Less: Cash Dividends Declared	$20,000		
Transfer to Appropriation for			
Plant Expansion	10,000	30,000	
Total Unappropriated Retained Earnings			245,000
Total Retained Earnings			$360,000

6.11 Based on the following information, prepare a retained earnings statement for the Mann Company for the year ended December 31, 19X1.

As of January 1, 19X1:

(1) The balances of the Unappropriated Retained Earnings account was $200,000 and Appropriation for Contingencies was $130,000.

(2) Four quarterly dividends of $10,000 each have been declared.

(3) The Mann Company earned a net profit of $52,000 for the year.

(4) Other affected accounts appear below.

Appropriation for Contingencies		Appropriation for Bonded Indebtedness	
Dec. 31 30,000	Jan. 1 Bal. 130,000		Jan. 1 Bal. 110,000

Mann Company

Statement of Retained Earnings

Year Ended December 31, 19X1

Appropriated Retained Earnings

_____

_____

_____

_____

Unappropriated Retained Earnings

_____

_____

_____

_____

_____

_____

Total Retained Earnings

SOLUTION

Mann Company		
Statement of Retained Earnings		
Year Ended December 31, 19X1		
Appropriated Retained Earnings		
Appropriation for Contingencies, Jan. 1 Balance	$130,000	
Less: Transfer to Retained Earnings	30,000	$100,000
Appropriation for Bonded Indebtedness, Jan. 1		110,000
Total Appropriated Retained Earnings		$210,000
Unappropriated Retained Earnings		
Balance, Jan. 1	$200,000	
Add: Transfer from Appropriation		
for Contingencies	$30,000	
Net Income	52,000	82,000
		$282,000
Less: Cash Dividends Declared		40,000
Total Unappropriated Retained Earnings		242,000
Total Retained Earnings		$452,000

6.12 At its latest meeting, the board of directors of the Conoway Corporation decided to reduce the par value of its common stock from $10 to $5 per share, thus increasing the number of shares outstanding from 100,000 to 200,000. (*a*) If the market price of the stock before the stock split was $12 per share, present the entry to record this stock split. (*b*) What price could a share of stock be expected to sell for immediately after the split?

SOLUTION

(*a*) No entry is required, because there are no changes in the balances of the corporate accounts. However, the stockholders' ledger would be changed to record the increased number of shares issued.

(*b*) $6 ($12 ÷ 2).

6.13 What effect (increase, decrease, no effect) do the following transactions have on assets, liabilities, and stockholders' equity?

	Assets	Liabilities	Stockholders' Equity
Receipt of subscription to stock at par			
Receipt of cash for stock subscription			
Issue of stock fully subscribed			
Receipt of donated stock			
Sale of donated stock			
Purchase of treasury stock			
Sale of treasury stock above par			
Declaration of cash dividend			
Payment of cash dividend			
Declaration of stock dividend			
Payment of stock dividend			
Setting date of record of cash dividend			
Increasing appropriation for expansion			
Decreasing appropriation for contingencies			

SOLUTION

	Assets	Liabilities	Stockholders' Equity
Receipt of subscription to stock at par	Increase	No effect	Increase
Receipt of cash for stock subscription	No effect	No effect	No effect
Issue of stock fully subscribed	No effect	No effect	No effect
Receipt of donated stock	No effect	No effect	No effect
Sale of donated stock	Increase	No effect	Increase
Purchase of treasury stock	Decrease	No effect	Decrease
Sale of treasury stock above par	Increase	No effect	Increase
Declaration of cash dividend	No effect	Increase	Decrease
Payment of cash dividend	Decrease	Decrease	No effect
Declaration of stock dividend	No effect	No effect	No effect
Payment of stock dividend	No effect	No effect	No effect
Setting date of record of cash dividend	No effect	No effect	No effect
Increasing appropriation for expansion	No effect	No effect	No effect
Decreasing appropriation for contingencies	No effect	No effect	No effect

6.14 Based on the balances of the accounts below, prepare a classified balance sheet.

Accounts Receivable	$ 82,000	Equipment	$148,000
Accounts Payable	22,000	Goodwill	40,000
Accumulated Depreciation, Building	14,000	Income Tax Payable	16,000
		Land	50,000
Accumulated Depreciation, Equipment	62,000	Merchandise Inventory	102,000
		Mortgage Payable	124,000
Allowance for Uncollectible Accounts	6,000	Notes Payable	28,000
Building	124,000	Preferred Stock, 6%, $100 par (2,000 shares authorized and issued)	200,000
Cash	245,000	Premium on Common Stock	25,000
Common Stock, $50 par (10,000 shares authorized, 5,000 shares issued)	250,000	Prepaid Insurance	16,000
		Retained Earnings	80,000
Discount on Preferred Stock	20,000		

ASSETS

Current Assets

Total Current Assets

Fixed Assets

Total Fixed Assets

Intangible Assets			
Total Assets			

LIABILITIES
Current Liabilities

Total Current Liabilities			
Long-Term Liabilities			
Total Liabilities			

STOCKHOLDERS' EQUITY
Paid-in Capital

Total Paid-in Capital			
Retained Earnings			
Total Stockholders' Equity			
Total Liabilities and Stockholders' Equity			

SOLUTION

ASSETS			
Current Assets			
Cash		$245,000	
Accounts Receivable	$ 82,000		
Less: Allowance for Uncollectible Accounts	6,000	76,000	
Merchandise Inventory		102,000	
Prepaid Insurance		16,000	
Total Current Assets			$439,000
Fixed Assets			
Equipment	$148,000		
Less: Accumulated Depreciation, Equipment	62,000	86,000	
Building	$124,000		
Less: Accumulated Depreciation, Building	14,000	110,000	
Land		50,000	
Total Fixed Assets			246,000
Intangible Assets			
Goodwill			40,000
Total Assets			$725,000

LIABILITIES

Current Liabilities			
Accounts Payable	$22,000		
Notes Payable	28,000		
Income Tax Payable	16,000		
Total Current Liabilities		$ 66,000	
Long-Term Liabilities			
Mortgage Payable		124,000	
Total Liabilities			$190,000

STOCKHOLDERS' EQUITY

Paid-in Capital			
Preferred Stock, 6%, $100 par			
(2,000 shares authorized and issued)	$200,000		
Less: Discount on Preferred Stock	20,000	$180,000	
Common Stock, $50 par (10,000 shares			
authorized, 5,000 shares issued)	$250,000		
Add: Premium on Common Stock	25,000	275,000	
Total Paid-in Capital		$455,000	
Retained Earnings		80,000	
Total Stockholders' Equity			535,000
Total Liabilities and Stockholders' Equity			$725,000

Chapter 7

The Corporation: Issuing Bonds

7.1 CHARACTERISTICS OF BONDS

A corporation may obtain funds by selling stock or by borrowing through long-term obligations. An issue of bonds is a form of long-term debt in which the corporation agrees to pay interest periodically and to repay the principal at a stated future date.

Bond denominations are commonly multiples of $1,000. A bond issue normally has a term of 10 or 20 years, although some issues may have longer lives. The date at which a bond is to be repaid is known as the *maturity date*. In an issue of *serial bonds*, the maturity dates are spread in a series over the term of the issue. This relieves the corporation of the impact of total payment at one date.

7.2 SECURITY

Mortgages

One method for protecting the investor in bonds is to back the bonds by mortgages on the corporation's property. These are *chattel mortgages*, if placed on movable items such as equipment and machinery, or else *real estate mortgages*.

Trust Indentures

A trustee, usually a trust company or large bank, is chosen by the corporation to safeguard the investors' interest. In an agreement (*indenture*) between the trustee and the corporation, the trustee certifies that the bonds are existent and are genuine. He or she also promises to hold collateral to be used for the issue, and to collect money from the corporation to pay interest and eventually the principal.

Collateral trust bonds are bonds backed by investments held by the issuing corporation. These investments (securities of other corporations) can be sold by the trustee if the corporation defaults on the payment of either interest or principal.

Sinking fund bonds. The issuing corporation deposits annual amounts with the trustee. Together with earnings on sinking fund investments, these deposits add up to the amount due at maturity.

EXAMPLE 1

A $1 million issue of 10-year sinking fund bonds does not require the issuing corporation to set aside $100,000 a year for 10 years ($1,000,000 ÷ 10 years). The deposit per year can be much smaller because of substantial interest earned through compounding. (More on sinking fund bonds is found in Section 8.2.)

Unsecured Bonds

If a firm does not need security to back its bonds, the bonds are known as *debentures*; they are based on the general credit of the company. U.S. government bonds are an example.

7.3 PAYMENT OF INTEREST. OPTIONS

Bonds are divided into two categories according to the way interest is paid.

(1) *Registered bonds.* A registered bond states the name of the owner on the face of the bond. The corporation maintains a register or list of the bond owners and forwards payments to them as interest becomes due.

(2) *Coupon bonds.* Coupon bonds contain no evidence of ownership. Interest is paid to the party who presents a dated coupon attached to the bond.

Certain bonds carry options for conversion or recall:

Convertible bonds. Convertible bonds may be exchanged at a future date for other securities of the issuing corporation, at the option of the *bondholder*. (See Section 8.1.)

Callable bonds. Callable bonds may be recalled before they mature, at the option of the *issuing corporation*. (See Section 8.1.)

7.4 FUNDING BY STOCK VERSUS FUNDING BY BONDS

The major differences between stocks and bonds may be summarized as follows:

	Stocks	**Bonds**
Representation	Ownership in the corporation	A debt of the corporation
Inducement to holders	Dividends	Interest
Accounting treatment	Dividends are a distribution of profits	Interest is an expense
	Stocks are equity	Bonds are a long-term liability
Repayment	—	On a predetermined date

These differences give rise to alternative methods of financing, as in Examples 2 and 3 below.

EXAMPLE 2

The board of directors of a new company has decided that $1,000,000 is needed to begin operations. The controller presents three different methods of financing:

	Method 1 Common Stock	Method 2 (Preferred and Common Stock)	Method 3 (Bonds, Preferred and Common Stock)
Bonds, 5%	—	—	$ 500,000
Preferred stock, 6%, $100 par	—	$ 500,000	250,000
Common stock, $100 par	$1,000,000	500,000	250,000
Total	$1,000,000	$1,000,000	$1,000,000

Subsequent profits before interest on bonds and before taxes are estimated at $300,000; taxes are estimated at 50%.

	Method 1	Method 2	Method 3
Profit	$300,000	$300,000	$300,000
Less: Interest on bonds	—	—	25,000
Net income before taxes	$300,000	$300,000	$275,000
Less: Income taxes	150,000	150,000	137,500
Net income after taxes	$150,000	$150,000	$137,500
Less: Dividends on preferred stock	—	30,000	15,000
Common stock balance	$150,000	$120,000	$122,500
Number of common shares	÷10,000*	÷5,000†	÷2,500‡
Earnings per common share	$15	$24	$49

*$1,000,000/$100

†$500,000/$100

‡$250,000/$100

For the common stockholders, Method 3 (called *debt and equity funding*) is clearly the best. It shows greater earnings because bond interest is deducted for income tax purposes.

EXAMPLE 3

As the amount of profit becomes smaller, Method 1 of Example 2 becomes the best financing method. Assume that the same three methods of funding are under consideration for an anticipated net income of $60,000 before interest and taxes.

	Method 1	Method 2	Method 3
Profit	$60,000	$60,000	$60,000
Less: Interest on bonds	–	–	25,000
Net income before taxes	$60,000	$60,000	$35,000
Less: Income taxes	30,000	30,000	17,500
Net income	$30,000	$30,000	$17,500
Less: Dividends on preferred stock	–	30,000	15,000
Common stock balance	$30,000	–	$ 2,500
Earnings per common share	$3	–0–	$1

7.5   RECORDING AUTHORIZED BOND TRANSACTIONS

A corporation's charter may require that a bond issue receive the prior approval of the stockholders. When the necessary approvals are received and the bonds issued, a memorandum entry is made to record the authorization.

EXAMPLE 4

On December 15, 19X1, the Phillips Corporation authorizes the issue of $100,000 in 5%, 10-year bonds, with interest payable semiannually on June 30 and December 31. A memorandum entry should be made.

Memo: $100,000 in 5%, 10-year bonds authorized

On January 1, 19X2, $75,000 of the $100,000 authorized bond issue is sold to the public. (The reason for authorizing more than the amount issued is that if additional funds are needed later, the unissued bonds can be used.)

Cash	75,000	
Bonds Payable		75,000

The balance sheet presentation of the above information would be:

Long-Term Liabilities:
5%, 10-Year Bonds Payable

Authorized	$100,000	
Less: Unissued	25,000	
Issued		$75,000

If, at a later date, the corporation decides to sell the remaining authorized bonds, the entry to record this additional sale would be:

Cash	25,000	
Bonds Payable		25,000

and the balance sheet liability section would then show a long-term liability of $100,000 for 5%, 10-year bonds payable, authorized and issued.

7.6 PREMIUM AND DISCOUNT ON BONDS

Just as the par value of stock does not measure its market value, the face value of a bond does not represent its market value. The rate of interest that bonds pay helps determine how much investors are willing to pay for the bonds.

EXAMPLE 5

A corporation may issue bonds carrying an interest rate of 6%, while similar bonds on the market pay 7%. Thus investors may not be willing to pay *face* value for the bonds. Conversely, if bonds on the market are paying only 5%, investors may be willing to pay more than the face value of the bonds.

The interest rate paid by the corporation on its bonds depends on (1) the security that the corporation offers, (2) its credit standing, and (3) the current level of bond interest rates. When the corporation issues bonds, it states the rate of interest it will pay (*contract rate*). In the period of time between the authorization and the sale of the bond issue, market interest rates may have changed from their contract rate. Because of this, bonds may be sold at a price above or below their face value.

The difference between the proceeds from the sale of the bonds and their face value is recorded as Premium on Bonds Payable (if issue price exceeds face value) or Discount on Bonds Payable (if issue price is less than face value).

Premium or discount is reflected in the price of bonds, which is stated as a percentage of face value.

EXAMPLE 6

A $1,000 bond issued "at 105" costs $1,050 ($1,000 × 105%); issued "at 98," the same bond costs $980 ($1,000 × 98%).

EXAMPLE 7   Issue at a Premium

When a corporation offers an issue with the interest rate higher than the market rate, buyers will normally pay a premium for the bonds. Suppose than on January 1 the Phillips Corporation sells a $100,000 issue of 10-year, 7% bonds at 104 ($104,000), with interest payable semiannually on June 30 and December 31. The entry to record the sale would be:

Jan. 1	Cash	104,000	
	Bonds Payable		100,000
	Premium on Bonds Payable		4,000

The entries to record the semiannual interest payments would be:

June 30	Interest Expense	3,500	
	Cash		3,500
Dec. 31	Interest Expense	3,500	
	Cash		3,500

Although the interest expense account has a balance of $7,000, this is not the true amount of interest expense for the year. The $4,000 premium received by the corporation should not be treated as income, but rather as interest collected in advance, an adjustment of the contract rate. Thus, the interest expense each year should be reduced by $4,000/10 = $400. The adjusting entry needed to record this spreading out (amortization) of the premium over the life of the bond would be:

Dec. 31	Premium on Bonds Payable	400	
	Interest Expense		400
	To amortize 1/10 of the premium		

and the balance of the Interest Expense account as of December 31 will be $6,600:

Interest Expense

June 30 Interest 3,500	Dec. 31 Premium 400
Dec. 31 Interest 3,500	

Immediately after the sale of the bonds the balance sheet of the Phillips Corporation shows unamortized premium of $4,000:

Long-Term Liabilities:		
Bonds Payable, 5%, 10-year	$100,000	
Add: Unamortized Premium	4,000	$104,000

EXAMPLE 8   Issue at a Discount

If a corporation offers a rate of interest below the market rate, buyers will normally pay less than face value for the bonds. Assume that the Schneider Corporation offers a $1,000,000 issue of 6%, 10-year bonds, while the market rate is 7%. Since the prevailing rate is more than 6%, the highest bid for the bonds, $970,000, was less than face value. Interest is paid annually on December 31.

Cash	970,000	
Discount on Bonds Payable	30,000	
Bonds Payable		1,000,000

The $30,000 discount is treated as extra interest expense that is amortized over the 10-year life of the bonds (compare with Example 7). Hence the entry to record the interest payment each year would be:

Dec. 31	Interest Expense	60,000	
	Cash		60,000
	To record interest charges (6% × $1,000,000)		

and the adjusting entry would be:

Dec. 31	Interest Expense	3,000	
	Discount on Bonds Payable		3,000
	To amortize 1/10 of the discount		

The annual charges to Interest Expense will then appear as:

Interest Expense

Dec. 31 Interest	60,000	
Dec. 31 Discount	3,000	

Immediately after the sale of the bonds, the corporation's balance sheet shows unamortized discount of $30,000:

Long-Term Liabilities:
| Bonds Payable, 6%, 10-year | $1,000,000 | |
| Deduct: Unamortized Discount | 30,000 | $970,000 |

7.7 ACCRUED INTEREST

At times bonds are sold between interest payment dates. This means that a purchaser of the bonds will be charged for the interest that has accrued since the last interest payment. He will, however, recover the accrued interest at the next payment date, when he will receive interest for the *full* period. This procedure frees the corporation from keeping a record of each bond sold and its accrued interest.

EXAMPLE 9

Assume that on January 1 a corporation authorizes $1,000,000 of 6% bonds on which interest is payable on January 1 and July 1. The bonds are not sold to the public until February 1.

Feb. 1	Cash	1,005,000	
	Bonds Payable		1,000,000
	Bond Interest Expense		5,000*

*$1,000,000 × 6% = $60,000
$60,000 ÷ 12 months = $5,000 per month

Five months later, on July 1, the semiannual interest payment will be made for the *full* 6 months. This will include both the 5 months' interest earned by the bondholders and the 1 months' interest that was collected in advance. The entry to record the payment would be:

| July 1 | Bond Interest Expense | 30,000 | |
| | Cash | | 30,000 |

The $25,000 balance interest in the interest expense account is shown below:

Interest Expense	
July 1 30,000	Feb. 1 5,000

We have, till now, assumed that interest was paid in January and July of the same year. However, as the interest period may not coincide with the accounting period, an adjusting entry for accrued interest may be required at the end of each accounting period.

EXAMPLE 10

On March 1, 19X1, the M. Bradley Corporation issues $100,000 of 6%, 10-year bonds, with interest payable semiannually on March 1 and September 1.

Mar. 1, 19X1	Cash	100,000	
	Bonds Payable		100,000
	To record the sale of bonds		

Sept. 1, 19X1	Interest Expense	3,000	
	Cash		3,000
	To record semiannual interest		

Dec. 31, 19X1	Interest Expense	2,000	
	Interest Payable		2,000*
	To record adjustment of interest payable		

*September 1 to December 31 = 4 months
4/6 × $3,000 = $2,000

When the interest is paid on March 1 of the following year, the entry to record the payment would be:

Mar. 1, 19X2	Interest Expense	1,000	
	Interest Payable	2,000	
	Cash		3,000

The above entry is made if no reversing entry occurred. If the reversing-entry method is used, the following entries would be required instead:

Jan. 1, 19X2	Interest Payable	2,000	
	Interest Expense		2,000
	Reversing entry required for interest payable		

Mar. 1, 19X2	Interest Expense	3,000	
	Cash		3,000
	To record interest payment		

Solved Problems

7.1 Three companies have the following structures:

	G Company	H Company	I Company
Bonds Payable, 5%	$1,000,000	$ 600,000	—
Preferred Stock, 6%, $100 par	—	600,000	$1,000,000
Common Stock, $100 par	1,000,000	800,000	1,000,000
Total	$2,000,000	$2,000,000	$2,000,000

Assuming a tax rate of 50% of income, determine the earnings per share of common stock if the net income of each company before bond interest and taxes was (a) $140,000; (b) $500,000.

(a)

	G Company	H Company	I Company

(b)

	G Company	H Company	I Company

SOLUTION

(a)

	G Company	H Company	I Company
Income	$140,000	$140,000	$140,000
Less: Bond Interest	50,000	30,000	—
Income before Taxes	$ 90,000	$110,000	$140,000
Less: Taxes (50%)	45,000	55,000	70,000
Net Income	$ 45,000	$ 55,000	$ 70,000
Less: Preferred Dividend	—	36,000	60,000
To Common Stock	$ 45,000	$ 19,000	$ 10,000
Number of Common Shares	÷10,000	÷8,000	÷10,000
Earnings per Share	$4.50	$2.38	$1.00

(b)

	G Company	H Company	I Company
Income	$500,000	$500,000	$500,000
Less: Bond Interest	50,000	30,000	—
Income before Taxes	$450,000	$470,000	$500,000
Less: Taxes (50%)	225,000	235,000	250,000
Net Income	$225,000	$235,000	$250,000
Less: Preferred Dividend	—	36,000	60,000
To Common Stock	$225,000	$199,000	$190,000
Number of Common Shares	÷10,000	÷8,000	÷10,000
Earnings per Share	$22.50	$24.88	$19.00

7.2 Shapot Industries has 12,000 shares of common stock outstanding. The board decides to expand existing facilities at a projected cost of $3,000,000. *Method I*: Issue of $3,000,000 in common stock, $50 par. *Method II*: Issue of $1,500,000 in preferred stock, 6%, $100 par, and $1,500,000 in common stock, $50 par. *Method III*: Issue of $1,500,000 in 6% bonds, $750,000 in preferred stock, 6%, $100 par, and $750,000 in common stock, $50 par. Assuming that the net income before bond interest and taxes (50%) will be increased to $300,000, find the earnings per share of common stock under each method.

	Method I	Method II	Method III

SOLUTION

	Method I	Method II	Method III
Income	$300,000	$300,000	$300,000
Less: Bond Interest	—	—	90,000
Income before Taxes	$300,000	$300,000	$210,000
Less: Taxes	150,000	150,000	105,000
Net Income	$150,000	$150,000	$105,000
Less: Preferred Dividend	—	90,000	45,000
To Common Stock	$150,000	$ 60,000	$ 60,000
Number of Common Shares	÷72,000	÷42,000	÷27,000
Earnings per Share	$2.08	$1.43	$2.22

7.3   Rework Problem 7.2 for an expected income of $180,000.

	Method I	Method II	Method III

SOLUTION

	Method I	Method II	Method III
Income	$180,000	$180,000	$180,000
Less: Bond Interest	—	—	90,000
Income before Taxes	$180,000	$180,000	$ 90,000
Less: Taxes	90,000	90,000	45,000
Net Income	$ 90,000	$ 90,000	$ 45,000
Less: Preferred Dividend	—	90,000	45,000
To Common Stock	90,000	—	—
Number of Common Shares	÷72,000		
Earnings per Share	$1.25	—	—

7.4   On March 1, Terry Corporation authorizes $4,000,000 in 9%, 25-year bonds. On April 1, it issues three-fourths of them and 4 months later issues the balance.

(*a*) Present the entries needed to record the above information.

(*b*) Present the liabilities section of the balance sheet as of (1) April 30; (2) August 31.

(*a*)

Apr. 1		
Aug. 1		

(b)   (1)

      (2)

SOLUTION

(a)

Apr. 1 Cash	3,022,500	
Bonds Payable		3,000,000
Interest Expense		22,500*

Aug. 1 Cash	1,037,500	
Bonds Payable		1,000,000
Interest Expense		37,500†

*3,000,000 × 9% per year × 1/12 year = $22,500 per month

†1,000,000 × 9% per year × 5/12 year = $7,500 per month; 7,500 × 5 months = 37,500

(b)

(1) Long-Term Liabilities:		
25-year Bonds Payable Authorized	$4,000,000	
Less: Unissued	1,000,000	
Total Issued		$3,000,000

(2) Long-Term Liabilities:		
25-year, 9% Bonds Payable		
Authorized and Issued		$4,000,000

7.5   On January 1, Spiro, Inc., issued $100,000 in 20-year, 5% bonds at 104, interest payable semiannually on June 30 and December 31. Present entries to record (a) sale of the bonds, (b) payment of interest on June 30, (c) payment of interest on December 31, and (d) amortization of the premium.

(a)   Jan. 1

(b)   June 30

(c)   Dec. 31

(d)   Dec. 31

SOLUTION

(a)

Jan. 1 Cash	104,000	
Bonds Payable		100,000
Premium on Bonds Payable		4,000

(b)	June 30 Interest Expense	2,500	
	Cash		2,500
(c)	Dec. 31 Interest Expense	2,500	
	Cash		2,500
(d)	Dec. 31 Premium on Bonds Payable	200*	
	Interest Expense		200

*$4,000 premium ÷ 20 years.

7.6   Based on the information in Problem 7.5, present the liabilities section of the balance sheet as of (a) January 31; (b) December 31.

(a)

(b)

SOLUTION

(a)	Long-Term Liabilities:		
	Bonds Payable, 5%, 20-year	$100,000	
	Add: Unamortized Premium	4,000	$104,000
(b)	Long-Term Liabilities:		
	Bonds Payable, 5%, 20-year	$100,000	
	Add: Unamortized Premium	3,800	$103,800

7.7   Assume that Spiro, Inc. (Problem 7.5) issued the bonds at 96 instead of 104. Present the entries to record (a) sale of the bonds, (b) payment of interest on June 30, (c) payment of interest on December 31, and (d) amortization of the discount.

(a)	Jan. 1		
(b)	June 30		
(c)	Dec. 31		
(d)	Dec. 31		

SOLUTION

(a)	Jan. 1	Cash	96,000	
		Discount on Bonds Payable	4,000	
		Bonds Payable		100,000
(b)	June 30	Interest Expense	2,500	
		Cash		2,500
(c)	Dec. 31	Interest Expense	2,500	
		Cash		2,500
(d)	Dec. 31	Interest Expense	200	
		Discount on Bonds Payable		200*

*$4,000 discount ÷ 20 years = $200 per year

7.8 Based on the information in Problem 7.7, present the liabilities section of the balance sheet as of (a) January 31; (b) December 31.

(a)

(b)

SOLUTION

(a)	Long-Term Liabilities:		
	Bonds Payable	$100,000	
	Less: Unamortized Discount	4,000	$96,000
(b)	Long-Term Liabilities:		
	Bonds Payable	$100,000	
	Less: Unamortized Discount	3,800	$96,200

7.9 On January 1 the Stevens Company authorized the issuance of $100,000 in 10-year, 6% bonds paying interest semiannually on June 30 and December 31, but it did not sell them until March 1 of that year. Prepare entries to record (a) the authorization, (b) the sale, (c) the first interest payment, and (d) the second interest payment.

(a)

(b)

(c)

(d)

SOLUTION

(a)

Memo: Authorized $100,000 in 10-year, 6% bonds with		
semiannual interest payable June 30 and Dec. 31		

(b)

Cash	101,000	
Bonds Payable		100,000
Interest Expense		1,000*

*$100,000 × 6% per year × 2/12 year = $1,000

The purchaser of a bond will be charged for the interest that has accrued during January and February. This interest, however, will be repaid to him or her (see the following entry).

(c)

Interest Expense	3,000	
Cash		3,000

Payment is made of the full 6 months (4 months' interest earned by purchaser and 2 months' interest collected in advance).

(d)

Interest Expense	3,000	
Cash		3,000

Chapter 8

The Corporation:
Redemption of Bonds

8.1 REDEMPTION OF BONDS

Callable Bonds

Many bonds are issued with the notice that they may be redeemed at the option of the corporation within a specific period of time and at a price specified, usually above face value. This is done because corporations may, at times, find themselves in a market where interest rates are declining. To profit from this situation, the corporation may sell new bonds carrying the lower interest rate and use the funds to redeem the original, higher paying issue.

EXAMPLE 1

The Wakefield Corporation exercises its option by calling in all of its bonds for $103,000. The ledger balances prior to the redemption were:

Bonds Payable		Premium on Bonds Payable	
	100,000	1,800	6,000

The entry to record the recall of the bonds would be:

Bonds Payable	100,000	
Premium on Bonds Payable	4,200	
Cash		103,000
Gain on Redemption of Bonds		1,200

EXAMPLE 2

The Wakefield Corporation (see Example 1) decides to call in only 25% of its outstanding bonds. The entry to record the redemption would be:

Bonds Payable	25,000	
Premium on Bonds Payable	1,050	
Cash		25,750
Gain on Redemption of Bonds		300

Convertible Bonds

An option offered to the bondholder is the right to exchange his or her bonds for a specific number of common stock shares. Convertible bonds offer the purchaser security in the initial stage of ownership, with an option of taking more risks if the company prospers. In other words, if the market price of common stock increases, the bondholder can convert to common stock and share in the increase.

EXAMPLE 3

The R. Tobey Corporation has $100,000 in convertible bonds outstanding, with $6,000 of related unamortized premiums. The bonds are convertible at the rate of 30 shares of $25 par common stock for each $1,000 bond. Assuming that all bonds have been presented for conversion, the entry is:

Bonds Payable	100,000	
Premium on Bonds Payable	6,000	
Common Stock		75,000*
Premium on Common Stock		31,000†

*100 bonds $\times$ (30 shares/bond) $\times$ \$25 per share

†\$100,000 + \$6,000 − \$75,000

8.2 BOND SINKING FUNDS. RESTRICTION OF DIVIDENDS

A *sinking fund* is created under the supervision of a trustee for the purpose of accumulating funds for the payment of bonds at maturity. The trustee invests the cash in the sinking fund in securities whose income, together with periodic payments into the fund by the corporation, is expected to produce an amount sufficient to retire the bonds when they mature. The new accounts to be established when a bond sinking fund is created include *Sinking Fund Cash* (cash of the corporation transferred to the sinking fund), *Sinking Fund Investments* (investments purchased with sinking fund cash), and *Sinking Fund Income Investments* (investments purchased with sinking fund cash), and *Sinking Fund Income* (income from the sinking fund investments).

EXAMPLE 4

A corporation issues \$100,000 of 6%, 10-year bonds and agrees to deposit with a sinking fund trustee equal amounts for the 10 years so that the accumulated amount plus interest will be sufficient to retire the bonds at maturity. The following sinking fund transactions are representative:

Annual deposit into the sinking fund:

Sinking Fund Cash	8,200	
Cash		8,200

[A yearly deposit of \$10,000 (\$100,000 ÷ 10 years) is not needed, as substantial interest will be earned.]

Purchase of investments:

Sinking Fund Investments	8,200	
Sinking Fund Cash		8,200

Income from investments:

Sinking Fund Cash	500	
Sinking Fund Income		500

Sale of investments:

Sinking Fund Cash	91,000	
Sinking Fund Investments		89,000
Gain on Sale of Investments		2,000

Payment at maturity:

Bonds Payable	100,000	
Sinking Fund Cash		100,000

With this last entry, the sinking fund is closed. If the final balance of Sinking Fund Cash had been more than $100,000, the excess would be returned to the Cash account; if the amount had been less than $100,000, additional cash would be needed to retire the bonds.

To prevent a corporation from using all its assets either to pay out sinking fund deposits or for the payment of earnings, a trustee may restrict the dividends of the corporation while the bonds are outstanding.One way of doing this would be to require that the corporation appropriate retained earnings each year equal to the sinking fund requirements.

EXAMPLE 5

For the bond issue of Example 4, the entry to record the annual appropriation would be:

Retained Earnings	10,000	
Appropriation for Bonded Indebtedness		10,000

At maturity the appropriation would be returned to the unappropriated Retained Earnings account:

Appropriation for Bonded Indebtedness	100,000	
Retained Earnings		100,000

8.3 REVIEW OF EQUITY AND DEBT FINANCING

In the last four chapters we have examined accounting areas of the corporation involving equity (stock) and debt (bond) financing. The balance sheet below illustrates the reporting of the types of financial information which have been discussed.

Cashier Corporation
Balance Sheet
December 19X1

ASSETS

Current Assets			
Cash		$ 25,000	
Securities (market value, $52,000)			
at Cost		46,000	
Accounts Receivable	$112,000		
Less: Allowance for Doubtful			
Accounts	3,300	108,700	
Merchandise Inventory (First-in,			
First-out)		104,200	
Common Stock Subscriptions			
Receivable		25,000	
Prepaid Expenses		6,000	
Total Current Assets			$314,900
Long-Term Investments			
Bond Sinking Fund		$ 35,000	
XYZ Common Stock		15,000	
Total Long-Term Investments			50,000

Fixed Assets

Building	$200,000		
Less: Accumulated Depreciation	120,000	$ 80,000	
Equipment	$100,000		
Less: Accumulated Depreciation	30,000	70,000	
Land		100,000	
Total Fixed Assets			250,000

Intangible Assets

Goodwill	$ 20,000	
Organization Costs	40,000	
Total Intangible Assets		60,000
Total Assets		$674,900

LIABILITIES

Current Liabilities

Notes Payable	$ 40,000	
Accounts Payable	60,000	
Income Tax Payable	21,000	
Total Current Liabilities		$121,000

Long-Term Liabilities

Sinking Fund, 6%, 10-Year Bonds	$100,000	
Add: Unamortized Premium	8,000	108,000
Total Liabilities		$229,000

STOCKHOLDERS' EQUITY

Paid-in Capital

Common Stock, $50 par (10,000 shares authorized, 6,000 shares issued)	$300,000	
Premium on Common Stock	10,000	
Common Stock Subscribed	10,000	
Total Paid-in Capital		$320,000

Retained Earnings

Appropriated Retained Earnings

For Bonded Indebtedness	$25,000		
For Contingencies	15,000	$ 40,000	
Unappropriated Retained Earnings		125,900	
Total Retained Earnings		165,900	
Total		$485,900	
Less: Treasury Stock (1,000 shares at cost)		40,000	
Total Stockholders' Equity			445,900
Total Liabilities and Stockholders' Equity			$674,900

Summary: Chapters 7 and 8

1. Most bonds are issued in units of $ _____ .

2. The market price of a bond is commonly given as a _____ of the face value.

3. A fund established to retire bonds by means of fixed annual deposits is known as a _____ .

4. Bonds that may be exchanged at a future date at the option of the bondholder are termed _____ bonds, while bonds that may be recalled at the option of the corporation are termed _____ bonds.

5. Bond premium (or discount) appears in the balance sheet as an addition to (or deduction from) _____ .

6. Bonds sold between interest payment dates are said to be sold plus _____ .

7. A mortgage placed on movable items is known as a _____ .

8. An account used to restrict dividends while bonds are outstanding is _____ .

9. A bond based on the general credit of the company is known as a _____ .

10. Capital stock is known as _____ capital, while bonds are termed _____ capital.

Answers: (1) 1,000; (2) percentage; (3) sinking fund; (4) convertible, callable; (5) bonds payable; (6) accrued interest; (7) chattel mortgage; (8) Appropriation for Bonded Indebtedness; (9) debenture; (10) equity, debt

Solved Problems

8.1   Match the items in Column A with the appropriate phrases from Column B.

Column A	Column B
1. Trust indentures	(a) Bonds backed by investments held by the issuing corporation
2. Serial bonds	(b) Corporation deposits annual amounts to make up the amount due at maturity
3. Sinking fund bonds	
4. Chattel mortgages	(c) A trustee is chosen by the corporation to safeguard investors' interest
5. Collateral trust bonds	
6. Registered bonds	(d) Mortgages placed on movable items
7. Callable bonds	(e) Bonds mature in different years
8. Convertible bonds	(f) Bondholder has option to exchange bonds for other securities
	(g) Corporation has option to call in bonds
	(h) Owner's name is stated on the face of the bond

SOLUTION

1. *c*; 2. *e*; 3. *b*; 4. *d*; 5. *a*; 6. *h*; 7. *g*; 8. *f*

8.2   Prior to redeeming its obligations at 104, Gallagher Company had the following ledger balances:

Bonds Payable		Discount on Bonds Payable	
	1,000,000	40,000	25,000

(a) Present the entry necessary to record the redemption.

(b) If it were decided to redeem only half the bonds, what entry would be needed?

(a) _____

(b) _____

SOLUTION

(a)	Bonds Payable	1,000,000	
	Loss on Redemption of Bonds	55,000	
	Cash		1,040,000
	Discount on Bonds Payable		15,000
(b)	Bonds Payable	500,000	
	Loss on Redemption of Bonds	27,500	
	Cash		520,000
	Discount on Bonds Payable		7,500

8.3   The Whalstom Corporation has the following balances in its ledger regarding its convertible bonds:

Bonds Payable		Premium on Bonds Payable	
	1,000,000	50,000	60,000

All bondholders exercise their option and convert their holdings at the ratio of 16 shares of $50 par common stock for each $1,000 bond. Present the entry for the conversion.

SOLUTION

Bonds Payable	1,000,000	
Premium on Bonds Payable	10,000	
Common Stock		800,000*
Premium on Common Stock		210,000

*1,000 bonds × (16/1) × $50 = $800,000

8.4 The Davis Company issues $2,000,000 in 5%, 10-year, sinking fund bonds and agrees to deposit annually with a trustee equal amounts sufficient to retire the bond issue at maturity. Transactions for three selected years appear below.

1st Year	Jan. 1	Sold the bonds at 103.
	Dec. 31	Deposited $176,000 in the bond sinking fund.
5th Year	Mar. 21	Purchased investments with sinking fund cash for $100,000.
	Dec. 31	Deposited $176,000 in the bond sinking fund.
	Dec. 31	Received $5,620 of income on sinking fund investments.
10th Year	Oct. 20	Sold the sinking fund investments for $108,000.
	Dec. 31	Paid the bonds at maturity. At this time the Sinking Fund Cash account has a balance of $2,024,000.

Present entries to record all information relating to the bond issue.

1st Year	Jan. 1		
	Dec. 31		
5th Year	Mar. 21		
	Dec. 31		
	Dec. 31		
10th Year	Oct. 20		
	Dec. 31		

SOLUTION

1st Year	Jan. 1	Cash ($2,000,000 × 103%)	2,060,000	
		Bonds Payable		2,000,000
		Premium on Bonds Payable		60,000
	Dec. 31	Sinking Fund Cash	176,000	
		Cash		176,000
5th Year	Mar. 21	Sinking Fund Investments	100,000	
		Sinking Fund Cash		100,000
	Dec. 31	Sinking Fund Cash	176,000	
		Cash		176,000

Dec. 31	Sinking Fund Cash		5,620	
		Sinking Fund Income		5,620
10th Year Oct. 20	Sinking Fund Cash		108,000	
		Sinking Fund Investments		100,000
		Gain on Sale of Investments		8,000
Dec. 31	Bonds Payable		2,000,000	
	Cash		24,000	
		Sinking Fund Cash		2,024,000

8.5   During 19X1 and 19X2, Beckworth Industries had the following transactions:

19X1	Mar. 31	Issued $100,000 in 10-year, 6% bonds at 105. Interest to be paid semiannually on Mar. 31 and Sept. 30.
	Sept. 30	Paid the semiannual interest on bonds payable.
	Dec. 31	Recorded the accrued interest on bonds payable.
	Dec. 31	Recorded the amortization of premium on bonds.
	Dec. 31	Closed the interest expense account.
19X2	Jan. 1	Reversed the adjusting entry for accrued interest.
	Mar. 31	Paid the semiannual interest.
	Sept. 30	Paid the semiannual interest.
	Dec. 31	Recorded the accrued interest on bonds payable.
	Dec. 31	Recorded the amortization of premium on bonds.
	Dec. 31	Closed the interest expense account.

Prepare entries to record the foregoing transactions.

19X1	Mar. 31		
	Sept. 30		
	Dec. 31		
	Dec. 31		
	Dec. 31		
19X2	Jan. 1		
	Mar. 31		

	Sept. 30			
	Dec. 31			
	Dec. 31			
	Dec. 31			

SOLUTION

19X1	Mar. 31	Cash	105,000	
		Bonds Payable		100,000
		Premium on Bonds Payable		5,000
	Sept. 30	Interest Expense	3,000	
		Cash		3,000
	Dec. 31	Interest Expense	1,500	
		Interest Payable		1,500*

*3 months' interest ($100,000 × 6% × 3/12 = $1,500).

	Dec. 31	Premium on Bonds Payable	375†	
		Interest Expense		375

†Mar. 31 to Dec. 31 = (9/12) year; ($5,000 premium/10 years) × (9/12) year = $375.

	Dec. 31	Expense and Income Summary	4,125	
		Interest Expense		4,125
19X2	Jan. 1	Interest Payable	1,500	
		Interest Expense		1,500
	Mar. 31	Interest Expense	3,000	
		Cash		3,000
	Sept. 30	Interest Expense	3,000	
		Cash		3,000
	Dec. 31	Interest Expense	1,500	
		Interest Payable		1,500
	Dec. 31	Premium on Bonds Payable	500	
		Interest Expense		500
	Dec. 31	Expense and Income Summary	5,500	
		Interest Expense		5,500

8.6 Below are the balance sheet accounts and balances for Stevemarc Corporation as of December 31, 19X1. Prepare a classified balance sheet.

Accounts Receivable	$ 128,400
Accounts Payable	102,000
Accumulated Depreciation, Building	120,000
Accumulated Depreciation, Equipment	26,000
Allowance for Doubtful Accounts	4,600
Appropriation for Plant Expansion	68,000
Appropriation for Treasury Stock	42,000
Bonds (6%, 10-year debentures)	1,000,000
Building	696,700
Cash	1,655,000
Common Stock, $25 par (40,000 shares authorized, 30,000 shares issued)	750,000
Common Stock Subscribed	100,000
Common Stock Subscriptions Receivable	60,000
Discount on Preferred Stock	60,000
Equipment	216,000
Goodwill	125,000
Land	30,000
Merchandise Inventory	442,500
Notes Payable	38,000
Notes Receivable	75,000
Organization Costs	15,000
Paid-in Capital from Sale of Treasury Stock	22,000
Preferred Stock, 6%, $100 par (20,000 shares authorized, 10,000 shares issued)	1,000,000
Premium on Bonds Payable	36,000
Premium on Common Stock	15,000
Prepaid Expenses	32,000
Taxes Payable	24,000
Treasury Stock (at cost)	42,000
Unappropriated Retained Earnings	230,000

Stevemarc Corporation
Balance Sheet
December 31, 19X1

ASSETS
Current Assets

Fixed Assets

Intangible Assets

Total Assets

LIABILITIES
Current Liabilities

Long-Term Liabilities

Total Liabilities

STOCKHOLDERS' EQUITY
Paid-in Capital

Retained Earnings

Total Stockholders' Equity		
Total Liabilities and Stockholders' Equity		

SOLUTION

Stevemarc Corporation
Balance Sheet
December 31, 19X1

ASSETS

Current Assets

Cash		$1,655,000	
Accounts Receivable	$ 128,400		
Less: Allowance for Doubtful Accounts	4,600	123,800	
Notes Receivable		75,000	
Merchandise Inventory		442,500	
Common Stock Subscriptions Receivable		60,000	
Prepaid Expenses		32,000	
Total Current Assets			$2,388,300

Fixed Assets

Building	$ 696,700		
Less: Accumulated Depreciation,			
Building	120,000	$ 576,700	
Equipment	$ 216,000		
Less: Accumulated Depreciation,			
Equipment	26,000	190,000	
Land		30,000	
Total Fixed Assets			796,700

Intangible Assets

Goodwill		$ 125,000	
Organization Costs		15,000	
Total Intangible Assets			140,000
Total Assets			$3,325,000

LIABILITIES

Current Liabilities

Notes Payable		$ 38,000	
Accounts Payable		102,000	
Taxes Payable		24,000	
Total Current Liabilities			$ 164,000

Long-Term Liabilities

Bonds (6%, 10-year debentures)		$1,000,000	
Add: Premium on Bonds Payable		36,000	
Total Long-Term Liabilities			1,036,000
Total Liabilities			$1,200,000

STOCKHOLDERS' EQUITY

Paid-in Capital			
Preferred Stock, 6%, $100 par (20,000 shares			
authorized, 10,000 shares issued)	$1,000,000		
Less: Discount on Preferred Stock	60,000	$ 940,000	
Common Stock, $25 (40,000 shares			
authorized, 30,000 shares issued)	$ 750,000		
Add: Premium on Common Stock	15,000	765,000	
Common Stock Subscribed		100,000	
From Sale of Treasury Stock		22,000	
Total Paid-in Capital			$1,827,000
Retained Earnings			
Appropriated Retained Earnings;			
For Plant Expansion	$ 68,000		
For Treasury Stock	42,000		
Total Appropriated Retained Earnings		$ 110,000	
Unappropriated Retained Earnings		230,000	
Total Retained Earnings		340,000	
Total		$2,167,000	
Less: Treasury Stock (at cost)		42,000	
Total Stockholders' Equity			2,125,000
Total Liabilities and Stockholders' Equity			$3,325,000

EXAMINATION I

Chapters 1–8

1. Brian and Craig have decided to form a partnership. Brian invests the following business assets at their agreed valuations, and transfers his liabilities to the new firm.

	Brian's Ledger Balances	Agreed Valuations
Cash	$10,000	$10,000
Accounts Receivable	8,200	7,200
Allowance for Doubtful Accounts	600	300
Merchandise Inventory	20,200	15,000
Equipment	8,000	6,200
Accumulated Depreciation	1,000	
Accounts Payable	5,500	5,500
Notes Payables	2,600	2,600

Craig agrees to invest $30,000 in cash. What entries are needed to record the investments of Brian and Craig?

2. The abbreviated income statement of Rothchild and Quick for December 31, 19X1, is as follows:

Sales (net)	$350,000
Less: Cost of Goods Sold	110,000
Gross Income	$240,000
Less: Expenses	140,000
Net Income	$100,000

The profit and loss agreement specifies that:

(1) Interest of 5% is to be allowed on capital balances (Rothchild, $50,000; Quick, $25,000).

(2) Salary allowances to Rothchild and Quick to be $8,000 and $7,000, respectively.

(3) A bonus is to be given to Rothchild equal to 20% of net income without regard to interest or salary.

(4) Remaining profits and losses are to be divided equally.

(a) Present the distribution of net income. (b) Present the journal entry required to close the books.

3. Able, Baker, and Con, who share income and losses in the ratio of 2:1:1, decide to liquidate their business on May 31. As of that date, their post-closing trial balance reveals the following balances:

Cash	$ 48,000	
Other Assets	72,000	
Liabilities		$ 40,000
Able, Capital		30,000
Baker, Capital		30,000
Con, Capital		20,000
	$120,000	$120,000

Present the entries to record the following liquidating transactions:

122

(a) Sold the noncash assets for $10,000.

(b) Distributed the loss to the partners.

(c) Paid the liabilities.

(d) Allocated the available cash to the partners.

(e) The partner with the debit balance pays the amount he owes.

(f) Any additional money is distributed.

4. The outstanding stock of the Gersten Corporation consists of 10,000 shares of 6%, $100-par cumulative preferred stock and 30,000 shares of $50-par common stock. The company pays out as dividends all of its net income. Over the last four years the company's earnings record has been: first year, $20,000; second year, $50,000; third year, $120,000; fourth year, $210,000. Determine the dividend per share on each class of stock for each of the four years.

5. The Agin Corporation agrees to issue 20,000 shares of common stock in exchange for equipment valued at $500,000. What journal entry must be made if the par value is (a) $25? (b) $20? (c) $30?

6. On January 1 the Rakosi Corporation was organized with an authorization for 10,000 shares of preferred 6% stock, $100 par, and 20,000 shares of common stock, $25 par. Record the following transactions:

Jan. 10   Sold half of the common stock at $30 for cash.
Jan. 15   Issued 3,000 shares of preferred stock and 1,000 shares of common stock at par in exchange for land and building with fair market values of $200,000 and $125,000, respectively.
Mar. 16   Sold the balance of the preferred stock at $105 for cash.

7. On September 1 the Marc Corporation received subscriptions to 50,000 shares of $10-par common stock at $16, collecting one-half of the subscription price immediately. Three months later the balance due was received and the stock issued. (a) Present the necessary entries. (b) Present the balance sheet as of September 30.

8. The board of directors of the Anit Corporation presented to the stockholders a plan to expand facilities at a cost of $1,000,000. This sum was to come from:

(a) An issue of $10,000 shares of preferred stock at par ($50)

(b) A loan of $200,000 by the bank

(c) A donation of 10% of all common stock outstanding (100,000 shares authorized and issued, par value $20)

Prepare entries to record the transactions above, assuming that the treasury stock in (c) was sold for $30 per share.

9. Listed below are the data from two different corporations labeled (a) and (b). Determine for each corporation the equity per share of preferred and common stock.

(a)		
Preferred stock, 8%, $100 par		$480,000
Premium on preferred stock		60,000
Common stock, $50 par		350,000
Discount on common stock		30,000
Retained earnings		180,000

(b) Dividends on preferred stock are in arrears for two years including the present year. Preferred stock is entitled to par plus payment of dividends in arrears regardless of the availability of retained earnings.

Preferred stock, 8%, $100 par	$600,000
Premium on preferred stock	26,000
Common stock, $60 par	480,000
Discount on common stock	16,000
Retained earnings	90,000

10. The retained earnings accounts of Weis Company appear below.

Appropriation for Contingencies	Appropriation for Plant Expansion	Retained Earnings
80,000	100,000	320,000

During the month of December the board of directors decided to:

(1) Increase the appropriation for contingencies *by* $30,000

(2) Decrease the appropriation for plant expansion *to* $90,000

(3) Establish an appropriation for bonded indebtedness requiring an annual deposit of $20,000

(4) Declare cash dividends of $80,000

(*a*) Present entries to record the decisions of the board. (*b*) Prepare a retained earnings statement.

11. Three companies have the following financial structures.

	A Company	B Company	C Company
Bonds payable, 6%	$1,000,000	$ 500,000	—
Preferred stock, 7%, $100 par	—	500,000	$1,000,000
Common stock, $50 par	1,000,000	1,000,000	1,000,000
Total	$2,000,000	$2,000,000	$2,000,000

Assuming a tax rate of 50% of income, determine the earnings per share for common stock of each company, if the net income of each before bond interest and taxes was (*a*) $100,000; (*b*) $500,000.

12. On January 1, 19X1, Hope Corporation authorized and issued $100,000 of 9%, 10-year bonds at 98, interest to be paid semiannually on June 30 and December 31. Prepare all entries through December 31.

13. On January 1, R. Bertash Corporation authorizes $1,000,000 in 6%, 20-year bonds. On February 1 it issues half of them, and 3 months later it issues the balance.

(*a*) Present the entries needed to record the above information

(*b*) Present the liabilities section of the balance sheet as of (1) February 28; (2) May 31.

14. During 19X1 and 19X2, Aliano Corp. completed the following transactions:

19X1   Mar. 31   Issued $1,000,000 in 10-year, 8% bonds at 104. Interest to be paid semiannually on Mar. 31 and Sept. 30.

           Sept. 30   Paid the semiannual interest on bonds payable.

           Dec. 31   Recorded the accrued interest on bonds payable.

           Dec. 31   Recorded the amortization of premium on bonds.

19X2   Jan.   1   Reversed the adjusting entry for accrued interest.
           Mar. 31 Paid the semiannual interest.
           Sept. 30 Paid the semiannual interest.
           Dec. 31 Recorded the accrued interest on bonds payable.
           Dec. 31 Recorded the amortization of premium on bonds.

Prepare entries to record the foregoing transactions.

15. On April 1, 19X1, the T. Baker Corporation authorized the issuance of $1,000,000 in 10-year, 10% bonds paying interest quarterly on March 31, June 30, September 30, and December 31. The bonds were sold on June 1 of the same year. Prepare entries to record (*a*) the authorization, (*b*) the sale, and (*c*) the first interest payment.

16. The board of directors of the Philip Company decides to issue $1,000,000 in 6%, 20-year sinking fund bonds and to deposit annually with a trustee equal amounts sufficient to retire the bond issue at maturity. Transactions for three separate years appear below.

1st Year   Jan.   1   Sold the bonds at 102.
             Dec. 31 Deposited $46,000 in the bond sinking fund.
10th Year   Mar. 21 Purchased securities with sinking fund cash for $95,000.
             Dec. 31 Deposited $46,000 in the bond sinking fund.
             Dec. 31 Received $2,600 of income on sinking fund securities.
20th Year   Oct. 20 Sold the sinking fund securities for $100,000.
             Dec. 31 Paid the bonds at maturity; at this time the sinking fund cash account has a balance of $1,120,000.

Present entries to record all information relating to the bond issue.

Answers to Examination I

1.

Cash		10,000	
Accounts Receivable		7,200	
Merchandise Inventory		15,000	
Equipment		6,200	
Allowance for Doubtful Accounts			300
Accounts Payable			5,500
Notes Payable			2,600
Brian, Capital			30,000
Cash		30,000	
Craig, Capital			30,000

2. (*a*)

	Rothchild	Quick	Total
Interest	$ 2,500	$ 1,250	$ 3,750
Salary	8,000	7,000	15,000
Bonus	20,000	—	20,000
	$30,500	$ 8,250	$ 38,750
Balance	30,625	30,625	61,250
Net income	$61,125	$38,875	$100,000

(b)

Expense and Income Summary	100,000	
Rothchild, Capital		61,125
Quick, Capital		38,875

3. (a)

Cash	10,000	
Loss on Realization	62,000	
Other Assets		72,000

(b)

Able, Capital	31,000	
Baker Capital	15,500	
Con, Capital	15,500	
Loss on Realization		62,000

(c)

Liabilities	40,000	
Cash		40,000

(d)

Baker, Capital	14,000	
Con, Capital	4,000	
Cash		18,000

(e)

Cash	1,000	
Able, Capital		1,000

(f)

Baker, Capital	500	
Con, Capital	500	
Cash		1,000

Summary of Transactions

Transaction	Cash	Other Assets	Liabilities	Able, Capital	Baker, Capital	Con, Capital
Balance	$48,000	$72,000	$40,000	$30,000	$30,000	$20,000
(a), (b)	+ 10,000	−72,000		−31,000	−15,500	−15,500
	$58,000		$40,000	($1,000)	$14,500	$ 4,500
(c)	−40,000		−40,000			
	$18,000			($1,000)	$14,500	$ 4,500
(d)	−18,000				−14,000	−4,000
				($1,000)	$ 500	$ 500
(e)	+ 1,000			+ 1,000		
	$ 1,000				$ 500	$ 500
(f)	−1,000				−500	−500

4.

	Total Distributed	Per Share Preferred	Per Share Common
First year	$ 20,000	$ 2.00	—
Second year	50,000	5.00	—
Third year	120,000	11.00	$0.33
Fourth year	210,000	6.00	5.00

5. (*a*)

Equipment	500,000	
Common Stock		500,000

(*b*)

Equipment	500,000	
Common Stock		400,000
Premium on Common Stock		100,000

(*c*)

Equipment	500,000	
Discount on Common Stock	100,000	
Common Stock		600,000

6.

Jan. 10

Cash	300,000	
Common Stock		250,000
Premium on Common Stock		50,000

Jan. 15

Land	200,000	
Building	125,000	
Preferred Stock		300,000
Common Stock		25,000

Mar. 16

Cash	735,000	
Preferred Stock		700,000
Premium on Preferred Stock		35,000

7. (*a*)

Sept. 1

Common Stock Subscriptions Receivable	800,000	
Common Stock Subscribed		500,000
Premium on Common Stock		300,000

Sept. 1

Cash	400,000	
Common Stock Subscriptions Receivable		400,000

Dec. 1

Cash	400,000	
Common Stock Subscriptions Receivable		400,000

Dec. 1

Common Stock Subscribed	500,000	
Common Stock		500,000

(*b*)

ASSETS		STOCKHOLDERS' EQUITY	
Cash	$400,000	Paid-in Capital	
Common Stock Subscriptions Receivable	400,000	Common Stock Subscribed	$500,000
		Premium on Common Stock	300,000
Total Assets	$800,000	Total Stockholders' Equity	$800,000

8. (*a*)

Cash	500,000	
Preferred Stock		500,000

(*b*)

Cash	200,000	
Notes Payable		200,000

(c)   Memo: Received 10,000 shares of common stock as a donation

               Cash   300,000
                    Donated Capital   300,000

9.   (a)   **Preferred Stock**   **Common Stock**

         $480,000 $350,000   Common stock
         $100 per share   60,000   Premium on preferred
         4,800 shares   (30,000)   Discount of common stock
                                            180,000   Retained earnings
                                           $560,000   To common stock
                                           $ 80   Per share
                                           7,000 shares

(b)   **Preferred Stock**   **Common Stock**

         $600,000   Preferred stock $480,000   Common stock
           96,000   Dividends in arrears 26,000   Premium on preferred
         $696,000   To preferred stock (16,000)   Discount on common
         $116 per share   9,000   Retained earnings
         6,000 shares   (96,000)   Preferred dividends arrears
                                           $484,000   To common stock
                                           $ 60.50
                                           8,000 shares

10. (a)   (1)   Retained Earnings   30,000
                          Appropriation for Contingencies   30,000

         (2)   Appropriation for Plant Expansion   10,000
                          Retained Earnings   10,000

         (3)   Retained Earnings   20,000
                          Appropriation for Bonded Indebtedness   20,000

         (4)   Retained Earnings   80,000
                          Cash Dividend Payable   80,000

(b)   *Weis Company*
                        Statement of Retained Earnings
                            December 31, 19X1

Appropriated Retained Earnings
   Appropriation for Contingencies,
      Balance $ 80,000
   Add: Appropriation Increase   30,000 $110,000
   Appropriation for Plant Expansion,
      Balance $100,000
   Less: Appropriation Decrease   10,000   90,000
   Appropriation for Bonded
      Indebtedness   20,000
Total Appropriated Retained Earnings $220,000

Unappropriated Retained Earnings

Balance	$320,000	
Add: Transfer from Appropriation for Plant Expansion	10,000	$330,000
Less: Transfer to Appropriation for Contingencies	$ 30,000	
Transfer to Appropriation for Bonded Indebtedness	20,000	
Cash Dividends Declared	80,000	130,000
Total Unappropriated Retained Earnings		200,000
Total Retained Earnings		$420,000

11. (*a*)

	A Company	B Company	C Company
Income	$100,000	$100,000	$100,000
Less: Bond interest	60,000	30,000	—
	$ 40,000	$ 70,000	$100,000
Less: Tax (50%)	20,000	35,000	50,000
Net income	$ 20,000	$ 35,000	$ 50,000
Less: Preferred dividend	—	35,000	50,000
To common	$ 20,000	–0–	–0–
Per-share distribution	$1	–0–	–0–

(*b*)

	A Company	B Company	C Company
Income	$500,000	$500,000	$500,000
Less: Bond interest	60,000	30,000	—
	$440,000	$470,000	$500,000
Less: Tax (50%)	220,000	235,000	250,000
Net income	$220,000	$235,000	$250,000
Less: Preferred dividend	—	35,000	70,000
To common	$220,000	$200,000	$180,000
Per-share distribution	$11	$10	$9

12.

Jan. 1	Memo: Authorized $100,000, 10-year, 9% bonds with semiannual interest payable on June 30 and Dec. 31			
Jan. 1	Cash	98,000	
	Discount on Bonds Payable	2,000	
	Bonds Payable		100,000
June 30	Interest Expense	4,500	
	Cash		4,500
Dec. 31	Interest Expense	4,500	
	Cash		4,500
Dec. 31	Interest Expense	200*	
	Discount on Bonds Payable		200*

*(2,000 discount/10 years) × 1 full year

13. (*a*) Jan. 1   (No entry; memorandum noting authorization of $1,000,000 in 6%, 20-year bonds)

Feb. 1   Cash   502,500
                 Bonds Payable   500,000
                 Interest Expense   2,500*

May 1   Cash   510,000
                 Bonds Payable   500,000
                 Interest Expense   10,000†

---

*$500,000 × 6% per year × 1/12 year = $2,500 interest per month

†$2,500 × 4 = $10,000

(*b*) (1)   Long-Term Liabilities:
                 20-year, 6% Bonds Payable Authorized $1,000,000
                 Less: Unissued   500,000
                 Total Issued $ 500,000

(2)   Long-Term Liabilities:
                 20-year, 6% Bonds Payable Authorized and Issued $1,000,000

14.   19X1   Mar. 31   Cash   1,040,000
                                       Bond Payable   1,000,000
                                       Premium on Bonds Payable   40,000

                         Sept. 30   Interest Expense   40,000
                                       Cash   40,000

                         Dec. 31   Interest Expense   20,000
                                       Interest Payable   20,000*

                         Dec. 31   Premium on Bonds Payable   3,000†
                                       Interest Expense   3,000

             19X2   Jan. 1   Interest Payable   20,000
                                       Interest Expense   20,000

                         Mar. 31   Interest Expense   40,000
                                       Cash   40,000

                         Sept. 30   Interest Expense   40,000
                                       Cash   40,000

                         Dec. 31   Interest Expense   20,000
                                       Interest Payable   20,000

                         Dec. 31   Premium on Bonds Payable   4,000
                                       Interest Expense   4,000

---

*3 months' interest.

†Mar. 31 to Dec. 31 = 9/12 year; ($40,000 premium/10 years) × 9/12 year = $3,000

15. *(a)*   Memo: authorized $1,000,000 in 10-year 10% bonds with quarterly interest
                              payable on Mar. 31, June 30, Sept. 30, and Dec. 31

(b)   Cash   1,016,666.66
                    Bonds Payable   1,000,000.00
                    Interest Payable   16,666.66

(c)   Interest Expense   25,000.00
                    Cash   25,000.00

16.   1st year   Jan. 1   Cash   1,020,000
                                                    Bonds Payable   1,000,000
                                                    Premium on Bonds Payable   20,000

                              Dec. 31   Sinking Fund Cash   46,000
                                                    Cash   46,000

          10th Year   Mar. 21   Sinking Fund Securities   95,000
                                                    Sinking Fund Cash   95,000

                              Dec. 31   Sinking Fund Cash   46,000
                                                    Cash   46,000

                              Dec. 31   Sinking Fund Cash   2,600
                                                    Sinking Fund Income   2,600

          20th Year   Oct. 20   Sinking Fund Cash   100,000
                                                    Sinking Fund Securities   95,000
                                                    Gain on Sale of Securities   5,000

                              Dec. 31   Bonds Payable   1,000,000
                                                    Cash   120,000
                                                    Sinking Fund Cash   1,120,000

Chapter 9

Manufacturing Accounting: Accounts and Statements

9.1 MANUFACTURING ACCOUNTS

A merchandising company provides services or buys and sells articles without changing their form. A manufacturing company, by contrast, converts raw materials into finished goods, in the process incurring labor and overhead costs. Because of this difference in nature, a manufacturing company requires additional asset and expense accounts. These may be summarized as follows:

Inventories. Instead of the single inventory account used by a merchandising company, a manufacturing company will need three separate inventory accounts: Raw Materials (or Direct Materials), Work in Process, and Finished Goods.

Plant and equipment (fixed assets). The equipment used in manufacturing is varied, numerous, and costly. Thus it is desirable to maintain a subsidiary plant ledger in which the individual items are recorded and to have a general ledger account, Plant and Equipment, to control the subsidiary ledger.

Manufacturing or production cost. As described in Section 9.2, manufacturing cost is made up of the cost of raw materials, direct labor costs, and factory overhead. Each of these three elements requires an account. If there are two or more products, subsidiary records may be used to list the production costs by product. For factory overhead a separate account is set up for each type of expense, such as depreciation, repairs, or taxes.

9.2 ANALYSIS OF MANUFACTURING COST

Each unit of finished goods includes the three elements of manufacturing cost—raw materials (also known as direct materials), direct labor, and factory overhead.

Raw Materials

This represents the *cost* of raw materials that become part of the finished product. Purchases of raw materials go into inventory, from which goods are issued and placed in production. The cost of raw materials used is obtained by adding the beginning inventory to the purchases for the period to arrive at the total raw materials available for use. Of this amount, part is used during, and part is on hand at the end of, the period. By taking a physical count at the end of the period the final inventory can be determined; the balance is presumed to have been used. The cost of raw materials is the invoice cost, plus transportation-in, less any returns or allowances received from the vendor.

EXAMPLE 1

Raw Materials Inventory		Transportation-in	
Jan. 1 20,000		4,000	
Dec. 31 23,000			

Raw Materials Purchases	
75,500	

Raw Materials Returns	
	5,000

132

From the above ledger accounts, the cost of raw materials used is computed as follows:

Beginning Inventory		$20,000
Purchases	$75,500	
Less: Returns and Allowances	5,000	70,500
Transportation-in		4,000
Raw Materials Available for Use		$94,500
Less: Ending Inventory		23,000
Cost of Raw Materials Used		$71,500

Direct Labor

This represents the amount of wages paid to factory employees who work *directly on the product*; it is charged to Work in Process. Included are the wages of machine operators, assemblers, and others. The work of employees such as supervisors, janitors, and timekeepers is indirect labor and their wages are included in factory overhead.

EXAMPLE 2

At the end of the month, labor costs are summarized and posted to the general ledger, usually according to direct and indirect costs, as shown by the following entry:

Work in Process	20,000	
Factory Overhead	6,000	
Wages Payable		26,000

Factory Overhead

This includes all factory costs other than raw materials and direct labor. Each overhead item is recorded in an individual account, but a single predetermined overhead rate is used in computing estimates and bids for jobs and for recording costs. If actual cost exceeds estimated cost, factory overhead is *underapplied*; otherwise it is *overapplied*. This simplifying procedure enables management to determine the total cost of a job as soon as the job is finished and to find out if the job resulted in a profit or a loss.

9.3 INVENTORIES

To calculate manufacturing cost and the cost of goods sold, it is generally necessary to find the amount of inventory at the end of the period. This amount is determined by (1) the *unit cost*, or manufacturing cost per item, and (2) the number of units on hand.

EXAMPLE 3

Assume that the unit cost of this month's production of alarm clocks was $6.52 for 1,000 clocks. Assume also that at the beginning of the month there were on hand 200 clocks that had been produced last month at a unit cost of $6.20, and 100 clocks that had been produced two months previously at $5.80 a clock. If 400 clocks were sold during the month, the cost of the clocks sold would be $2,472 by the FIFO method or $2,608 by the LIFO method.

Periodic Inventory Method

Under the periodic method the costs of individual sales are not recorded, and to find the amount of the closing inventory it is necessary to count and price the items on hand at the end of the period. If units of a product were on hand at the beginning of the period and additional units were produced during that period, the sum of the two is the number of units available for sale during the period. Of this number, some units were sold and some are still on hand. In most cases it is easier to count the items on hand at the end of the period and to apply a cost using LIFO, FIFO, or some other costing basis (see *Schaum's Outline of*

Accounting I). The amount so obtained is then subtracted from the total goods available for sale to derive the amount of Cost of Goods Sold.

The periodic inventory method, while much simpler than keeping track of hundreds or thousands of receipts and issues throughout the period, has some disadvantages. It is time-consuming, and since it is applied only at intervals, usually once a year, there are sometimes errors in counting, pricing, or compiling the total.

Perpetual Inventory Method

Continuous individual records are usually maintained to keep closer control of high-price manufactured items or to assure that a sufficient quantity of raw materials is on hand for production. For expensive products, especially where there are not a great many transactions, it is desirable to know at all times how many units have been sold and how many are on hand—and also how many should be on hand. In the case of automobiles or large appliances, each unit will carry a serial number which appears on the purchase invoice. It is then a simple matter to list from purchase invoices the serial numbers of those units that were not sold and should be on hand. If any unit is missing, it is usually easy to trace by serial number the receipt, shipment, or location of the particular item.

Critical raw materials do not bear serial numbers. However, it is necessary to keep perpetual records of receipts, issues, and quantity on hand to prevent shortages that might halt production and be very costly.

9.4 COST OF GOODS MANUFACTURED

The *cost of goods manufactured* is the manufacturing cost (raw materials + direct labor + factory overhead) of the products *finished* during the period. It is to be distinguished from *total manufacturing cost*, which also includes work in process.

As illustrated in Example 4 below, the balance of Cost of Goods Manufactured is carried in the manufacturing summary account, from which it is transferred to Expense and Income Summary. To keep the income statement from becoming overly long, a separate *statement of cost of goods manufactured* is prepared. This statement expands on the manufacturing summary, providing the additional operating details required by management. Two or more periods may be included on the statement to show the changes from one period to another.

EXAMPLE 4

The development of the statement of cost of goods manufactured for the Chamberlain Manufacturing Company is shown in Exhibit A below.

Manufacturing Summary

19X1		19X1	
Work in Process Inv., Jan. 1	15,000	Work in Process Inv., Dec. 31	12,500
Raw Materials Inv., Jan. 1	20,000	Raw Materials Inv., Dec. 31	23,000
Purchases and Transportation	74,500	Bal. to Exp. and Inc. Sum.	173,300
Direct Labor	57,500		
Factory Overhead	41,800		
	208,800		208,800

Expense and Income Summary

19X1		19X1	
Finished Goods Inv., Jan. 1	27,600	Finished Goods Inv., Dec. 31	32,500
From Manufacturing Sum.	173,300	Cost of Goods Sold	168,400
	200,900		200,900

Exhibit A
Chamberlain Manufacturing Company
Statement of Cost of Goods Manufactured
For Year Ended December 31, 19X1

Work in Process Inventory, Jan. 1, 19X1			$ 15,000
Raw Materials			
Inventory, Jan. 1		$20,000	
Purchases	$75,500		
Less: Returns and Allowances	5,000	70,500	
Transportation-in		4,000	
Raw Materials Available for Use		$94,500	
Less: Inventory, Dec. 31		23,000	
Cost of Raw Materials Used		$71,500	
Direct Labor		57,500	
Factory Overhead			
Indirect Labor	$12,200		
Heat, Light, and Power	10,500		
Property Taxes	2,250		
Insurance	1,500		
Depreciation	11,500		
Miscellaneous	3,850		
Total Factory Overhead		41,800	
Total Manufacturing Cost			170,800
Total Work in Process During Period			$185,800
Less: Work in Process Inventory, Dec. 31			12,500
Cost of Goods Manufactured			$173,300

9.5 INCOME STATEMENT

The income statement for a manufacturing company is similar to that for a merchandising company, except for the terminology in the cost of goods sold section. Below is shown a comparison of the terms.

Merchandising Company	Manufacturing Company
Beginning Inventory of Merchandise	Beginning Inventory of Finished Goods
+	+
Purchases of Merchandise	Cost of Goods Manufactured
−	−
Ending Inventory of Merchandise	Ending Inventory of Finished Goods
=	=
Cost of Goods Sold	Cost of Goods Sold

In most cases the caption in the income statement of manufacturing costs is shown as "Cost of Goods Manufactured (see Exhibit A)." Thus, attention is directed to the cost statement that supports the total figure shown in the income statement.

EXAMPLE 5

In the income statement of the Chamberlain Manufacturing Company (Example 4), the sales and cost of goods sold sections would appear as:

Chamberlain Manufacturing Company
Income Statement
For Year Ended December 31, 19X1

Sales		$256,700
Cost of Goods Sold		
Finished Goods Inventory, Jan. 1, 19X1	$ 27,600	
Cost of Goods Manufactured (see Exhibit A)	173,300	
Goods Available for Sale	$200,900	
Less: Finished Goods Inventory, Dec. 31, 19X1	32,500	
Cost of Goods Sold		168,400

Solved Problems

9.1 The Robert Benson Company manufactures one product, Egypt Balm, which is processed in four departments. During December, $56,700 of direct materials was put into production and $68,500 of direct labor was incurred in Department 1. The factory overhead rate is 75% of direct labor cost. Work in process in Department 1 was $36,200 at the beginning of the month and $32,600 at the end of the month. Prepare general journal entries to record (a) direct materials, (b) direct labor, (c) factory overhead, and (d) cost of the production transferred to Department 2.

(a)

(b)

(c)

(d)

SOLUTION

(a)	Work in Process, Department 1	56,700	
	Materials		56,700
(b)	Work in Process, Department 1	68,500	
	Wages Payable		68,500

(c)	Work in Process, Department 1	51,375	
	Factory Overhead, Department 1		51,375
(d)	Work in Process, Department 2	180,175	
	Work in Process, Department 2		180,175

9.2 Ray's Company budgeted amounts for the current year included 80,000 direct labor hours and $560,000 of factory overhead cost. Actual direct labor hours were 75,000, and actual factory overhead cost was $550,000. (a) Compute the estimated factory overhead rate based on direct labor hours. (b) Compute the amount of factory overhead applied to production. (c) Determine the amount of overhead overapplied or underapplied.

SOLUTION

(a) Estimated overhead rate = $560,000 ÷ 80,000 direct labor hours = $7 per direct labor hour.

(b) Factory overhead applied = $7 × 75,000 = $525,000.

(c) $550,000 (actual overhead) − $525,000 (applied overhead) = $25,000 underapplied overhead.

9.3 The following balances appeared in Rose Company's ledger prior to closing entries for 19X1 and 19X2.

	12/31/X1	12/31/X2
Raw Materials Inventory	$ 26,000	$ 25,000
Work in Process Inventory	10,000	8,000
Finished Goods Inventory	12,000	18,000
Raw Materials Purchases (net)	100,000	110,000
Direct Labor	80,000	105,000
Manufacturing Overhead	200,000	220,000

(a) Compute the cost of raw materials used in 19X2.

(b) Compute the cost of goods manufactured in 19X2.

(c) Compute the cost of goods sold in 19X2.

SOLUTION

(a) $110,000 + $26,000 − $25,000 = $111,000.

(b) $111,000 + $105,000 + $220,000 + $10,000 − $8,000 = $438,000.

(c) $438,000 + $12,000 − $18,000 = $432,000.

9.4 The James Harold Manufacturing Company has the following accounts in its preclosing trial balance at December 31:

Raw Materials Purchases	$ 75,700	Finished Goods Inventory	$ 85,000
Raw Materials Inventory	29,500	Sales	360,000
Direct Labor	113,500	Selling Expense (control)	18,000
Factor Overhead (control)	76,000	General Expense (control)	12,000
Work in Process Inventory	35,000		

Inventories at December 31 were:

Raw Materials	$31,400
Work in Process	28,200
Finished Goods	80,000

Prepare a statement of cost of goods manufactured.

Statement of Cost of Goods Manufactured

_____

SOLUTION

Statement of Cost of Goods Manufactured

Work in Process Inventory, Jan. 1		$ 35,000
Raw Materials		
Inventory, Jan. 1	$ 29,500	
Purchases	75,700	
Available for Use	$105,200	
Less: Inventory, Dec. 31	31,400	
Put in Production	$ 73,800	
Direct Labor	113,500	
Factory Overhead	76,000	
Total Manufacturing Costs		263,300
Total Work in Process during Period		$298,300
Less: Work in Process Inventory, Dec. 31		28,200
Cost of Goods Manufactured		$270,100

9.5   Prepare an income statement based on the information in Problem 9.4.

Income Statement

_____

SOLUTION

Income Statement

Sales		$360,000
Cost of Goods Sold		
Finished Goods Inventory, Jan. 1	$ 85,000	
Cost of Goods Manufactured	270,100	
Cost of Finished Goods Available for Sale	$355,100	
Less: Finished Goods Inventory, Dec. 31	80,000	
Cost of Goods Sold		275,100
Gross Profit		$ 84,900
Less: Selling Expense (control)	$ 18,000	
General Expense (control)	12,000	
Total Expenses		30,000
Net Income		$ 54,900

9.6 Based on the data in Problem 9.4, show the journal entries for December 31 needed (*a*) to adjust the inventory accounts; (*b*) to close the accounts to Manufacturing Summary; and (*c*) to close Manufacturing Summary.

(*a*)

(*b*)

(*c*)

SOLUTION

(*a*)	Manufacturing Summary	64,500	
	Work in Process Inventory		35,000
	Raw Materials Inventory		29,500

	Work in Process Inventory	28,200	
	Raw Materials Inventory	31,400	
	Manufacturing Summary		59,600
	Expense and Income Summary	85,000	
	Finished Goods Inventory		85,000
	Finished Goods Inventory	80,000	
	Expense and Income Summary		80,000
(b)	Manufacturing Summary	265,200	
	Raw Materials Purchases		75,700
	Direct Labor		113,500
	Factory Overhead		76,000
(c)	Expense and Income Summary	270,100	
	Manufacturing Summary		270,100

9.7 Before closing, Schmidt Manufacturing has the following accounts in its trial balance at December 31:

Raw Materials Purchases	$192,000	Finished Goods Inventory	$ 50,250
Raw Materials Inventory	39,200	Sales	645,750
Direct Labor	181,500	Selling Expense (controlling)	70,275
Factory Overhead (controlling)	89,650	General Expense (controlling)	65,400
Work in Process Inventory	38,500		

Inventories at December 31:

   Raw Materials $42,300   Work in Process $40,600   Finished Goods $56,400

Prepare (a) a statement of cost of goods manufactured; (b) an income statement.

(a)

Schmidt Manufacturing Company

Statement of Cost of Goods Manufactured

For Year Ended December 31, 19X1

(b)

Schmidt Manufacturing Company
Income Statement
For Year Ended December 31, 19X1

SOLUTION

(a)

Schmidt Manufacturing Company
Statement of Cost of Goods Manufactured
For Year Ended December 31, 19X1

Work in Process Inventory, Jan. 1		$ 38,500
Raw Materials		
Inventory, Jan. 1	$ 39,200	
Purchases	192,000	
Cost of Materials Available for Use	$231,200	
Less: Inventory, Dec. 31	42,300	
Cost of Materials Put in Production	$188,900	
Direct Labor	181,500	
Factory Overhead	89,650	
Total Manufacturing Costs		460,050
Total Work in Process during Period		$498,550
Less: Work in Process Inventory, Dec. 31		40,600
Cost of Goods Manufactured		$457,950

(b)

Schmidt Manufacturing Company
Income Statement
For Year Ended December 31, 19X1

Sales		$645,750
Cost of Goods Sold		
Finished Goods Inventory, Jan. 1	$ 50,250	
Cost of Goods Manufactured	457,950	
Cost of Finished Goods Available for Sale	$508,200	
Less: Finished Goods Inventory, Dec. 31	56,400	
Cost of Goods Sold		451,800
Gross Profit on Sales		$193,950

Operating Expenses		
Selling Expenses	$ 70,275	
General Expenses	65,400	
Total Operating Expenses		135,675
Net Income before Taxes		$ 58,275

9.8 At the end of the first month of the current fiscal year P & T Mahoney Company has the following trial balance:

Cash	$ 34,750	
Marketable Securities	15,000	
Accounts Receivable	41,300	
Allowance for Doubtful Accounts		$ 2,200
Finished Goods, Product A	32,400	
Finished Goods, Product B	56,200	
Work in Process, Department 1	22,900	
Work in Process, Department 2	22,600	
Raw Materials	25,400	
Prepaid Expenses	5,800	
Machinery and Equipment	115,700	
Accumulated Depreciation, Machinery and Equipment		35,000
Buildings	257,000	
Accumulated Depreciation, Buildings		55,000
Land	50,000	
Accounts Payable		48,600
Wages Payable		6,500
Income Tax Payable		4,200
Mortgage Note Payable (due 19X6)		75,000
Common Stock, $25 par		350,000
Retained Earnings		85,400
Sales		175,800
Cost of Goods Sold	115,600	
Factory Overhead, Department 1	300	
Factory Overhead, Department 2	50	
Factory Overhead, Department 3		100
Selling Expenses	24,600	
General Expenses	13,500	
Interest Expense	650	
Interest Income		150
Income Tax	4,200	
	$837,950	$837,950

Prepare (*a*) an income statement, and (*b*) a balance sheet.

(a)

P & T Mahoney Company

Income Statement

Month Ended January 31, 19X1

(b)

P & T Mahoney Company

Balance Sheet

January 31, 19X1

ASSETS

Current Assets

Total Current Assets

	Cost	Accumulated Depreciation	Book Value
Plant Assets			

Total Plant Assets

Deferred Charge

Total Assets

LIABILITIES

Current Liabilities

Total Current Liabilities
Long-Term Liabilities

Total Liabilities

STOCKHOLDERS' EQUITY

Stockholders' Equity
Total Liabilities and Stockholders' Equity

SOLUTION

(a)

P & T Mahoney Company
Income Statement
Month Ended January 31, 19X1

Sales		$175,800
Less: Cost of Goods Sold		115,600
Gross Profit on Sales		$ 60,200
Operating Expenses		
Selling Expenses	$24,600	
General Expenses	13,500	38,100
Income from Operations		$ 22,100
Other Expenses (net)		
Interest Expense	$ 650	
Less: Interest Income	150	500
Income before Income Tax		$ 21,600
Income Tax		4,200
Net Income		17,400

(b)

P & T Mahoney Company
Balance Sheet
January 31, 19X1

ASSETS

Current Assets			
Cash		$ 34,750	
Marketable Securities		15,000	
Accounts Receivable	$41,300		
Less: Allowance for Doubtful Accounts	2,200	39,100	
Inventories			
Finished Goods	$88,600		
Work in Process	45,500		
Raw Materials	25,400	159,500	
Prepaid Expenses		5,800	
Total Current Assets			$254,150

	Cost	Accumulated Depreciation	Book Value	
Plant Assets				
Mach. & Equip.	$115,700	$35,000	$ 80,700	
Buildings	257,000	55,000	202,000	
Land	50,000		50,000	
Total Plant Assets	$422,700	$90,000		332,700
Deferred Charge				
Factory Overhead Underapplied				250
Total Assets				$587,100

LIABILITIES

Current Liabilities		
Accounts Payable	$ 48,600	
Wages Payable	6,500	
Income Tax Payable	4,200	
Total Current Liabilities		$ 59,300
Long-Term Liabilities		
Mortgage Note Payable (due 19X6)		75,000
Total Liabilities		$134,300

STOCKHOLDERS' EQUITY

Common Stock, $25 par	$350,000	
Retained Earnings	102,800*	
Stockholders' Equity		452,800
Total Liabilities and Stockholders' Equity		$587,100

*Balance per trial balance	$ 85,400
Net income for January	17,400
Balance, Jan. 31	$102,800

Chapter 10

Manufacturing Accounting:
Worksheets and Joint and By-products

10.1 WORKSHEETS

As in nonmanufacturing companies, the financial statements can be prepared more quickly and accurately if a worksheet is used. The form of the worksheet for a manufacturing company is derived from the form for a merchandising company by merely adding a pair of columns to provide the data needed for the statement of cost of goods manufactured (see Section 9.4). The preparation of the worksheet for the Allison Company is illustrated on the next page. For simplicity, only those adjustments for cost of manufacturing and inventories are made.

Adjustment Data
Inventories at December 31, 19X1

Finished Goods	$74,150
Work in Process	49,250
Raw Materials	43,500

The statement of cost of goods manufactured and the income statement, based on the information obtained from the worksheet, follow on page 148.

10.2 JOINT PRODUCTS

Where two or more products are obtained from a common process, they are usually referred to as *joint products* if all are of significant value. Typical of joint products are gasoline, kerosene, and naphtha, which are all obtained from the refining of crude oil. Generally, one joint product cannot be produced without the others, and only the total revenue of the entire group and the total production cost are relevant. However, for inventory purposes it is necessary to make an allocation of costs among the joint products. The usual method of allocating cost is on the sales value of the various products.

EXAMPLE 1

Assume that 5,000 units of Product A and 20,000 units of Product B were produced at a total cost of $30,000.

Joint Product	Units Produced	Unit Sales Price	Sales Value	Percent of Total
A	5,000	$4.00	$20,000	40%
B	20,000	1.50	30,000	60%
			$50,000	

Allocation of Joint Cost

A	40%	$12,000
B	60%	18,000
		$30,000

Unit Cost

A: $12,000 ÷ 5,000 units = $2.40
B: 18,000 ÷ 20,000 units = .90
    $30,000

Allison Company
Worksheet
Year Ended December 31, 19X1

Account Title	Trial Balance Dr.	Trial Balance Cr.	Adjustments Dr.	Adjustments Cr.	Cost of Manufacturing Statement Dr.	Cost of Manufacturing Statement Cr.	Income Statement Dr.	Income Statement Cr.	Balance Sheet Dr.	Balance Sheet Cr.
Cash	51,000								51,000	
Accounts Receivable	68,850								68,850	
Allow. for Doubtful Acct.		1,200								1,200
Finished Goods	71,300		74,150	71,300					74,150	
Work in Process	47,500		49,250	47,500					49,250	
Raw Materials	42,000		43,550	42,000					43,550	
Prepaid Expense (controlling)	19,700								19,700	
Plant Assets (controlling)	807,900								807,900	
Accum. Depr., Plant Asset (cont.)		287,900								287,900
Accounts Payable		40,200								40,200
Common Stock ($20 par)		550,000								550,000
Retained Earnings		100,500								100,500
Income Summary			71,300	74,150			71,300	74,150		
Manufacturing Summary			47,500	49,250	47,500	49,250				
			42,000	43,550	42,000	43,550				
Sales		808,600						808,600		
Raw Materials Purchases	210,850				210,850					
Direct Labor	188,400				188,400					
Factory Overhead (control)	95,600				95,600					
Selling Expenses (control)	114,250						114,250			
General Expenses (control)	71,050						71,050			
	1,788,400	1,788,400	327,750	327,750		92,800	256,600		1,114,400	979,800
Cost of Goods Manufactured						491,550	491,550			
					584,350	584,350	748,150	882,750		
Net Income							134,600			134,600
							882,750	882,750	1,114,400	1,114,400

147

Allison Company
Statement of Cost of Goods Manufactured
For Year Ended December 31, 19X1

Work in Process Inventory, Jan. 1		$ 47,500
Raw Materials		
Inventory, Jan. 1	$ 42,000	
Purchases	210,850	
Cost of Materials Available for Use	$252,850	
Less: Inventory, Dec. 31	43,550	
Cost of Materials Put in Production	$209,300	
Direct Labor	188,400	
Factory Overhead	95,600	
Total Manufacturing Costs		493,300
Total Work in Process during Period		$540,800
Less: Work in Process Inventory, Dec. 31		49,250
Cost of Goods Manufactured		$491,550

Allison Company
Income Statement
For Year Ended December 31, 19X1

Sales		$808,600
Cost of Goods Sold		
Finished Goods Inventory, Jan. 1	$ 71,300	
Cost of Goods Manufactured	491,550	
Cost of Finished Goods Available for Sale	$562,850	
Less: Finished Goods Inventory, Dec. 31	74,150	
Cost of Goods Sold		488,700
Gross Profit on Sales		$319,900
Operating Expenses		
Selling Expenses	$114,250	
General Expenses	71,050	
Total Operating Expenses		185,300
Net Income		$134,600

10.3 BY-PRODUCTS

A product is referred to as a *by-product* if it has a limited value in relation to the principal product. Generally a by-product is merely incidental to the manufacture of the principal product.

An example of a by-product would be leftover material such as sawdust in a lumber mill. Generally, the sales value of the by-product, less any processing or selling costs, is deducted from Work in Process of the principal product and transferred to a finished goods account.

EXAMPLE 2

Assume that costs accumulated in Work in Process, Production Department, were $18,600, including the by-product, Product B, with an estimated value of $400. The entry would be as follows:

| Finished Goods, Product B | 400 | |
| Work in Process, Production Department | | 400 |

The accounts would appear as below:

Work in Process, Production Department			Finished Goods, Product B	
18,600	400		400	

Summary: Chapters 9 and 10

1. The three kinds of manufacturing costs included in finished goods are _____ , _____ , and _____ .

2. Indirect materials, indirect labor, factory manager's salary, machinery repairs are all examples of _____ .

3. Three principal inventory accounts for a manufacturing business are _____ , _____ , and _____ .

4. The value of inventory is determined through counting and pricing under the _____ method, and through individual records under the _____ method.

5. The manufacturing summary account is amplified in the _____ .

6. To calculate _____ , we add the opening work in process inventory, the direct materials placed in production, and the direct labor and factory overhead for the period, and then subtract the ending work in process inventory.

7. The total production cost of two joint products would usually be divided between them in the ratio of their _____ .

8. If two or more products are obtained from a common process, the products are known as _____ .

9. If a product produced is merely incidental to the principal product, it is called a _____ .

10. The sales value of a by-product is generally subtracted from _____ of the principal product.

Answers: (1) direct materials, direct labor, factory overhead; (2) factory overhead; (3) Finished Goods, Work in Process, Raw Materials; (4) periodic, perpetual; (5) statement of cost of goods manufactured; (6) cost of goods manufactured; (7) sales values; (8) joint products; (9) by-product; (10) work in process.

Solved Problems

10.1 Shown below is the trial balance for Van Horn Chemicals, Inc. (For account groups for which subsidiary ledgers are maintained, only the control balances are listed.)

Cash	$ 44,750	
Accounts Receivable	35,300	
Allowance for Doubtful Accounts		$ 1,250
Finished Goods	60,300	
Work in Process	25,600	
Raw Materials	22,100	
Prepaid Expenses (control)	7,500	
Plant Assets (control)	545,450	
Accumulated Depreciation, Plant Assets		138,400
Accounts Payable		32,500
Common Stock, $15 par		450,000
Retained Earnings		50,500
Sales		510,000
Raw Materials Purchases	160,800	
Direct Labor	145,000	
Factory Overhead (control)	46,750	
Selling Expenses (control)	41,000	
General Expenses (control)	35,600	
Interest Expense	500	
Income Tax	12,000	
	$1,182,650	$1,182,650

Adjustments data for the current year are as follows:

(1) Prepaid insurance of $4,000 has expired during the year, 80% being applicable to factory operations and 20% to general operations.

(2) An analysis of accounts receivable shows that the Allowance for Doubtful Accounts should be $2,000.

(3) Unpaid payroll amounts at the end of the year are: direct labor, $2,200; factory supervision, $300.

(4) Depreciation for the year was $20,000, chargeable 90% to factory operations and 10% to general operations.

(5) Inventories at December 31, 19X1, are: Finished Goods, $43,100; Work in Process, $31,500; Raw Materials, $27,600.

(6) The opening inventories are to be closed out to the appropriate summaries.

(7) The estimated federal income tax for the year is $15,000.

Prepare (*a*) a ten-column worksheet; (*b*) a statement of cost of goods manufactured; and (*c*) an income statement.

(a)

Van Horn Chemicals, Inc.
Worksheet
Year Ended December 31, 19X1

Accounts	Trial Balance		Adjustments		Cost of Goods Manufactured		Income Statement		Balance Sheet	
	Dr.	Cr.	Dr.	Cr.	Dr.	Cr.	Dr.	Cr.	Dr.	Cr.

(b)

Van Horn Chemicals, Inc.

Statement of Cost of Goods Manufactured

Year Ended December 31, 19X1

(c)

Van Horn Chemicals, Inc.

Income Statement

Year Ended December 31, 19X1

SOLUTION

(a) See the worksheet on the next page.

(a)

Van Horn Chemicals, Inc.
Worksheet
Year Ended December 31, 19X1

Accounts	Trial Balance Dr.	Trial Balance Cr.	Adjustments Dr.	Adjustments Cr.	Cost of Goods Manufactured Dr.	Cost of Goods Manufactured Cr.	Income Statement Dr.	Income Statement Cr.	Balance Sheet Dr.	Balance Sheet Cr.
Cash	44,750								44,750	
Accounts Receivable	35,300								35,300	
Allow. for Doubtful Acct.		1,250		(2) 750						2,000
Finished Goods	60,300		(5) 43,100	(6) 60,300					43,100	
Work in Process	25,600		(5) 31,500	(6) 25,600					31,500	
Raw Materials	22,100		(5) 27,600	(6) 22,100					27,600	
Prepaid Expenses (control)	7,500			(1) 4,000					3,500	
Plant Assets (control)	545,450								545,450	
Accum. Depr., Plant Assets		138,400		(4) 20,000						158,400
Accounts Payable		32,500								32,500
Income Tax Payable				(7) 3,000						3,000
Accrued Liabilities				(3) 2,500						2,500
Common Stock, $15 par		450,000								450,000
Retained Earnings		50,500								50,500
Income Summary			(6) 60,300	(5) 43,100			60,300	43,100		
Manufacturing Summary			(6) 25,600	(5) 31,500	25,600	31,500				
Manufacturing Summary			(6) 22,100	(5) 27,600	22,100	27,600				
Sales		510,000						510,000		
Direct Materials Purchases	160,800				160,800					
Direct Labor	145,000		(3) 2,200		147,200					
Factory Overhead (control)	46,750		(1) 3,200		68,250					
Factory Overhead (control)			(3) 300							
Factory Overhead (control)			(4) 18,000							
Selling Expenses (control)	41,000		(1) 800				41,000			
General Expenses (control)	35,600		(4) 750				39,150			
			(4) 2,000							
Interest Expense	500						500			
Income Tax	12,000		(7) 3,000				15,000			
	1,182,650	1,182,650	240,450	240,450		59,100				
Cost of Goods Manufactured						364,850	364,850			
					423,950	423,950	520,800	553,100	731,200	698,900
Net Income							32,300			32,300
							553,100	553,100	731,200	731,200

153

(b)

Van Horn Chemicals, Inc.
Statement of Cost of Goods Manufactured
Year Ended December 31, 19X1

Work in Process Inventory, Jan. 1		$ 25,600
Raw Materials		
Inventory, Jan. 1	$ 22,100	
Purchases	160,800	
Available for Use	$182,900	
Less: Inventory, Dec. 31	27,600	
Cost Put in Production	$155,300	
Direct Labor	147,200	
Factory Overhead	68,250	
Total Manufacturing Costs		370,750
Total Work in Process during Period		$396,350
Less: Work in Process Inventory, Dec. 31		31,500
Cost of Goods Manufactured		$364,850

(c)

Van Horn Chemicals, Inc.
Income Statement
Year Ended December 31, 19X1

Sales		$510,000
Cost of Goods Sold		
Finished Goods Inventory, Jan. 1	$ 60,300	
Cost of Goods Manufactured	364,850	
Goods Available for Sale	$425,150	
Less: Finished Goods Inventory,		
Dec. 31	43,100	
Cost of Goods Sold		382,050
Gross Profit on Sales		$127,950
Operating Expenses		
Selling Expenses	$ 41,000	
General Expenses	39,150	
Total Operating Expenses		80,150
Income from Operations		$ 47,800
Other Expense		
Interest Expense		500
Income before Income Tax		$ 47,300
Income Tax		15,000
Net Income		$ 32,300

10.2   The account Work in Process, Department B, for the Lanuto Electric Company shows dollar charges and units of products completed as follows:

Work in Process, Department B

From Department A	8,600	By-product M (1,000 units)
Direct Labor	17,777	Joint Product X (6,000 units)
Factory Overhead	22,223	Joint Product Y (8,000 units)

The value of M is $0.60 a unit; X sells for $12 a unit and Y sells for $3 a unit. Work in Process has no inventory at either the beginning or the end of the period. (a) Allocate the costs to the three products. (b) Compute the unit cost for each joint product.

SOLUTION

(a)

Total cost to be allocated	$48,600
Less: Value of by-product M (1,000 × $0.60)	600
Cost to be allocated to joint products	$48,000

Joint Product	Sales Value
X (6,000 units @ $12)	$72,000
Y (8,000 units @ $3)	24,000
Total sales value	$96,000

$$\text{Cost of X:} \quad \frac{72,000}{96,000} \times \$48,000 = \$36,000$$

$$\text{Cost of Y:} \quad \frac{24,000}{96,000} \times \$48,000 = \$12,000$$

Allocation Summary

M	$ 600
X	36,000
Y	12,000
Total Cost	$48,600

(b)

Unit cost of X:	$36,000 ÷ 6,000 units = $6.00
Unit cost of Y:	$12,000 ÷ 8,000 units = $1.50

10.3 On December 1 the Kuezek Auto Company had the following inventory balances: Materials, $25,000; Work in Process, $40,000; Finished Goods, $20,000. Representative transactions for the month of December are:

(1) Materials were purchased for $18,500.

(2) Parts in the amount of $20,000 were issued from the storeroom for production.

(3) Requisitions for indirect materials and supplies amounted to $2,500.

(4) Labor costs for December were $28,000, including salespeople's salaries of $5,000 and office salaries of $3,000. Income taxes of $2,500 and Social Security taxes of $1,500 were deducted.

(5) Miscellaneous manufacturing expenses during the month were $7,500.

(6) The factory overhead rate is 75% of direct labor cost.

(7) The cost of production completed in December was $65,500 and finished goods inventory at December 31 was $8,100.

(8) Sales, all on account, for the month were $95,600.

Prepare journal entries (a) to record the above transactions, (b) to close the various accounts to Expense and Income Summary and to close the net income to Retained Earnings.

(a)

(1)

(2)

(3)

(4)

(5)

(6)

(7)

(8)

(b)

SOLUTION

(a)	(1)	Materials	18,500	
		Accounts Payable		18,500
	(2)	Work in Process	20,000	
		Materials		20,000
	(3)	Factory Overhead Control	2,500	
		Materials		2,500

(4)	Work in Process (Direct Labor)	20,000	
	Selling Expenses Control (Salespeople's Salaries)	5,000	
	General Expenses Control (Office Salaries)	3,000	
	Federal Income Taxes Withheld		2,500
	Social Security Taxes Withheld		1,500
	Cash		24,000
(5)	Factory Overhead Control	7,500	
	Accounts Payable		7,500
(6)	Work in Process	15,000	
	Factory Overhead Applied		15,000
(7)	Finished Goods	65,500	
	Work in Process		65,500
(8)	Accounts Receivable	95,600	
	Sales		95,600
	Cost of Goods Sold	77,400*	
	Finished Goods		77,400

*Finished goods inventory, Dec. 1	$20,000
December production	65,500
Goods available for sale	$85,500
Less: Finished goods inventory, Dec. 31	8,100
	$77,400

(b)	Sales	95,600	
	Expense and Income Summary		95,600
	Expense and Income Summary	85,400	
	Cost of Goods Sold		77,400
	Selling Expenses		5,000
	General Expenses		3,000
	Expense and Income Summary	10,200	
	Retained Earnings		10,200

10.4　The Cameo Baking Company produces Cameo Crispies and Cameo Creamies. Initially materials are put into process in Department A and on completion are transferred to Department B, where further materials are added. After processing in Department B, the finished goods are ready for sale. The two service departments are Maintenance & Repair and Factory Office. Manufacturing transactions for January are:

(1)　Materials purchased on account, $15,000.

(2)　Materials issued from inventory: Department A, $13,600 (of which $11,000 is direct materials); Department B, $10,050 (of which $8,650 is direct materials); Maintenance & Repair, $600.

(3)　Miscellaneous costs and expenses payable: Department A, $700; Department B, $450; Maintenance & Repair, $350; Factory Office, $235.

(4) Labor costs: Department A, $8,850 (of which $8,250 is direct costs); Department B, $6,400 (of which $6,000 is direct costs); Maintenance & Repair, $950; Factory Office, $750.

(5) Prepaid expenses used up: Department A, $80; Department B, $60; Maintenance & Repair, $150; Factory Office, $65.

(6) Depreciation on plant assets: Department A, $500; Department B, $900; Maintenance & Repair, $250; Factory Office, $150.

(7) Factory office costs are allocated on the basis of total labor hours worked in each department: Department A, 400 labor hours; Department B, 600 labor hours; Maintenance & Repair, 200 labor hours.

(8) Maintenance and repair costs are allocated on the basis of services given: Department A, 70%; Department B, 30%.

(9) Factory overhead is applied at predetermined rates: Department A, 80% of direct labor costs; Department B, 75% of direct labor costs.

(10) Completed production, Department A, 2,000 units.

(11) Completed production, Department B, 1,500 units of Cameo Crispies and 2,000 units of Cameo Creamies. The unit sales price is $12 for Cameo Crispies and $18 for Cameo Creamies.

Additional data: Finished goods inventories at January 1: Cameo Crispies, 400 units @ $8; Cameo Creamies, 600 units @ $14. There was no work in process inventory at the beginning or at the end of the month.

Prepare general journal entries to record the above transactions.

(1)		
(2)		
(3)		
(4)		
(5)		

(6)		
(7)		
(8)		
(9)		
(10)		
(11)		

SOLUTION

(1)	Materials	15,000	
	Accounts Payable		15,000
(2)	Work in Process, Department A	11,000	
	Work in Process, Department B	8,650	
	Factory Overhead, Department A	2,600	
	Factory Overhead, Department B	1,400	
	Maintenance & Repair	600	
	Materials		24,250
(3)	Factory Overhead, Department A	700	
	Factory Overhead, Department B	450	
	Maintenance & Repair	350	
	Factory Office	235	
	Accounts Payable		1,735

(4)	Work in Process, Department A	8,250	
	Work in Process, Department B	6,000	
	Factory Overhead, Department A	600	
	Factory Overhead, Department B	400	
	Maintenance & Repair	950	
	Factory Office	750	
	Wages Payable		16,950

(5)	Factory Overhead, Department A	80	
	Factory Overhead, Department B	60	
	Maintenance & Repair	150	
	Factory Office	65	
	Prepaid Expenses		355

(6)	Factory Overhead, Department A	500	
	Factory Overhead, Department B	900	
	Maintenance & Repair	250	
	Factory Office	150	
	Accumulated Depreciation, Plant Assets		1,800

(7)	Factory Overhead, Department A (400 labor hours)	400	
	Factory Overhead, Department B (600 labor hours)	600	
	Maintenance & Repair (200 labor hours)	200	
	Factory Office		1,200*

(8)	Factory Overhead, Department A (70%)	1,750	
	Factory Overhead, Department B (30%)	750	
	Maintenance & Repair		2,500†

(9)	Work in Process, Department A	6,600	
	Work in Process, Department B	4,500	
	Factory Overhead, Department A (80%)		6,600
	Factory Overhead, Department B (75%)		4,500

| (10) | Work in Process, Department B | 25,850 | |
| | Work in Process, Department A | | 25,850‡ |

(11)	Finished Goods, Cameo Crispies	15,000	
	Finished Goods, Cameo Creamies	30,000	
	Work in Process, Department B		45,000**

Allocation of Joint Costs in the Ratio of Sales Values

Joint Product	Units Produced	Unit Sales Price	Sales Value	Ratio	Joint Cost	Unit Cost
Cameo Crispies	1,500	$12	$18,000	1/3	$15,000	$10
Cameo Creamies	2,000	18	36,000	2/3	30,000	15
			$54,000		$45,000	

*235 + 750 + 65 + 150   ‡11,000 + 8,250 + 6,600

†600 + 350 + 950 + 150 + 250 + 200   **8,650 + 6,000 + 4,500 + 25,850

10.5   The Augusta Dairy had the following data on its books for January 19X1:

Inventories, January 1	
Raw Materials	$35,000
Work in Process, Materials	12,000
Work in Process, Labor	15,000
Work in Process, Factory Overhead	10,000
Finished Goods	20,000
Transactions during January	
Materials Purchased	$90,000
Direct Labor Cost	75,000
Factory Overhead (80% of direct labor cost)	60,000
Inventories, January 31	
Raw Materials	$25,000
Work in Process, Materials	20,000
Work in Process, Labor	18,000
Work in Process, Factory Overhead	15,000
Finished Goods	33,000

Prepare T accounts showing the flow of cost of goods manufactured and sold. (Use three work in process accounts.)

Finished Goods

Inv., 1/1	20,000		

Work in Process, Materials

Inv., 1/1	12,000		

Work in Process, Labor

Inv., 1/1	15,000		

Work in Process, Factory Overhead

Inv., 1/1	10,000		

Raw Materials

Inv., 1/1	35,000		

Cost of Goods Sold

SOLUTION

Finished Goods

Inv., 1/1	20,000	Transf.	206,000	(3)
(2) Transf.	219,000	Inv., 1/31	33,000	
	239,000		239,000	

Work in Process, Materials

Inv., 1/1	12,000	Transf.	92,000	(2)
(1) Transf.	100,000	Inv., 1/31	20,000	
	112,000		112,000	

Work in Process, Labor

Inv., 1/1	15,000	Transf.	72,000	(2)
Incurred	75,000	Inv., 1/31	18,000	
	90,000		90,000	

Work in Process, Factory Overhead

Inv., 1/1	10,000	Transf.	55,000	(2)
Applied	60,000	Inv., 1/31	15,000	
	70,000		70,000	

Raw Materials				**Cost of Goods Sold**	
Inv., 1/1	35,000	Transf.	100,000 (1)	(3)	206,000
Purchased	90,000	Inv., 1/31	25,000		
	125,000		125,000		

Flow of Costs

(1) Raw Materials to Work in Process

(2) Work in Process to Finished Goods

(3) Finished Goods to Cost of Goods Sold

Chapter 11

Cost Systems: Job Order

11.1 INTRODUCTION

A *cost system* is a method of accumulating and assigning costs. It is essential that a manufacturing company know quickly the cost of making a product, performing a factory operation, or carrying out any other activity of the business. Decisions of the highest importance depend on the accuracy of the cost data. For example, an understatement in the cost of producing an automobile would result in a lower selling price than warranted and cause losses of perhaps millions of dollars. Trading and service companies, as well, have developed cost systems for their operations.

A good cost system also provides a means of *cost control*. Thus, management can compare cost data with budgets and standards to effectively plan and control all business activities.

In Sections 11.2 and 11.3 we outline the two principal cost systems: job order cost and process cost. The procedures given in Chapters 9 and 10 for the procurement and issue of materials, the compiling of labor costs, and the application of overhead generally applies to both systems.

11.2 JOB-ORDER COST SYSTEM

Under the job-order cost system the cost of raw materials, direct labor, and factory overhead are accumulated according to the particular job order or lot number. To arrive at the average unit cost the total cost is divided by the number of completed units.

Generally, the job-order cost system is most suitable where the product is made to individual customer's specifications and where the price quoted is closely tied to the cost (for instance, cost plus 15%).

EXAMPLE 1

The accounting cycle will be completed for the Smith Manufacturing Company, which uses a job-order cost system. The company's fiscal year ends December 31. The trial balance at November 30, 19X1, is shown below.

Cash	$ 30,000	
Accounts Receivable	31,000	
Finished Goods	25,000	
Work in Process	15,000	
Raw Materials	10,000	
Prepaid Expenses	3,000	
Plant Assets	244,000	
Accumulated Depreciation, Plant Assets		$ 85,000
Accounts Payable		30,000
Wages Payable		16,000
Common Stock		200,000
Retained Earnings		27,000
	$358,000	$358,000

Opening Balances

The inventory details for the above control accounts at November 30 are as follows:

Finished Goods		Work in Process		Raw Materials	
Product M	$12,000	Job #99	$10,000	Material x	$ 5,000
Product N	8,000	Job #100	5,000	Material y	3,000
Product O	5,000			Material z	2,000
	$25,000		$15,000		$10,000

163

Transactions for the Month

Cost-related transactions for December are summarized below, the general journal entry being given after each transaction. Three jobs are in process—Job #101, Job #102, and Job #103—and these use Material x, Material y, and Material z, in varying proportions.

(1) *Purchases of materials*

	Material x	$12,000	
	Material y	16,000	
	Material z	3,000	
		$31,000	

| Raw Materials | 31,000 | |
| Accounts Payable | | 31,000 |

(2) *Materials requisitioned and placed in production*
Raw materials, $28,000; indirect materials, $2,000

Job	Amount	Material	Amount
#101	$ 8,000	x	$10,000
102	14,000	y	15,000
103	6,000	z	3,000
	$28,000		$28,000

Work in Process	28,000	
Factory Overhead	2,000	
Raw Materials		30,000

(3) *Payroll for the period*
Direct labor, $50,000; supervision and administration, $15,000

Job	Amount
#101	$30,000
102	15,000
103	5,000
	$50,000

Work in Process	50,000	
Factory Overhead	15,000	
Wages Payable		65,000

(4) *Accounts payable for costs incurred*

| Factory Overhead | 23,000 | |
| Accounts Payable | | 23,000 |

(5) *Prepaid expenses used up*

| Factory Overhead | 600 | |
| Prepaid Expenses | | 600 |

(6) *Depreciation for the period*

| Factory Overhead | 4,000 | |
| Accumulated Depreciation, Plant Assets | | 4,000 |

(7) **Factory overhead**
Applied at departmental rate of direct labor cost

Rate	Job	Amount
90%	#101	$27,000
80%	102	12,000
120%	103	6,000
		$45,000

Work in Process   45,000
    Factory Overhead   45,000

(8) **Jobs completed**

Job	Amount	Product	Amount
# 99	$ 10,000	M	$ 75,000
100	5,000	N	46,000
101	65,000		$121,000
102	41,000		
	$121,000		

Finished Goods   121,000
    Work in Process   121,000

(9) **Cost of goods sold**

Product	Amount
M	$ 73,000
N	43,000
O	2,000
	$118,000

Cost of Goods Sold   118,000
    Finished Goods   118,000

Ledger Accounts

The opening balances at November 30 and the transactions for December have been posted to the control accounts:

Raw Materials				Work in Process			
Bal.	10,000	28,000	(2)	Bal.	15,000	121,000	(8)
(1)	31,000			(2)	28,000		
	41,000			(3)	50,000		
Bal.	13,000			(7)	45,000		
					138,000		
				Bal.	17,000		

Finished Goods			
Bal.	25,000	118,000	(9)
(8)	121,000		
	146,000		
Bal.	28,000		

and to the subsidiary ledgers:

Materials Ledger

Material x

Bal.	5,000	10,000	(2)
(1)	12,000		
	17,000		
Bal.	7,000		

Material y

Bal.	3,000	15,000	(2)
(1)	16,000		
	19,000		
Bal.	4,000		

Material z

Bal.	2,000	3,000	(2)
(1)	3,000		
	5,000		
Bal.	2,000		

Cost Ledger

Job #99

Bal.	10,000	10,000	(8)

Job #100

Bal.	5,000	5,000	(8)

Job #101

(2)	8,000	65,000	(8)
(3)	30,000		
(7)	27,000		
	65,000		

Job #102

(2)	14,000	41,000	(8)
(3)	15,000		
(7)	12,000		
	41,000		

Job #103

(2)	6,000		
(3)	5,000		
(7)	6,000		
Bal.	17,000		

Finished Goods Ledger

Product M

Bal.	12,000	73,000	(9)
(8)	75,000		
	87,000		
Bal.	14,000		

Product N

Bal.	8,000	43,000	(9)
(8)	46,000		
	54,000		
Bal.	11,000		

Product O

Bal.	5,000	2,000	(9)
Bal.	3,000		

and to the factory overhead account:

Factory Overhead

(2)	2,000	45,000	(7)
(3)	15,000		
(4)	23,000		
(5)	600		
(6)	4,000		
	44,600	45,000	
	400		
	45,000	400	Bal.

It is seen that factory overhead was *overapplied* for the month; that is, the estimated overhead ($45,000) exceeded the actual charges ($44,600). The resulting credit balance ($400) will be included in the balance sheet as a liability. Had factory overhead been *underapplied*, there would have been a debit balance, which would be shown as a deferred charge on the balance sheet. At the end of the period any amount of underapplied or overapplied overhead would be closed out to Cost of Goods Sold.

Agreement of Subsidiary and Control Accounts

Observe the agreement between the subsidiary ledger balances and the control account balances:

Control Accounts		Subsidiary Ledgers	
Raw Materials	$13,000	Material x	$ 7,000
		Material y	4,000
		Material z	2,000
Work in Process	17,000	Job #103	17,000
Finished Goods	28,000	Product M	14,000
		Product N	11,000
		Product O	3,000

Solved Problems

11.1   The Hebb Manufacturing Company has the following estimated costs for the current year:

	Department A	Department B
Estimated direct labor cost	$60,000	$48,000
Estimated factory overhead cost	75,000	—
Estimated machine hours	—	24,000

Factory overhead is applied to jobs on the basis of direct labor dollars in Department A and on machine hours in Department B. Departmental accounts are kept for work in process and factory overhead. Following are the actual costs for March:

	Department A	Department B
Actual direct labor cost	$5,500	—
Actual factory overhead cost	7,000	$3,600
Actual machine hours	—	2,000

(a) Compute the factory overhead rate for each department.

(b) Prepare the general journal entries to apply overhead to March production.

(c) Determine the departmental factory overhead balances and show whether they are underapplied or overapplied as of March 31.

(a)

(b)

(c)

	Actual	Standard	Balance	
			Underapplied	Overapplied
Department A				
Department B				

SOLUTION

(a)

Department A: $75,000 ÷ $60,000 = 125% of direct labor cost

Department B: $48,000 ÷ $24,000 = $2 per machine hour

(b)

Work in Process, Department A	6,875	
Factory Overhead, Department A ($5,500 × 125%)		6,875
Work in Process, Department B	4,000	
Factory Overhead, Department B ($2 × 2,000)		4,000

(c)

	Actual	Standard	Balance	
			Underapplied	Overapplied
Department A	7,000	6,875	125	
Department B	3,600	4,000		400

11.2 The Klussman Manufacturing Company produces special equipment made to customer specifications. Below is the data for Job #86.

Description: 20 pattern cutters, Style B

Date started: Sept. 1

Date promised: Sept. 15

Materials used, Department 1: $4,800

Direct labor rate, Department 1: $4.20 per hour

Labor hours used, Department 1: 1,200

Direct labor rate, Department 2: $2.00 per hour

Labor hours used, Department 2: 300

Machine hours, Department 2: 400

Applied factory overhead, Department 1: $4.00 per labor hour

Applied factory overhead, Department 2: $1.80 per hour

Compute (*a*) the cost for Job #86; (*b*) the cost per unit.

(*a*)

	Department 1	Department 2	Total

(*b*)

SOLUTION

(*a*)

	Department 1	Department 2	Total
Materials	$ 4,800		$ 4,800
Direct labor			
Department 1 ($4.20 × 1,200)	5,040		5,040
Department 2 ($2.00 × 300)		$ 600	600
Factory overhead			
Department 1 ($4.00 × 1,200)	4,800		4,800
Department 2 ($1.80 × 400)		720	720
Total	$14,640	$1,320	$15,960

(*b*)   Cost per unit: $15,960 ÷ 20 = $798

11.3   The Plastine Manufacturing Corporation, which produces special plastic compounds, uses a job order cost system. Subsidiary ledger balances on October 31, the end of the first month of the current fiscal year, were as follows.

Finished Goods Subsidiary Ledger

Polyester (500 lbs.), $2,500; Epoxy (6,000 lbs.), $30,000; Urethane (3,000 lbs.), $12,000

Work in Process Subsidiary Ledger

Job #690, $8,600; Job #691, $11,400

Raw Materials Subsidiary Ledger

Petroleum Resin, $25,250; Benzine, $12,050; Lubricating Grease, $5,000

The corporation's trial balance as of October 31 was:

Cash	$148,300	
Accounts Receivable	140,000	
Materials Inventory	42,300	
Work in Process Inventory	20,000	
Finished Goods Inventory	44,500	
Prepaid Insurance	5,000	
Plant and Equipment	170,080	
Accounts Payable		$ 54,260
Accrued Wages Payable		10,600
Accumulated Depreciation, Plant and Equipment		115,210
Capital Stock		250,000
Retained Earnings		120,300
Sales		108,100
Cost of Goods Sold	72,000	
Factory Overhead		410
Marketing and Administrative Expenses	16,700	
	$658,880	$658,880

The following transactions took place during November.

(1) Materials purchased on account: petroleum resin, $17,300; benzine, $8,400; lubricating grease, $3,500.

(2) Materials issued during the month

Job #690: petroleum resin, $11,300; benzine, $6,300	$17,600
Job #691: petroleum resin, $7,000; benzine, $4,700	11,700
Job #692: petroleum resin, $4,400; benzine, $2,100	6,500
Supplies issued to factory	
Lubricating grease	740

(3) Payroll for the month: Job #690, $12,400; Job #691, $9,900; Job #692, $4,300; Indirect labor, $3,300.

(4) Factory overhead expenses of $20,600 were incurred on account.

(5) Insurance of $850 expired on the prepaid insurance account.

(6) Marketing and administrative expenses of $17,300 were incurred on account.

(7) Factory payroll checks amounting to $34,600 were distributed.

(8) Payments of accounts payable totaled $64,300.

(9) Depreciation for the month on plant and equipment was $1,500.

(10) Factory overhead is charged to production jobs at 100% of direct labor cost.

(11) Jobs finished during the month: Job #690, 10,000 lbs. of polyester; Job #691, 8,500 lb. of epoxy.

(12) Sales on account were $120,000, covering 9,000 lb. of polyester @ $7.67, 5,500 lb. of epoxy @ $7.50, and 1,620 lb. of urethane @ $6.00. FIFO is used to compute cost of goods sold.

(a) Set up general ledger T accounts, and subsidiary T accounts for Work in Process, Finished Goods, and Materials. Insert opening dollar balances and include quantities in the finished goods ledger. Prepare general journal entries for the month of November. Post to general ledger T accounts and subsidiary ledger T accounts, using numbers 1–12 to identify transactions.

(b) Check the general ledger account balances with appropriate balances in the subsidiary ledgers.

(c) Prepare a trial balance as of November 30.

(a)   *General Ledger*

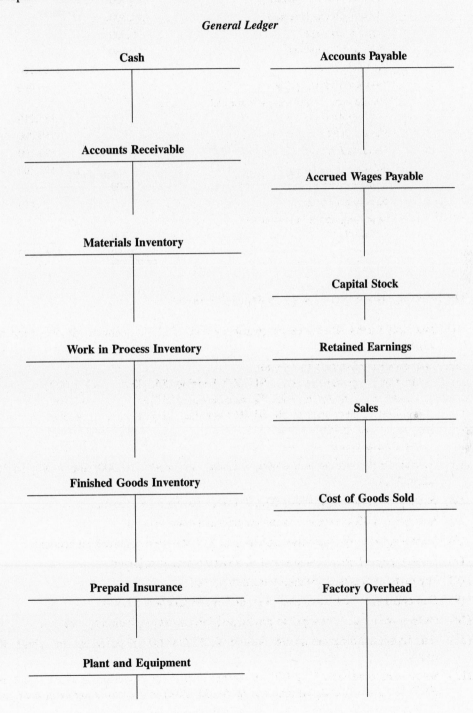

Accumulated Deprec., Plant and Equip.

Market and Administrative Exp.

Finished Goods Ledger

Polyester

Urethane

Epoxy

Work in Process Ledger

Job #690

Job #692

Job #691

Materials Ledger

Petroleum Resin

Lubricating Grease

Benzine

(1)		
(2)		
(3)		

(4)

(5)

(6)

(7)

(8)

(9)

(10)

(11)

(12)

(b)   *Finished Goods Ledger*

                         Work in Process Ledger

                          Materials Ledger

(c)

_____
_____
_____
_____
_____
_____
_____
_____
_____
_____
_____
_____
_____
_____
_____
_____
_____
_____
_____
_____
_____
_____

SOLUTION

General Ledger

Cash

Bal.	148,300	34,600	(7)
		64,300	(8)
Bal.	49,400	98,900	

Accounts Receivable

Bal.	140,000
(12)	120,000
Bal.	260,000

Materials Inventory

Bal.	42,300	36,540	(2)
(1)	29,200		
	71,500		
Bal.	34,960		

Work in Process Inventory

Bal.	20,000	93,900	(11)
(2)	35,800		
(3)	26,600		
(10)	26,600		
	109,000		
Bal.	15,100		

Finished Goods Inventory

Bal.	44,500	79,830	(12)
(11)	93,900		
	138,400		
Bal.	58,570		

Accounts Payable

(8)	64,300	54,260	Bal.
		29,200	(1)
		20,600	(4)
		17,300	(6)
		121,360	
		57,060	Bal.

Accrued Wages Payable

(7)	34,600	10,600	Bal.
		29,900	(3)
		40,500	
		5,900	Bal.

Capital Stock

250,000	Bal.

Retained Earnings

120,300	Bal.

Sales

108,100	Bal.
120,000	(12)
228,100	Bal.

Cost of Goods Sold

Bal.	72,000
(12)	79,830
Bal.	151,830

Prepaid Insurance

Bal.	5,000	850	(5)
Bal.	4,150		

Plant and Equipment

Bal.	170,080		

Accumulated Deprec., Plant and Equip.

		115,210	Bal.
		1,500	(9)
		116,710	Bal.

Factory Overhead

(2)	740	410	Bal.
(3)	3,300	26,600	(10)
(4)	20,600	27,010	
(5)	850	20	Bal.
(9)	1,500		
	26,990		

Market and Administrative Exp.

Bal.	16,700		
(6)	17,300		
Bal.	34,000		

Finished Goods Ledger

Polyester

Bal.	500 lb	2,500	45,850	9,000 lb	(12)
(11)	10,000 lb	51,000			

Urethane

Bal.	3,000 lb	12,000	6,480	1,620 lb	(12)

Epoxy

Bal.	6,000 lb	30,000	27,500	5,500 lb	(12)
(11)	8,500 lb	42,900			

Work in Process Ledger

Job #690

Bal.	8,600	51,000	(11)
(2)	17,600		
(3)	12,400		
(10)	12,400		
	51,000	51,000	

Job #692

(2)	6,500		
(3)	4,300		
(10)	4,300		

Job #691

Bal.	11,400	42,900	(11)
(2)	11,700		
(3)	9,900		
(10)	9,900		
	42,900	42,900	

Materials Ledger

Petroleum Resin

Bal.	25,250	22,700	(2)
(1)	17,300		

Lubricating Grease

Bal.	5,000	740	(2)
(1)	3,500		

Benzine

Bal.	12,050	13,100	(2)
(1)	8,400		

(1)	Materials	29,200	
	Accounts Payable		29,200
(2)	Work in Process	35,800	
	Factory Overhead	740	
	Materials Inventory		36,540
(3)	Work in Process	26,600	
	Factory Overhead	3,300	
	Accrued Wages Payable		29,900
(4)	Factory Overhead	20,600	
	Accounts Payable		20,600
(5)	Factory Overhead	850	
	Prepaid Insurance		850
(6)	Marketing and Administrative Expenses	17,300	
	Accounts Payable		17,300
(7)	Accrued Wages Payable	34,600	
	Cash		34,600
(8)	Accounts Payable	64,300	
	Cash		64,300
(9)	Factory Overhead	1,500	
	Accumulated Depreciation, Plant and Equipment		1,500
(10)	Work in Process (100% of Direct Labor)	26,600	
	Factory Overhead Applied		26,600
(11)	Finished Goods	93,900*	
	Work in Process		93,900

*Job #690: $51,000
Job #691: $42,900

(12)	Accounts Receivable	120,000	
	Sales		120,000
	Cost of Goods Sold	79,830*	
	Finished Goods		79,830

*Polyester (9,000 lbs.) $45,850
 Epoxy (5,500 lbs.)   27,500
 Urethane (1,620 lbs.)   6,480
                        $79,830

(b)

Finished Goods Ledger

Polyester	$ 7,650	
Epoxy	45,400	
Urethane	5,520	
	$58,570	

Balance in control account is $58,570.

Work in Process Ledger

Job #692	$15,100

Balance in control account is $15,100.

Materials Ledger

Petroleum Resin	$19,850
Benzine	7,350
Lubricating Grease	7,760
	$34,960

Balance in control account is $34,960.

(c)

Cash	$ 49,400	
Accounts Receivable	260,000	
Materials Inventory	34,960	
Work in Process Inventory	15,100	
Finished Goods Inventory	58,570	
Prepaid Insurance	4,150	
Plant and Equipment	170,080	
Accounts Payable		$ 57,060
Accrued Wages Payable		5,900
Accumulated Depreciation, Plant and Equipment		116,710
Capital Stock		250,000
Retained Earnings		120,300
Sales		228,100
Cost of Goods Sold	151,830	
Factory Overhead		20
Marketing and Administrative Expenses	34,000	
	$778,090	$778,090

Chapter 12

Cost Systems: Process

12.1 PROCESS COST SYSTEM

Under a process cost system, the costs are accumulated according to each department or process for a given time period. Thus the average unit departmental cost for a day, week, month, or year is arrived at by dividing the total departmental cost by the number of units (or tons, gallons, etc.) produced in the particular period.

The process cost system is used by manufacturers of goods such as paper and steel, which are produced in large volumes on a continuous basis. Section 12.5 gives a detailed illustration of this system.

12.2 SUPPLEMENTARY COSTING PRACTICES

Either of the following two procedures can be used in conjunction with the job order system or with the process cost system.

Standard Costs

A large number of manufacturers determine representative costs ahead of time and use them to predict actual costs. Special variance accounts are provided to pinpoint the discrepancies between standard and actual. Standard costs, and the related subject of *budgets*, are discussed in Chapter 13.

Direct (Variable) Costing

Under the direct (variable) costing procedure, only costs that increase in direct proportion to the volume produced become part of the cost of the product. Thus, raw materials costs, direct labor cost, and some items of overhead are included; but items such as rent and administrative salaries, which do not change with the quantity produced, are excluded.

Direct costing brings the cost of goods sold into closer relation with the sales for the period. When full costs—that is, variable plus fixed costs—are used, the average cost per unit goes down as more units are produced. This might suggest higher profits than is the case; actually, a larger portion of the fixed costs is now included in the inventory cost.

12.3 FLOW OF GOODS. EQUIVALENT UNITS

Usually the products for which process costing is employed will have a number of different production operations performed on them. Thus, the goods pass from one department to another and the costs applied to date are maintained in the cost records.

EXAMPLE 1

The Wamo Manufacturing Company has two departments, a machining department and an assembly department. In the machining department the various parts are cut from steel bars. In the assembly department the parts are secured and bolted to a frame to make up the finished product. Suppose that the parts for 5,000 units were transferred from machining to assembly during the month. The costs for raw materials and for the labor and overhead applied in the machining department amounted to $3.50 per unit.

Work in Process, Assembly Department

5,000 units from Mach. Dept. @ $3.50	17,500	5,000 units to Fin. Goods @ $6.00		30,000
Direct Labor	7,500			
Factory Overhead	5,000	12,500		
		30,000		

The unit cost passed on to Finished Goods is \$6.00; it is composed of \$3.50 for the machining department and \$2.50 = (\$7,500 + \$5,000)/5,000 for the assembly department. These costs can be compared with the unit costs for other periods and the causes of any differences found.

Example 1 represents a special situation, in that all units received by the assembly department during the month were completed and sent on within that same month. Usually, not all the work begun during the period will be finished at the end of the period: there will be an ending inventory of units in various stages of completion. Likewise, there will be an opening inventory of units only partially completed during the previous period. This more general situation is described by the flow equation

$$\text{Units available during period} = \text{units disposed of during period} \qquad (1)$$

$$\underbrace{}$$
$$\underbrace{\text{Opening inventory}}_{\text{+ units put into production}} \qquad \underbrace{\text{units transferred to next dept.}}_{\text{+ ending inventory}}$$

When any three terms in the flow equation are known, the missing piece of data can be computed from the equation itself.

EXAMPLE 2

As in Example 1, 5,000 units are put into production in the assembly department during the month. At the beginning of the month 1,500 units (2/3 completed) were on hand in the assembly department and 1,000 units (3/5 completed) were on hand at the end of the month. How many completed units were transferred to finished goods during the month?

$$\text{Units available} = \text{units disposed of}$$

$$\underbrace{1,500 + 5,000} \qquad \underbrace{\text{units transferred} + 1,000}$$

or
$$\text{Units transferred} = 1,500 + 5,000 - 1,000 = 5,500$$

To allocate costs when inventories of partially finished goods are involved, we need a common measure for all goods. Therefore, we express both the work in process and the finished goods in terms of completed units known as *equivalent units of production*.

EXAMPLE 3

(a) 1,500 units, 2/3 completed, are equivalent to 1,000 completed units.

(b) 1,000 units, 3/5 completed, are equivalent to 600 completed units.

(c) An inventory consists of 900 units, 1/3 completed; 600 units, 3/4 completed; and 100 fully completed units. The inventory contains $900(1/3) + 600(3/4) + 100(1) = 850$ equivalent completed units.

EXAMPLE 4

How many equivalent units were produced during the month by the assembly department in Example 2?

We reason this way: The work done by the department had two and only two effects: (1) it changed the inventory from $1,500 \times 2/3 = 1,000$ equivalent units (opening) to $1,000 \times 3/5 = 600$ equivalent units (ending); and (2) it brought into being $5,500(1) = 5,500$ equivalent units of finished goods. The net increase in equivalent units was thus

$$(600 - 1,000) + 5,500 = 5,100$$

and this must represent the production of the department.

The above reasoning is quite general, and we have analogous to the flow equation (1):

$$\begin{aligned}
\text{Equivalent units of production} = &\ \text{equivalent units of ending inventory} \\
&- \text{equivalent units of opening inventory} \\
&+ \text{equivalent units of finished goods} \qquad (2)
\end{aligned}$$

12.4   FLOW OF COSTS

With all inventories and production reduced to equivalent units, we can calculate unit costs for use in conjunction with FIFO, LIFO, weighted average, or some other inventory costing method. It should be emphasized that the number of equivalent units involved is determined solely by the manufacturing process and is independent of the choice of costing method.

EXAMPLE 5   FIFO

The physical data for the assembly department of the Wamo Manufacturing Company are as in Examples 2 and 4. If FIFO costing is used, the departmental work in process account for the current month appears as follows:

Work in Process, Assembly Department

Opening Inventory (1,500 units, 2/3 completed)	4,200	Finished Goods (5,500 units)	25,700
Put into Production		Ending Inventory (1,000 units, 3/5 completed)	3,800
Materials (5,000 units @ $2)	10,000		
Direct Labor 8,500			
Factory Overhead 6,800	15,300		
	29,500		29,500

Let us see how each cost was arrived at.

The number of equivalent units produced in the department has already been calculated in Example 4; it is 5,100. This gives a unit processing cost of $15,300/5,100 = $3. The unit materials cost is $2. Because only assembling is involved, even the uncompleted units will carry the full materials cost. We then have, under FIFO:

Opening inventory. There were 1,500 units that were 2/3 completed in the previous period and had costs applied of $4,200 at the end of that period.

Put into production. There were 5,000 new units put into production during the month with a related cost of $25,300. This cost consisted of $10,000 for materials, $8,500 for direct labor, and $6,800 for factory overhead.

Finished goods. There were 5,500 units of production finished this period and transferred to finished goods, at a total cost of $25,700, as shown below.

	Units	Subtotal	Amount
Opening inventory	1,500		
Balance, 2/3 completed		$ 4,200	
Processing cost (500 × $3)		1,500	
			$ 5,700
Started and completed during period	4,000		
Materials cost in period @ $2		$ 8,000	
Processing cost for period @ $3		12,000	
Total (Unit cost: $20,000 ÷ 4,000 = $5)			20,000
Goods finished in period	5,500		$25,700

Ending inventory. The ending inventory is composed of 1,000 units of materials at $2.00 per unit, or $2,000 (the full materials cost), and 600 equivalent units of processing cost (1,000 units, 3/5 completed) at $3.00 per unit, or $1,800, as shown below.

	Units	Amount
Ending inventory	1,000	
Materials cost in period @ $2		$2,000
Processing cost (600 × $3)		1,800
Total	1,000	$3,800

Different costs would be obtained in Example 5 under LIFO or weighted average. If LIFO is used, the 5,500 units transferred would be assumed to consist of the 5,000 units put into production during the month and 500 units from the opening inventory.

In the weighted average method, the cost of the opening inventory and the cost of goods put into production would be added, and the sum ($29,500) divided by the equivalent units of production (5,100). This would provide the unit cost, which would be applied to *both* the goods transferred and the ending inventory.

12.5 COMPREHENSIVE ILLUSTRATION OF PROCESS COSTS

The Brown Manufacturing Company uses a process cost system for Product X. All materials are placed in production in Department A. A by-product, Product Y, is also obtained in this department. Factory overhead is applied on the basis of direct labor cost, the rate being 90% in Department A and 50% in Department B. There are inventories of work in process *in Department B only*. Maintenance and Power are the two service departments.

The company has a fiscal year ending December 31. Following are the inventory balances on November 30:

Finished Goods, Product X	$ 5,000
Finished Goods, Product Y	400
Work in Process, Department B	9,400
Materials	10,000
	$24,800

The transactions for December are summarized in general journal form below.

(1) *Purchases of materials*

Materials	27,500	
Accounts Payable		27,500

(2) *Materials placed in production*

Power Department	500	
Maintenance Department	2,500	
Factory Overhead, Department A	1,500	
Factory Overhead, Department B	1,000	
Work in Process, Department A	20,000	
Materials		25,500

(3) *Factory payroll for the period*

Power Department	950	
Maintenance Department	1,800	
Factory Overhead, Department A	900	
Factory Overhead, Department B	600	
Work in Process, Department A	7,500	
Work in Process, Department B	14,400	
Wages Payable		26,150

(4) *Accounts payable for costs incurred*

Power Department	100	
Maintenance Department	200	
Factory Overhead, Department A	500	
Factory Overhead, Department B	300	
Accounts Payable		1,100

(5) *Prepaid expenses used up*

Power Department	150	
Maintenance Department	250	
Factory Overhead, Department A	600	
Factory Overhead, Department B	400	
Prepaid Expenses		1,400

(6) *Depreciation for the period*

Power Department	200	
Maintenance Department	400	
Factory Overhead, Department A	700	
Factory Overhead, Department B	1,000	
Accumulated Depreciation, Plant Assets		2,300

(7) *Distribution of power department costs to departments based on kilowatt-hours supplied*

Maintenance Department	200	
Factory Overhead, Department A	800	
Factory Overhead, Department B	900	
Power Department		1,900*

*500 + 950 + 100 + 150 + 200

(8) *Distribution of maintenance department costs to departments on the basis of maintenance services rendered*

Factory Overhead, Department A	2,600	
Factory Overhead, Department B	2,750	
Maintenance Department		5,350*

*2,500 + 1,800 + 200 + 250 + 400 + 200

(9) *Factory overhead applied*

Work in Process, Department A (90% of $7,500)	6,750	
Work in Process, Department B (50% of $14,400)	7,200	
Factory Overhead, Department A		6,750
Factory Overhead, Department B		7,200

In addition to the entries from the books of original entry, there are entries transferring goods from one department or process to the next, as illustrated below.

(a) Transfer of Production: Department A to Department B

There were 5,000 units of Product X fully processed and transferred to Department B. There were no inventories of Product X in Department A at the beginning or end of the month. There were 3,125 pounds of the by-product, Product Y, produced, which is to be valued at $0.40 a pound. Product Y is considered as finished goods since it would be sold in this form. From the total department cost of $34,250 is to be deducted the by-product cost of $1,250, leaving $33,000 applicable to Product X, as shown below.

Total cost, Department A	$34,250
Less: Product Y	1,250
Cost of Product X transferred	$33,000
Unit cost of Product X transferred ($33,000 ÷ 5,000)	$6.60

The journal entry is:

Work in Process, Department B	33,000	
Finished Goods, Product Y	1,250	
Work in Process, Department A		34,250

(b) Transfer of Production: Department B to Finished Goods

Opening inventory in process in Department B consisted of 1,200 units, 1/3 completed. There were 5,200 units completed during the month, and ending inventory in process was 1,000 units, 3/5 completed.

Equivalent units of production			
Ending inventory in process (1,000 × 3/5)	600		
Less: Opening inventory in process (1,200 × 1/3)	400	200	
Finished goods (5,200 × 1)		5,200	
Total equivalent units of production		5,400	
Processing costs			
Direct labor (3)	$14,400		
Factory overhead (9) (50%)	7,200		
Total processing costs	$21,600		
Unit processing cost of product transferred to Finished Goods ($21,600 ÷ 5,400)	$4.00		

On the basis of FIFO, costs are allocated to Department B as follows:

Opening inventory in process (1,200 units, 1/3 completed)	$ 9,400	
Processing costs in period (800 @ $4.00)	3,200	
Total (unit cost: $12,600 ÷ 1,200 = $10.50)		$12,600
Started and completed during period		
From Department A (4,000 @ $6.60)	$26,400	
Processing costs (4,000 @ $4.00)	16,000	
Total (unit cost: $42,400 ÷ 4,000 = $10.60)		$42,400
Total transferred to Finished Goods		$55,000
Ending inventory in process		
From Department A (1,000 @ $6.60)	$ 6,600	
Processing costs (600 @ $4.00)	2,400	
Total work in process (3/5 completed)		$ 9,000
Total costs charged to Department B		$64,000

The journal entry is:

Finished Goods, Product X	55,000	
Work in Process, Department B		55,000

(c) Cost of Goods Sold

The opening inventory of Finished Goods, Product X, was 500 units (unit cost: $5,000 \div 500 = $10.00) and there were 5,200 units of Product X completed during the month. Of the total 5,700 units, 4,700 were shipped out. Costing under FIFO is as follows:

Product X (4,700 units)		
500 units @ $10.00	$ 5,000	
1,200 units @ $10.50	12,600	
3,000 units @ $10.60	31,800	
Total cost of Product X sold		$49,400
Product Y (2,625 pounds @ $0.40)		1,050
Total cost of goods sold		$50,450

The journal entry is:

Cost of Goods Sold	50,450	
Finished Goods, Product X		49,400
Finished Goods, Product Y		1,050

The net underapplied factory overhead, $600 ($850 − $250), is shown as part of deferred charges. The balances in the inventory accounts at December 31 are:

Finished Goods, Product X	$10,600
Finished Goods, Product Y	600
Work in Process, Department B	9,000
Materials	12,000
	$32,200

Flow of Costs—Process Cost Accounts

Work in Process, Department A

(2)	20,000	34,250	(a)
(3)	7,500		
(9)	6,750		
	34,250	34,250	

Finished Goods, Product X

Bal.	5,000	49,400	(c)
(b)	55,000		
	60,000		
Bal.	10,600		

Work in Process, Department B

Bal.	9,400	55,000	(b)
(3)	14,400		
(9)	7,200		
(a)	33,000		
	64,000		
Bal.	9,000		

Finished Goods, Product Y

Bal.	400	1,050	(c)
(a)	1,250		
	1,650		
Bal.	600		

Factory Overhead, Department A

(2)	1,500	6,750	(9)
(3)	900		
(4)	500		
(5)	600		
(6)	700		
(7)	800		
(8)	2,600		
	7,600		
Bal.	850		

Factory Overhead, Department B

(2)	1,000	7,200	(a)
(3)	600		
(4)	300		
(5)	400		
(6)	1,000		
(7)	900		
(8)	2,750		
	6,950	250	Bal.

Power Department

(2)	500	1,900	(7)
(3)	950		
(4)	100		
(5)	150		
(6)	200		
	1,900		

Maintenance Department

(2)	2,500	5,350	(8)
(3)	1,800		
(4)	200		
(5)	250		
(6)	400		
(7)	200		
	5,350		

Summary: Chapters 11 and 12

1. The job-order cost system is most suitable if the product is _____ .

2. For which of the following would a job-order cost system be best: a steel mill, a printing shop, or a flour mill? _____ .

3. For the data below, the cost of materials issued to production under the first-in, first-out method is $ _____ .

Beginning balance	300 units at $2.00
Purchases	400 units at $2.25
Issued to production	200 units

4. For the data in Question 3, the cost of materials issued to production under the last-in, first-out method is $ _____ .

5. Under the job-order cost system, the costs are accumulated according to _____ .

6. Under the job-order cost system, the unit cost is determined by dividing the _____ by the _____ .

7. The process cost system is most suitable where the product is _____ .

8. Under the process cost system, the costs are accumulated according to _____ .

9. The number of equivalent units of production equals the number of _____ for a processing department in which there is no work in process at the beginning or end of the period.

10. Under the process cost system, goods are transferred from production departments to
_____ .

Answers: (1) custom made; (2) printing shop; (3) 400; (4) 450; (5) job orders; (6) cost of the job, number of completed
units; (7) mass produced; (8) departments or processes; (9) completed units; (10) finished goods

Solved Problems

12.1   The Hankinson Company manufactures one product that passes through three production departments
in a continuous process. For the month of July, $46,500 of direct materials were issued and $85,600
of direct labor cost was incurred in Department A. The factory overhead rate is 75% of direct labor
cost. The work in process in Department A was $26,200 at the beginning of the month and $22,400
at the end of the month. Prepare journal entries to show (*a*) the costs put into production for the
month, and (*b*) the transfer of production costs to Department B.

(*a*)

(*b*)

SOLUTION

(*a*)	Work in Process, Department A	46,500	
	Materials		46,500
	Work in Process, Department A	85,600	
	Wages Payable		85,600
	Work in Process, Department A	64,200	
	Factory Overhead, Department A		64,200
(*b*)	Work in Process, Department B	200,100	
	Work in Process, Department A		200,100*

*26,200 (beginning inventory) + 196,300 (production cost) − 22,400 (ending inventory)

12.2   The Farnell Company has the following entries at December 31:

Work in Process, Department A

2,000 units, 75% completed	17,400	To Department B (5,000 units)	64,800
Direct Materials (3,000 units @ $6)	18,000		
Direct Labor	19,600		
Factory Overhead	9,800		
	64,800		64,800

All raw materials are put into production at the beginning of the process. Compute (a) equivalent units of production; (b) processing cost per equivalent unit of production; (c) total and unit cost of product started in prior period and completed in current period; and (d) total and unit cost of product started and completed in current period.

(a)

(b)

(c)

(d)

SOLUTION

(a)	Ending inventory in process		–0–	
	Less: Opening inventory in process (2,000 units × 75%)		1,500	−1,500
	Finished goods (5,000 × 1)			5,000
	Total equivalent units of production			3,500

(b)	Direct labor	$19,600
	Factory overhead	9,800
	Total processing costs	$29,400
	Processing cost per equivalent	
	unit of production ($29,400 ÷ 3,500)	$8.40

(c)	Costs in prior period (2,000 units, 75% completed)	$17,400
	Processing costs in current period (500 @ $8.40)	4,200
	Total cost	$21,600
	Unit cost ($21,600 ÷ 2,000)	$10.80

(d)	Raw materials (3,000 units @ $6.00)	$18,000
	Processing costs (3,000 units @ $8.40)	25,200
	Total cost	$43,200
	Unit cost ($43,200 ÷ 3,000)	$14.40

12.3 The R. Strauss Company furnished the following information for the Assembly Department for the month of June: Work in Process Inventory, June 1 (2,500 units, 1/2 completed), $15,000; Materials from Machining Department (7,500 units), $60,000; Direct Labor, $18,375; Factory Overhead, $11,025. During June, 6,500 units of finished goods were assembled, and the work in process inventory on July 1 consisted of 3,500 units, 3/5 completed. Prepare a cost of production report for the Assembly Department for the month of June.

R. Strauss Company
Cost of Production, Assembly Department
Month of June, 19X1

Quantities

Units Accounted for

Equivalent Units of Production

Costs

Allocation of Costs

SOLUTION

R. Strauss Company		
Cost of Production, Assembly Department		
Month of June, 19X1		

Quantities		
Work in Process Inventory, June 1		2,500
Received from Machining Department		7,500
Total Units to Be Accounted for		10,000

Units Accounts for		
Transferred to Finished Goods		6,500
Work in Process Inventory, July 1		3,500
Total Units Accounted for		10,000

Equivalent Units of Production		
Ending Inventory in Process (3,500 × 3/5)	2,100	
Less: Opening Inventory in Process (2,500 × 1/2)	1,250	850
Finished Goods (6,500 × 1)		6,500
Total Equivalent Units of Production		7,350

Costs		
Work in Process Inventory, June 1		$ 15,000
Materials from Machining Department (7,500 units @ $8)		60,000
Processing Costs		
Direct Labor	$18,375	
Factory Overhead	11,025	
Total Processing Costs		
(unit cost: $29,400 ÷ 7,350 = $4)		29,400
Total Cost to Be Accounted for		$104,400

Allocation of Costs		
Transferred to Finished Goods		
2,500 Units [$15,000 + (2,500 × 1/2 × $4)]	$20,000	
4,000 Units @ $8 + $4 = $12	48,000	
Total Cost of Completed Units		$ 68,000
Work in Process Inventory, July 1		
Raw Materials (3,500 units @ $8)	$28,000	
Processing Costs (3,500 × 3/5 × $4)	8,400	36,400
Total Cost Accounted for		$104,400

12.4 Karl Gurken has recently patented a new machine for skinning cucumbers, which he calls Model SK-74. In the manufacture of this device, all materials are introduced at the beginning of the process; after passing through Department A and Department B, Model SK-74 is complete. On January 31, a report from Department B showed the following information:

Work in Process Inventory, Jan. 1	
(1,200 units, 2/3 completed)	$19,560
Finished Goods Inventory, Jan. 1	
(1,000 units @ $18)	18,000

Raw Materials in January	
(1,600 units @ $12.50)	20,000
Direct Labor in January	6,290
Factory Overhead in January	5,950
Work in Process Inventory, Jan. 31	
(800 units, 5/8 completed)	
Finished Goods Inventory, Jan. 31	
(350 units)	

The report went on further to show that a total of 2,000 units were transferred from work in process to finished goods. Sales of 2,650 units were reported.

(a) For Department B, calculate: (1) the equivalent units of production for January; (2) the processing cost per unit for January; (3) the total cost of production of completed units of Model SK-74; (4) work in process inventory at January 31; (5) cost of goods sold; (6) finished goods inventory at January 31. (Use FIFO costing.)

(b) Prepare a cost of production report.

(a)   (1)

        (2)

        (3)

        (4)

        (5)

        (6)

(b)

	Model SK-74
	Cost of Production, Department B
	Month Ended January 31, 19X1

Units

Costs

SOLUTION

(a) (1)

Ending inventory in process (800 × 5/8)	500		
Less: Opening inventory in process (1,200 × 2/3)	800		−300
Finished goods (2,000 × 1)			2,000
Total equivalent units of production			1,700

(2)

Direct labor	$ 6,290	
Factory overhead	5,950	
	$12,240 ÷ 1,700 units = $7.20 per unit	

(3)

1,200 units		
2/3 completed on Jan. 1	$19,560	
Cost to complete in Jan. (1,200 × 1/3 × $7.20)	2,880	
Total (unit cost: $22,440 ÷ 1,200 = $18.70)		$22,440
800 units		
Materials in Jan. (800 × $12.50)	$10,000	
Cost to complete in Jan. (800 × $7.20)	5,760	
Total (unit cost: $15,760 ÷ 800 = $19,70)		15,760
Total cost of completed units		$38,200

(4)	800 units		
	Materials in Jan. (800 × $12.50)	$10,000	
	Cost to partially complete in		
	Jan. (5/8 × 800 × $7.20)	3,600	
	Work in Process Inventory, Jan. 31		$13,600

(5)	1,000 units @ $18.00 = $18,000
	1,200 units @ $18.70 = 22,440
	450 units @ $19.70 = 8,865
	2,650 units sold $49,305

(6)	Finished Goods Inventory, Jan. 31 (350 units @ $19.70)	$6,895

(b)

Model SK-74
Cost of Production, Department B
Month Ended January 31, 19X1

Units

Work in Process Inventory, Jan. 1	1,200
Transferred into Department	1,600
Units to Be Accounted for	2,800
Transferred to Finished Goods	2,000
Work in Process Inventory, Jan. 31	800
Units Accounted for	2,800

Costs

Work in Process Inventory, Jan. 1		$19,560
Materials into Department		20,000
Direct Labor		6,290
Factory Overhead		5,950
Total Cost to Be Accounted for		$51,800
Transferred to Finished Goods		
1,200 Units @ $18.70	$22,440	
800 Units @ $19.70	15,760	$38,200
Work in Process Inventory, Jan. 31		
800 Units Materials @ $12.50	$10,000	
800 Units, 5/8 Completed, @ $7.20	3,600	13,600
Total Cost Accounted for		$51,800

12.5 The Martin Manufacturing Company uses a process cost system for Product N, which requires four processes. Work in Process, Department 4, shows the following entries for May:

Balance, May 1 (1,600 units, 1/4 completed)	$ 4,060
From Department 3 (4,300 units)	7,525
Direct Labor	12,250
Factory Overhead	3,185

Processing for the month of May consisted of completing the 1,600 units in process on May 1, completing the processing on 3,500 additional units, and leaving 800 units that are 1/4 completed.

During June the charges to Work in Process, Department 4, were:

From Department 3 (5,500 units)	$ 8,250
Direct Labor	11,760
Factory Overhead	2,940

By June 30, all beginning work in process units were completed; of the 5,500 new units, 1,500 were left only 1/5 completed.

(a) Prepare a work in process account for Department 4, beginning with the May 1 balance and working through to the beginning balances for July.

(b) Show supporting computations for both months—namely, the determination of the equivalent units, the processing costs per unit, costs of goods completed and available for transfer to finished goods, and the work in process inventory.

(a)   **Work in Process, Department 4**

May   May

Work in Process, Department 4

June   June

(b)   Equivalent Production for May

Unit Processing Cost for May

Cost of Goods Finished in May

Work in Process, May 31

_____

_____

_____

Equivalent Production for June

_____

_____

_____

_____

_____

Unit Processing Cost for June

_____

Cost of Goods Finished in June

_____

_____

_____

_____

_____

_____

_____

Work in Process, June 30

_____

_____

_____

SOLUTION

(a)

Work in Process, Department 4

May			May		
Bal. (1,600 units, 1/4 completed)	4,060		1,600 Units Completed	7,840	
4,300 Units from Dept. 3	7,525		3,500 Units Completed	17,150	
Direct Labor	12,250		800 Units, 1/4 Completed	2,030	
Factory Overhead	3,185				
	27,020			27,020	

Work in Process, Department 4

June			June		
Bal. (800 units, 1/4 completed)	2,030		800 Units Completed	3,830	
5,500 Units Introduced to System	8,250		4,000 Units Completed	18,000	
Direct Labor	11,760		Bal. (1,500 units, 1/5 completed)	3,150	
Factory Overhead	2,940				
	24,980			24,980	
July 1					
Bal. (1,500 units, 1/5 completed)	3,150				

(b)

Equivalent Production for May		
To Complete May 1 Inventory (1,600 × 3/4)	1,200	
Started and Completed During May	3,500	
To Partially Complete Units Remaining on		
May 31 (800 × 1/4)	200	
Equivalent Units of Production	4,900	

Unit Processing Cost for May		
($12,250 + $3,185) ÷ 4,900 = $3.15		

Cost of Goods Finished in May		
1,600 Units		
1/4 Completed at May 1	$ 4,060	
Cost to Complete in May (1,600 × 3/4 × $3.15)	3,780	
Total (unit cost: $7,840 ÷ 1,600 = $4.90)		$ 7,840
3,500 units		
Past Costs (3,500 × $1.75)	$ 6,125	
Cost Applied in May (3,500 × $3.15)	11,025	
Total (unit cost: $17,150 ÷ 3,500 = $4.90)		17,150
Cost of Goods Finished in May		$24,990

Work in Process, May 31		
800 Units		
Past Costs (800 × $1.75)	$ 1,400	
Cost to Partially Complete in May (800 × 1/4 × $3.15)	630	$ 2,030

Equivalent Production for June		
To Complete June 1 Inventory (800 × 3/4)	600	
Started and Completed During June	4,000	
To Partially Complete Units Remaining on June 30		
(1,500 × 1/5)	300	
Equivalent Units of Production	4,900	

Unit Processing Cost for June		
($11,760 + $2,940) ÷ 4,900 = $3.00		

Cost of Goods Finished in June		
800 units		
1/4 Completed at June 1	$ 2,030	
Cost to Complete in June (800 × 3/4 × $3.00)	1,800	
Total (unit cost: $3,830 ÷ 800 = $4.79)		$ 3,830
4,000 Units		
Past Costs (4,000 × $1.50)	$ 6,000	
Cost Applied in June (4,000 × $3.00)	12,000	
Total (unit cost: $18,000 ÷ 4,000 = $4.50)		18,000
Cost of Goods Finished in June		$21,830

Work in Process, June 30		
1,500 Units		
Past Costs (1,500 × $1.50)	$ 2,250	
Cost to Partially Complete in June (1,500 × 1/5 × $3.00)	900	$ 3,150

Chapter 13

Budgets: Income Statement

13.1 NATURE OF BUDGETING

A *budget* is a quantitative projection of business operations. It helps management (1) to set specific objectives and (2) to assure that actual operations conform to the established plan.

The budget preparation varies somewhat among companies, but there are a number of budget statements and forms that have become standardized and in general use. These may be grouped under *master budgets*, *income and expense budgets (operating budgets)*, and *balance sheet budgets (financial budgets)*.

13.2 MASTER BUDGET

The master budget is the overall, coordinated plan for all the budgets and is usually the responsibility of a special budget officer or budget department. The various income and expense budgets and balance sheet budgets are subsidiary parts of the master budget, as indicated below:

Master Budget

Budgeted income statement	*Budgeted balance sheet*
Sales budget	Cash budget
Cost of goods sold budget	Capital expenditures budget
Production budget	
Materials purchases budget	
Direct labor budget	
Factory overhead budget	
Operating expenses budget	
Selling expenses budget	
General expenses budget	

The various components of the master budget are discussed in Sections 13.3 and 13.4.

Generally, the sequence of procedures in preparing the master budget is: (1) develop objectives and long-range goals; (2) project sales for the period; (3) estimate operating costs (that is, cost of goods sold and operating expenses); (4) estimate the asset, liability, and equity accounts after giving effect to the projected income and expense budgets; (5) prepare an overall budget, including a projected income statement and a projected balance sheet with supporting component budgets.

13.3 BUDGETED INCOME STATEMENT

The budgeted income statement summarizes the various component projections of income and expense, usually for the coming fiscal year. However, for control purposes the budget is commonly divided into quarters, or even months or weeks, depending on the need. Many companies use a *moving budget*, or *continuous budget*, that shows four quarters or 12 months ahead at all times.

EXAMPLE 1

Bollett Company
Budgeted Income Statement
Year Ended December 31, 19X1

Sales		$879,200
Cost of Goods Sold		602,700
Gross Profit		$276,500
Operating Expenses		
Selling Expenses	$65,000	
General Expenses	57,500	122,500
Net Income Before Taxes		$154,000
Provision for Income Taxes		74,000
Net Income		$ 80,000

Sales Budget

The first budget to be prepared is usually the sales budget, since most other budgets will depend on the results of this projection. The sales budget begins with the estimated quantity of each product to be sold, broken down further by area and by salesperson. The estimates of quantity are based on past experience adjusted for expected changes in general business conditions, industry trends, etc. The quantities are extended by the unit price to arrive at the sales amount.

EXAMPLE 2

The sales figure in Example 1 is arrived at as follows.

Bollett Company
Sales Budget
Year Ended December 31, 19X1

	Quantity	Amount
Product A (unit price, $9)		
Area 1	30,200	$271,800
Area 2	20,600	185,400
Area 3	15,500	139,500
Total	66,300	$596,700
Product B (unit price, $5)		
Area 1	25,500	$127,500
Area 2	18,600	93,000
Area 3	12,400	62,000
Total	56,500	$282,500
Total Sales	122,800	$879,200

The actual sales for each area can be shown in relation to the budgeted sales. Any significant variances between budget and actual can be investigated and any needed corrective action taken.

Cost of Goods Sold Budget

The various supporting budgets, such as those for production, materials purchases, direct labor, and factory overhead, are used in developing the cost of goods sold budget.

EXAMPLE 3

Bollett Company
Cost of Goods Sold Budget
Year Ended December 31, 19X1

Finished Goods Inventory, Jan. 1			$ 85,600
Work in Process Inventory, Jan. 1		$ 6,500	
Raw Materials Used			
Inventory, Jan. 1	$ 25,900		
Materials Purchases	133,600		
Available for Use	$159,500		
Less: Budgeted Inventory, Dec. 31	18,000		
Raw Materials Used	$141,500		
Direct Labor	233,200		
Factory Overhead	215,400		
Manufacturing Cost		590,100	
Total Work in Process During Period		$596,600	
Less: Budgeted Work in Process, Dec. 31		8,200	
Cost of Goods Manufactured			588,400
Finished Goods Available for Sale			$674,000
Less: Budgeted Finished Goods Inventory, Dec. 31			71,300
Cost of Goods Sold			$602,700

Production budget. To meet the requirements of the sales and inventory projections, it is necessary to determine the number of units of each product to be produced. This is done by adding the desired closing inventory to the projected sales quantity and subtracting from that sum the opening inventory quantity (see Example 4).

EXAMPLE 4

From Example 2, the budgeted sales of Products A and B are 66,300 units and 56,500 units, respectively.

Bollett Company
Production Budget
Year Ended December 31, 19X1

	Units of A	Units of B
Sales	66,300	56,500
Desired Ending Inventory	10,200	8,000
	76,500	64,500
Less: Opening Inventory	9,500	8,000
Production Units Required	67,000	56,500

Materials purchases budget. The amount of raw materials to be purchased depends on the production budget and the desired inventory amounts. The required production plus the desired ending inventory, less the opening inventory, equals the purchases required.

EXAMPLE 5

Bollett Company's two products have the following compositions:

Product	Units of Material		
(1 unit)	x	y	z
A	1	2	0
B	1	1	1

From the production budget (Example 4), 67,000 units of A and 56,500 units of B are to be produced.

Bollett Company
Materials Purchases Budget
Year Ended December 31, 19X1

	Units of x	**Units of y**	**Units of z**
Production			
Product A (67,000 units)	67,000	134,000	—
Product B (56,500 units)	56,500	56,500	56,500
	123,500	190,500	56,500
Desired Ending Inventory	15,000	25,000	7,000
	138,500	215,500	63,500
Less: Opening Inventory	23,000	35,000	10,000
Units to Be Purchased	115,500	180,500	53,500
Unit Price	× $0.30	× $0.40	× $0.50
Materials Purchases	$34,650	$72,200	$26,750

It is seen that the total materials purchases for the three ingredients is $133,600. This amount is reflected in the cost of goods sold budget (Example 3).

Direct labor budget. The direct labor cost is calculated as the number of hours required to accomplish the budgeted production times the hourly labor rate.

EXAMPLE 6

Assume that Products A and B of the Bollett Company are produced in two departments, according to the following schedule:

Product	Hours in Department	
(1 unit)	#1	#2
A	0.2	0.3
B	0.1	0.2

Bollett Company
Direct Labor Budget
Year Ended December 31, 19X1

	Department #1	**Department #2**
Hours Required		
Product A (67,000 units)	13,400	20,100
Product B (56,500 units)	5,650	11,300
Total	19,050	31,400
Hourly Rate	× $4	× $5
Direct Labor Cost	$76,200	$157,000

The total direct labor cost amounting to $233,200 is carried to the cost of goods sold budget (Example 3).

Factory overhead budget. The factory overhead budget summarizes the projected cost for the many different components of factory overhead. Separate supporting schedules may be made for each department or cost center, according to the area of each foreman's responsibility.

EXAMPLE 7

Bollett Company
Factory Overhead Budget
Year Ended December 31, 19X1

Indirect Factory Labor	$ 82,000
Supervision	45,000
Supplies	15,000
Power, Heat, and Light	20,000
Depreciation of Plant and Equipment	25,000
Maintenance	14,000
Property Taxes	10,200
Insurance	4,200
Total Factory Overhead	$215,400

The total appears in the cost of goods sold budget (Example 3).

Operating Expenses Budget

The operating expenses budget shows the ordinary expenses involved in selling the products or in managing the business; they are chargeable against current income. Operating expenses will be supported by detailed schedules according to departmental responsibility. For example, there might be a separate schedule of advertising showing details of the various media used.

Operating expenses are usually separated into *selling expenses* and *general expenses*.

Selling expenses budget. A budget of selling expenses usually shows individual amounts for the items listed in Example 8.

EXAMPLE 8

Bollett Company
Selling Expenses Budget
Year Ended December 31, 19X1

Salaries and Commissions	$21,000
Travel and Entertainment	16,000
Advertising	14,000
Supplies	5,000
Shipping and Delivery	3,000
Rent	2,000
Utilities	1,500
Depreciation	1,000
Insurance	500
Telephone	800
Miscellaneous	200
Total Selling Expenses	$65,000

The cost of market research may also be included, or it may be separated into a marketing category under the responsibility of a market research manager. Often, for managerial control, selling expenses are classed as fixed or variable (Section 12.2), and standards are established for each class.

General expenses budget. The *general expenses budget* (sometimes called the *general and administrative expenses budget*) is similar to the selling expenses budget, but its items are less closely linked to specific activities.

EXAMPLE 9

Bollett Company
General Expenses Budget
Year Ended December 31, 19X1

Officers' Salaries	$32,000
General Office Salaries	15,000
Legal Services	4,000
Pensions	3,000
Payroll Taxes	2,000
Depreciation	600
Telephone	400
Insurance	300
Miscellaneous	200
Total General Expenses	$57,500

Solved Problems

13.1 The Kuezek Company is interested in developing a flexible budget for monthly operating expenses. Following is the information needed for each type of expense.

Salespeople's salaries	$30,000
Salespeople's commissions	8% of sales
Advertising expense	$15,000 for $300,000 sales
	$16,000 for $350,000 sales
	$17,000 for $400,000 sales
Miscellaneous selling expenses	1% of sales
Office salaries	$10,000
Office supplies	1/2 of 1% of sales
Miscellaneous general expenses	1% of sales

Prepare a flexible operating expenses budget based on sales of $300,000, $350,000, and $400,000.

Kuezek Company
Flexible Operating Expenses Budget
Monthly Volume, 19X1

SOLUTION

Kuezek Company *Flexible Operating Expenses Budget* *Monthly Volume, 19X1*			
Total Sales	$300,000	$350,000	$400,000
Selling Expenses			
Salespeople's Salaries	$ 30,000	$ 30,000	$ 30,000
Salespeople's Commissions	24,000	28,000	32,000
Advertising Expense	15,000	16,000	17,000
Miscellaneous Selling Expenses	3,000	3,500	4,000
	$ 72,000	$ 77,500	$ 83,000
General Expenses			
Office Salaries	$ 10,000	$ 10,000	$ 10,000
Office Supplies	1,500	1,750	2,000
Miscellaneous General Expenses	3,000	3,500	4,000
	$ 14,500	$ 15,250	$ 16,000
Total Operating Expenses	$ 86,500	$ 92,750	$ 99,000

13.2   The actual operating expenses for the Kuezek Company for October were as follows:

Salespeople's salaries	$32,000
Salespeople's commissions	25,500
Advertising expense	19,000
Miscellaneous selling expenses	4,000
Office salaries	10,500
Office supplies	1,650
Miscellaneous general expenses	3,300

Sales for the month were $350,000. Prepare a budget report for operating expenses, using the standard data developed in Problem 13.1.

Kuezek Company			
Budget Report, Operating Expenses			
October 19X1			
	Actual	**Budget**	**Over**	**Under**

SOLUTION

	Actual	Budget	Over	Under
Kuezek Company				
Budget Report, Operating Expenses				
October 19X1				
Salespeople's Salaries	$32,000	$30,000	$2,000	
Salespeople's Commissions	25,500	28,000		$2,500
Advertising Expense	19,000	16,000	3,000	
Miscellaneous Selling				
Expenses	4,000	3,500	500	
Office Salaries	10,500	10,000	500	
Office Supplies	1,650	1,750		100
Miscellaneous General				
Expenses	3,300	3,500		200
	$95,950	$92,750	$6,000	$2,800

13.3 The Benson Company has the following standard and actual costs for the current month. There were 4,000 units produced.

	Actual	**Standard**
Raw materials	14,000 units @ $2.10	15,000 units @ $2.00
Direct labor	8,000 hours @ $2.75	7,500 units @ $3.00
Factory overhead		
Variable	$13,500	$1.50 per hour
Fixed	$ 7,500	$ .75 per hour*

*Rate based on normal capacity of 10,000 labor hours

(*a*) For raw materials, compute the quantity variance, price variance, and total materials cost variance.
(*b*) For direct labor, compute the time variance, rate variance, and total direct labor cost variance.
(*c*) For factory overhead, compute the volume variance, controllable variance, and total factory overhead cost variance.

(*a*) **Quantity Variance** **Units**

Price Variance **Per Unit**

(*b*) **Time Variance** **Hours**

Rate Variance **Per Hour**

(*c*) **Volume Variance** **Hours**

Controllable Variance

SOLUTION

(*a*)

Quantity Variance	Units		
Standard quantity	15,000		
Actual quantity	14,000		
Variance (favorable)	1,000 × standard		
		price, $2.00	$2,000

Price Variance	Per Unit		
Actual price	$2.10		
Standard price	2.00		
Variance (unfavorable)	$0.10	× actual quantity,	
		14,000	1,400
Total raw materials cost variance (favorable)			$ 600

(b)

Time Variance	Hours		
Actual time	8,000		
Standard time	7,500		
Variance (unfavorable)	500	× standard rate,	
		$3.00	$1,500

Rate Variance	Per Hour		
Standard rate	$3.00		
Actual rate	2.75		
Variance (favorable)	$0.25	× actual time,	
		8,000 hours	2,000
Total direct labor cost variance (favorable)			$ 500

(c)

Volume Variance	Hours		
Normal capacity at 100%	10,000		
Standard for volume produced	7,500		
Capacity not used (unfavorable)	2,500	× standard rate,	
		$0.75	$1,875

Controllable Variance			
Actual factory overhead cost		$21,000	
Budgeted for standard production			
Variable (7,500 × $1.50)	$11,250		
Fixed (10,000 × $0.75)	7,500	18,750	
Variance (unfavorable)			2,250
Total factory overhead cost variance (unfavorable)			$4,125

13.4 The Reilly Corporation had the following factory overhead costs for January, in which 9,500 direct labor hours were used: indirect wages, $9,930; indirect materials, $4,570; utilities, $3,540; supervision, $8,520; depreciation, $4,150; insurance, $1,750; property taxes, $1,180. The monthly factory overhead budget, based on normal capacity of 10,000 direct labor hours, has been established as follows: indirect wages, $10,300; indirect materials; $4,700; utilities, $3,800; supervision, $8,520; depreciation, $4,150; insurance, $1,750; property taxes, $1,180. Present a factory overhead report for January based on 9,500 direct labor hours.

Reilly Corporation
Factory Overhead Variance Report
Month Ended January 31, 19X1

	Actual	Budget	Favorable	Unfavorable

SOLUTION

Reilly Corporation
Factory Overhead Variance Report
Month Ended January 31, 19X1

Normal Capacity	10,000			
Actual Production	9,500			
Below Standard (500 ÷ 10,000 = 5%)	500			

	Actual	Budget	Favorable	Unfavorable
Variable Costs				
Indirect Wages	$ 9,930	$ 9,785		$145
Indirect Materials	4,570	4,465		105
Utilities	3,540	3,610	$70	
Total Variable Costs	$18,040	$17,860	$70	$250
Fixed Costs				
Supervision	$ 8,520	$ 8,520		
Depreciation	4,150	4,150		
Insurance	1,750	1,750		
Property Taxes	1,180	1,180		
Total Fixed Costs	$15,600	$15,600		
Total Factory Overhead	$33,640	$33,460		
Total Controllable Variances			$70	$250
Net Controllable Variance (unfavorable)				$180
Volume Variance (unfavorable)				
Idle Hours at Standard Rate for				
Fixed Overhead (500 × $1.56)				780
Total Factory Overhead Variance (unfavorable)				$960

13.5 The B & G Clothing Manufacturing Company prepares monthly estimates of sales, production, and other operating data. Sales and production data for April are shown below.

Estimated sales for April
   Shirts: 35,500 @ $7
   Slacks: 22,000 @ $12
Estimated inventories on Apr. 1
  Direct materials
   Cloth: 3,500 yards
   Thread: 25 spools
   Buttons: 10,000
   Zippers: 1,100
  Finished products
   Shirts: 1,500
   Slacks: 1,000
Expected inventories at Apr. 30
  Direct materials
   Cloth: 4,000 yards
   Thread: 35 spools
   Buttons: 18,000
   Zippers: 1,000
  Finished products
   Shirts: 2,000
   Slacks: 1,500

Direct materials required for production
  To manufacture shirts
   Cloth: 1.5 yards per shirt
   Thread: 1 spool per 100 shirts
   Buttons: 8 buttons per shirt
  To manufacture slacks
   Cloth: 2.5 yards per pair of slacks
   Thread: 1 spool per 75 pairs
   Buttons: 2 buttons per pair
   Zippers: 1 zipper per pair
Expected purchase price for direct materials
  Cloth: $1.50 per yard
  Thread: $0.20 per spool
  Buttons: $0.01 each
  Zippers: $0.10 each

Direct labor required
  Shirts
   Cutting Department: 5 shirts per hour @ $5/hour
   Sewing Department: 4 shirts per hour @ $6/hour
   Inspection Department: 30 shirts per hour @ $4/hour
  Slacks
   Cutting Department: 3 pair per hour @ $5/hour
   Sewing Department: 2 pair per hour @ $6/hour
   Inspection Department: 20 pair per hour @ $4/hour

Prepare the following for April: (*a*) sales budget; (*b*) production budget; (*c*) direct materials purchases budget; (*d*) direct labor cost budget.

(*a*)

B & G Clothing Manufacturing Company
Sales Budget
Month Ended April 30, 19X1

Product	Unit Sales Volume	Unit Selling Price	Total Sales

(b)

B & G Clothing Manufacturing Company
Production Budget
Month Ended April 30, 19X1

	Shirts	Slacks

(c)

B & G Clothing Manufacturing Company
Direct Materials Purchases Budget
Month Ended April 30, 19X1

	Cloth (yards)	Thread (spools)	Buttons (each)	Zippers (each)

(d)

B & G Clothing Manufacturing Company
Direct Labor Cost Budget
Month Ended April 30, 19X1

	Cutting Department	Sewing Department	Inspection Department

SOLUTION

(a)

B & G Clothing Manufacturing Company
Sales Budget
Month Ended April 30, 19X1

Product	Unit Sales Volume	Unit Selling Price	Total Sales
Shirts	35,500	$ 7.00	$248,500
Slacks	22,000	$12.00	264,000
Total			$512,500

(b)

B & G Clothing Manufacturing Company
Production Budget
Month Ended April 30, 19X1

	Shirts	Slacks
Sales	35,500 units	22,000 units
Expected Inventory, Apr. 30	2,000	1,500
Total	37,500	23,500
Less: Estimated Inventory, Apr. 1	1,500	1,000
Total Production	36,000 units	22,500 units

(c)

B & G Clothing Manufacturing Company
Direct Materials Purchases Budget
Month Ended April 30, 19X1

	Cloth (yards)	Thread (spools)	Buttons (each)	Zippers (each)
Required for Production				
Shirts	54,000	360	432,000	0
Slacks	56,250	300	45,000	22,500
Expected Inventory, Apr. 30	4,000	35	18,000	1,000
Total	114,250	695	495,000	23,500
Less: Estimated Inventory, Apr. 1	3,500	25	10,000	1,100
Total Units to Be Purchased	110,750	670	485,000	22,400
Unit Price	× $1.50	× $0.20	× $0.01	× $0.10
Total Direct Materials				
Purchases	$166,125	$134	$4,850	$2,240

(d)

B & G Clothing Manufacturing Company
Direct Labor Cost Budget
Month Ended April 30, 19X1

	Cutting Department	Sewing Department	Inspection Department
Hours Required for Production			
Shirts	7,200	9,000	1,200
Slacks	7,500	11,250	1,125
Total	14,700	20,250	2,325
Hourly Rate	× $5	× $6	× $4
Total Direct Labor Cost	$73,500	$121,500	$9,300

13.6 The Newman Company has prepared the factory overhead budget for the Finishing Department for August as follows.

Direct Labor Hours	
Normal Productive Capacity	20,000
Hours Budgeted	16,000

Variable Costs		
Indirect Factory Wages	$7,500	
Indirect Materials	4,000	
Utilities	3,500	
Total Variable Costs		$15,000
Fixed Costs		
Supervisors' Salaries	$8,000	
Indirect Factory Wages	6,400	
Depreciation on Plant and Equipment	3,500	
Utilities	3,000	
Insurance	1,200	
Property Taxes	900	
Total Fixed Costs		23,000
Total Factory Overhead Cost		$38,000

For the month of September, actual factory overhead costs were:

Variable Costs	
Indirect Factory Wages	$ 7,000
Indirect Materials	3,000
Utilities	3,300
Fixed Costs	
Supervisors' Salaries	8,000
Indirect Factory Wages	6,400
Depreciation	3,500
Utilities	3,000
Insurance	1,200
Property Taxes	900
Total Overhead Budget	$36,300

(a) On the basis of the August budget, prepare a flexible budget for the month of September, with direct labor hours of 15,000, 18,000, 20,000, and 22,000. Determine also the standard factory overhead rate per direct labor hour.

(b) Prepare a standard factory overhead cost variance report for September. Direct labor hours in September for the Finishing Department were 18,000.

(a)

The Newman Company
Factory Overhead Cost Budget, Finishing Department
Month Ended September 30, 19X1

Percent of Normal Capacity	75%	90%	100%	110%
Budgeted Factory Overhead				
Variable Costs				
Total Variable Costs				

Fixed Costs				
Total Fixed Costs				
Total Factory Overhead Cost				

(b)

The Newman Company
Factory Overhead Cost Variance Report, Finishing Department
Month Ended September 30, 19X1

Normal Capacity for the Month
Actual Production for the Month

	Budget	**Actual**	**Favorable**	**Unfavorable**
Variable Costs				
Total Variable Costs				
Fixed Costs				
Total Fixed Costs				
Total Factory Overhead Costs				
Total Controllable Variance				
Net Controllable Variance				
Volume Variance				
Total Factory Overhead Cost Variance				

SOLUTION

(a)

The Newman Company
Factory Overhead Cost Budget, Finishing Department
Month Ended September 30, 19X1

Percent of Normal Capacity	75%	90%	100%	110%
Direct Labor Hours	15,000	18,000	20,000	22,000
Budgeted Factory Overhead				
Variable Costs				
Indirect Factory Wages	$ 5,625	$ 6,750	$ 7,500	$ 8,250
Indirect Materials	3,000	3,600	4,000	4,400
Utilities	2,625	3,150	3,500	3,850
Total Variable Costs	$11,250	$13,500	$15,000	$16,500

Fixed Costs				
Supervisors' Salaries	$ 8,000	$ 8,000	$ 8,000	$ 8,000
Indirect Factory Wages	6,400	6,400	6,400	6,400
Depreciation	3,500	3,500	3,500	3,500
Utilities	3,000	3,000	3,000	3,000
Insurance	1,200	1,200	1,200	1,200
Property Taxes	900	900	900	900
Total Fixed Costs	$23,000	$23,000	$23,000	$23,000
Total Factory Overhead Cost	$34,250	$36,500	$38,000	$39,500

Standard overhead rate per direct labor hour is $38,000 ÷ 20,000 = $1.90.

(b)

The Newman Company
Factory Overhead Cost Variance Report, Finishing Department
Month Ended September 30, 19X1

Normal Capacity for the Month	20,000 hours			
Actual Production for the Month	18,000 hours			
	Budget	**Actual**	**Favorable**	**Unfavorable**
Variable Costs				
Indirect Factory Wages	$ 6,750	$ 7,000		$ 250
Indirect Materials	3,600	3,000	$600	
Utilities	3,150	3,300		150
Total Variable Costs	$13,500	$13,300		
Fixed Costs				
Supervisors' Salaries	$ 8,000	$ 8,000		
Indirect Factory Wages	6,400	6,400		
Depreciation	3,500	3,500		
Utilities	3,000	3,000		
Insurance	1,200	1,200		
Property Taxes	900	900		
Total Fixed Costs	$23,000	$23,000		
Total Factory Overhead Costs	$36,500	$36,300		
Total Controllable Variance			$600	$ 400
Net Controllable Variance (favorable)			$200	
Volume Variance (unfavorable)				
Idle Hours at Standard Rate for Fixed Overhead				
(2,000 × $23,000/20,000)				$2,300
Total Factory Overhead Cost Variance (unfavorable)				$2,100

Chapter 14

Budgets: Balance Sheet and Standard Costs

14.1 BUDGETED BALANCE SHEET

The results of the various income and expense budgets are reflected in the budgeted balance sheet that is prepared at the end of the budget period. For this statement it is useful to adopt the financial position form, in which current liabilities are subtracted from current assets to arrive at net working capital. Some advantages of the budgeted balance sheet are that (1) it discloses possible unfavorable trends far in advance, so that steps can be taken for improvement; (2) it acts as a check on the accuracy of the various operating budgets; and (3) it provides the data for computing the return on investment.

EXAMPLE 1

Bollett Company
Budgeted Balance Sheet
December 31, 19X1

	Actual, Prior Year	Projected, Current Year	Increase or (Decrease)
CURRENT ASSETS			
Cash	$ 40,100	$ 50,600	$ 10,500
Receivables	60,300	78,500	18,200
Inventories	118,000	97,500	(20,500)
Total Current Assets	$218,400	$226,600	$ 8,200
LESS: CURRENT LIABILITIES			
Accounts Payable	$ 40,300	$ 67,500	$ 27,200
Accrued Expenses	8,900	5,500	(3,400)
Income Taxes Payable	14,100	18,400	4,300
Other Current Liabilities	4,000	7,500	3,500
	$ 67,300	$ 98,900	$ 31,600
Net Working Capital	$151,100	$127,700	$(23,400)
Plant and Equipment (net)	531,800	610,500	78,700
Other Assets	28,100	52,800	24,700
Total	$711,000	$791,000	$ 80,000
Less: Long-Term Liabilities	150,000	150,000	—
Total Net Assets	$561,000	$641,000	$ 80,000

Cash Budget

The expected receipts and disbursements of cash are shown by the cash budget. The components of this budget, such as collections from sales, expected outlays for manufacturing costs, operating expenses, and other expenses, must be carefully coordinated with other budgets. Also, long-term financing, dividend policies, and other financing that affects cash will have to be considered.

EXAMPLE 2

Bollett Company
Cash Budget
Quarter Ended March 31, 19X1

	January	February	March
ESTIMATED CASH RECEIPTS			
Cash Sales	$ 19,700	$ 25,500	$ 24,000
Collections of Receivables	52,800	75,000	58,300
Other Sources	2,500	3,000	8,200
Total Cash Receipts	$ 75,000	$103,500	$ 90,500
ESTIMATED CASH DISBURSEMENTS			
Manufacturing Costs	$ 50,500	$ 50,000	$ 65,500
Selling Expenses	5,500	4,500	5,500
General Expenses	5,000	5,000	5,000
Capital Expenditures	29,000	21,000	19,000
Other Disbursements	10,000	6,000	8,000
Total Cash Disbursements	$100,000	$ 86,500	$103,000
Net Increase or (Decrease)	$ (25,000)	$ 17,000	$ (12,500)
Balance at Beginning of Month	110,000	85,000	102,000
Balance at End of Month	$ 85,000	$102,000	$ 89,500
Minimum Cash Balance	60,000	60,000	60,000
Excess or (Deficiency)	$ 25,000	$ 42,000	$ 29,500

Capital Expenditures Budget

The amount required for capital expenditures may vary considerably from year to year. This change is due partly to the difference in amounts needed to replace machinery and equipment that has become worn out or obsolete. Also, new products or other expansion may require new machinery and equipment.

Since capital expenditures usually require large outlays and may require long-term financing, it is essential that close control be maintained, generally by means of the capital expenditures budget. Capital expenditures are projected for five to ten years, or longer.

EXAMPLE 3

Bollett Company
Capital Expenditures Budget
Five Years Ended December 31, 19X6

	19X2	19X3	19X4	19X5	19X6
Machinery					
Department 1	$ 40,000	$15,000	$ 65,000	$45,000	$10,000
Department 2	30,000	25,000	10,000	19,000	15,000
Office Equipment	22,000	15,000	25,000	18,000	20,000
Delivery Equipment	11,000	6,000	7,000	8,000	15,000
Total	$103,000	$61,000	$107,000	$90,000	$60,000

14.2 FLEXIBLE BUDGETS

Where the volume of operations is fairly stable the fixed-budget approach would be suitable. That is the approach of most companies. However, where substantial changes in volume occur, it is better to use a *flexible budget*, which gives separate treatment to fixed and variable costs (see Section 12.2) over a series of volume levels.

EXAMPLE 4

Bollett Company
Flexible Budget
Monthly Operations

Units of Production	10,000	11,000	12,000
Variable Costs per Unit			
Indirect Wages ($4.00)	$ 40,000	$ 44,000	$ 48,000
Indirect Materials ($3.00)	30,000	33,000	36,000
Electric Power ($1.50)	15,000	16,500	18,000
Total Variable Costs ($8.50)	$ 85,000	$ 93,500	$102,000
Per Unit	$8.50	$8.50	$8.50
Fixed Costs			
Supervision	$ 30,000	$ 30,000	$ 30,000
Depreciation, Plant	18,000	18,000	18,000
Property Taxes	10,000	10,000	10,000
Insurance	8,000	8,000	8,000
Electric Power	11,000	11,000	11,000
Total Fixed Costs	$ 77,000	$ 77,000	$ 77,000
Per Unit	$7.70	$7.00	$6.42
Total Factory Overhead	$162,000	$170,500	$179,000
Per Unit	$16.20	$15.50	$14.92

Observe that the total cost per unit decreases from $16.20 for 10,000 units to $14.92 for 12,000 units.

Electric power is shown under both Variable Costs and Fixed Costs; it is an example of a *semivariable (semifixed)* cost. For such items, there is a fixed charge for consumption up to a certain level, and a unit charge thereafter.

The relationship of fixed to variable costs is important in determining pricing and manufacturing policies. For instance, if total overhead costs are covered, the only additional costs in making longer runs of a single item would be the variable costs. Thus, it may be profitable to take special orders from chain stores and others at a lower price.

14.3 PERFORMANCE REPORTS

To be most effective, performance reports must be made available periodically to measure progress in meeting the budget goals. A part of the performance report should be comments explaining any significant variances from the budget. Steps to be taken to prevent the recurrence of unfavorable variances should be outlined. Below is shown one form of performance report.

EXAMPLE 5

Bollett Company
Budget Report
Factory Overhead, Department #1

	Budget	Actual	Over	Under
Indirect Factory Labor	$ 4,000	$ 4,200	$200	
Supervision	2,300	2,300		
Supplies	1,200	1,100		$100
Power, Heat, and Light	1,600	1,550		50
Depreciation of Plant and Equipment	1,400	1,400		
Property Taxes	1,100	1,200	100	
Insurance	900	950	50	
Maintenance	400	500	100	
Total Factory Overhead	$12,900	$13,200	$450	$150

14.4 STANDARD COSTS

Many companies compare the current month, quarter, or year with the same period of the previous year. But that approach presupposes that the previous year is typical, which may or may not be the case. A much better approach, especially for costing products, is the use of *standard costs*. Through these predetermined costs management can find out how much a product should cost and how much it actually costs. Then, by means of variance analysis (Section 14.5), management can pinpoint the *cause* of the difference between expected and actual costs.

Standard costs for a manufactured product are established after a study of the factory operations and of the expected costs for materials, labor, and factory overhead. If any of these factors change, the standard should be changed accordingly. It is desirable to make an annual review to ensure that the standards are up to date for the coming year.

Standard costs are used with either the job-order or process cost system. When many factory operations are carried on in a single department, specific cost centers, and not the department, should be assigned the standards.

14.5 ANALYSIS OF VARIANCES

When the actual cost of a product or department differs from the established standard cost the difference is called a *variance*. When actual cost is less than standard, the variance is *favorable*; otherwise it is *unfavorable*. Under the principle of "exceptions only," small variances are ignored, and thus most items will not have to be reviewed.

Direct materials variances. Standards are set up both for the quantity required to make one unit of product and for the price of material for one unit of product. It is possible to have a favorable quantity variance and an unfavorable price variance (or vice versa) at the same time, as can be seen in the following example.

EXAMPLE 6

During the month of November, 20,000 units of Product A were produced. There were 19,600 pounds of materials used at a cost of $1.03 per pound. The standards for that volume were 20,000 pounds of materials and a price of $1.00 per pound.

Bollett Company
Direct Materials Variances
Month of November 19X1

Quantity Variance		
Actual Quantity	19,600	
Standard Quantity	20,000	
Difference	400	
Standard Price	× $1.00	
Variance (favorable)		$400
Price Variance		
Actual Price	$1.03	
Standard Price	1.00	
Difference	$0.03	
Actual Quantity	× 19,600	
Variance (unfavorable)		588
Total Materials Variance (unfavorable)		$188*

*Check: (19,600 × $1.03) − (20,000 × $1.00) = 20,188 − 20,000 = 188

Direct labor variances. Standards are set up both for the number of labor hours required to make a unit of product and for the labor rate, or price per unit of product.

EXAMPLE 7

To produce the 20,000 units of Product A described in Example 6, there were 4,200 hours of labor used at a cost of $2.50 each. The standards for that quantity were 4,000 hours and a rate of $2.65 an hour.

Bollett Company
Direct Labor Variances
Month of November 19X1

Usage Variance		
Actual Hours	4,200	
Standard Hours	4,000	
Difference	200	
Standard Rate	× $2.65	
Variance (unfavorable)		$530
Rate Variance		
Actual Rate	$2.50	
Standard Rate	2.65	
Difference	$0.15	
Actual Hours	× 4,200	
Variance (favorable)		630
Total Direct Labor Variance (favorable)		$100*

*Check: (4,000 × $2.65) − (4,200 × $2.50) = $10,600 − $10,500 = $100

Factory overhead variances. An overhead variance will usually result from (1) operating above or below the normal capacity (*volume variance*) or (2) incurring a total cost different from the amount budgeted for the level of operations (*controllable variance*).

EXAMPLE 8

For the 20,000 units of Product A produced during November, the standard and actual data were as follows: *Standard:* 12,000 hours (90% capacity) and a total factory overhead of $31,850. *Actual:* variable factory overhead, $23,200; fixed factory overhead, $10,000.

Bollett Company
Factory Overhead Variance
Month of November, 19X1

Volume Variance		
Normal Capacity	13,300	
Standard for Volume Produced		
(90%)	12,000	
Productive Capacity Not Used	1,300	
Standard Fixed Overhead Rate	× $.50	
Variance (unfavorable)		$ 650
Controllable Variance		
Actual Factory Overhead	$33,200	
Standard Factory Overhead	31,850	
Variance (unfavorable)		1,350
Total Factory Overhead Variance		
(unfavorable)		$2,000

Summary: Chapters 13 and 14

1. A budget is a _____ .

2. All budgets are coordinated in the _____ .

3. The amount of raw materials to be purchased depends on the _____ and the desired _____ .

4. The cash budget shows the expected _____ and _____ for the period.

5. Alternative levels of operations are allowed for in a _____ budget.

6. Standard costs determine how much a product _____ cost and how much it _____ cost.

7. A variance is the difference between an _____ cost and a _____ cost.

8. The two variances for direct materials are _____ and _____ .

9. The two variances for direct labor are _____ and _____ .

10. The two variances for factory overhead are _____ and _____ .

Answers: (1) quantitative projection of operations; (2) master budget; (3) production budget, inventory amounts; (4) cash receipts, cash disbursements; (5) flexible; (6) should, does; (7) actual, standard; (8) quantity, price; (9) usage, rate; (10) volume, controllable

Solved Problems

14.1 From the information below, prepare a monthly cash budget for the next quarter (October–December) for the Golden Company.

	October	November	December
Sales	$750,000	$800,000	$900,000
Manufacturing Costs	450,000	480,000	540,000
Operating Expenses	225,000	240,000	270,000
Capital Expenditures	—	60,000	—

Golden Company expects 25% of its sales to be in cash, and of the accounts receivable, 70% will be collected within the next month. Depreciation, insurance, and property taxes comprise $25,000 of monthly manufacturing costs and $10,000 of the operating expenses. Insurance and property taxes are paid in February, June, and September. The rest of the manufacturing costs and operating expenses will be paid off, one-half in the month in which incurred and the rest in the following month. The current assets on October 1 are made up of

Cash, $70,000

Marketable securities, $50,000

Accounts receivable, $600,000 ($450,000 from September, $150,000 from August)

and current liabilities include

$60,000, 6%, 90-day note payable due October 18

Accounts payable for $200,000 for September manufacturing expenses

Accrued liabilities of $100,000 for September operating expenses

Dividends of $1,000 should be received in November. An income tax payment of $50,000 will be made in November.

	Golden Company		
	Cash Budget		
	Three Months Ended December 31, 19X1		
	October	November	December
Estimated Cash Receipts from:			
Total Cash Receipts			
Estimated Cash Disbursements for:			
Total Cash Disbursements			

Cash Increase or (Decrease)			
Cash Balance at Beginning of Month			
Cash Balance at End of Month			

SOLUTION

Golden Company
Cash Budget
Three Months Ended December 31, 19X1

	October	November	December
Estimated Cash Receipts from:			
Cash Sales	$187,500	$200,000	$225,000
Collections of Accounts			
Receivable*	465,000	528,750	588,750
Dividends Received	—	1,000	—
Total Cash Receipts	$652,500	$729,750	$813,750
Estimated Cash Disbursements for:			
Manufacturing Costs†	$425,000	$465,000	$510,000
Operating Expenses‡	212,500	232,500	255,000
Capital Expenditures	—	60,000	—
Other Purposes			
Notes Payable (including interest)	60,900	—	—
Income Tax	—	50,000	—
Total Cash Disbursements	$698,400	$807,500	$765,000
Cash Increase or (Decrease)	$ (45,900)	$ (77,750)	$ 48,750
Cash Balance at Beginning of Month	70,000	24,100	53,650
Cash Balance at End of Month	$ 24,100	$ (53,650)	$ (4,900)

*Computation:	October	November	December
August sales	$150,000		
September sales	315,000	$135,000	
October sales		393,750	$168,750
November sales			420,000
	$465,000	$528,750	$588,750

†Computation:	October	November	December
Payment of accounts payable,			
beginning of month balance	$200,000	$225,000	$240,000
Payment of current month's costs	225,000	240,000	270,000
	$425,000	$465,000	$510,000

‡Computation:	October	November	December
Payment of accrued expenses,			
beginning of month balance	$100,000	$112,500	$120,000
Payment of current month's costs	112,500	120,000	135,000
	$212,500	$232,500	$255,000

14.2   The Kelsch Company uses a standard cost system and maintains perpetual inventories for materials, work in process, and finished goods.

	Standard	Standard Cost per Unit
Raw materials	3 lbs. @ $2 per lb.	$ 6.00
Direct labor	3 hrs. @ $4 per hr.	12.00
Factory overhead	$3 per direct labor hour	9.00
		$27.00

There was no beginning or ending work in process inventory for January. The transactions for production completed during January are as follows:

(1) Raw materials bought on account, $33,000.

(2) $29,250 of raw materials was used; this is 15,000 lb @ $1.95.

(3) Direct labor was $59,450; this is 14,500 hours @ $4.10.

(4) Factory overhead for the month was: indirect labor, $15,000; depreciation, $9,000; utilities, $8,000; miscellaneous costs, $3,000. Utilities, indirect labor, and miscellaneous costs were paid during January. Of the total factory overhead costs of $35,000, fixed costs were $12,000 and variable costs were $23,000.

(5) Goods finished during January, 4,200 units.

(a) Prepare general journal entries to record the transactions, assuming that the work in process account is debited for actual production costs and credited with standard costs for completed goods.

(b) Set up a T account for work in process and post to the account, using the specified numbers.

(c) Show the variances for raw materials cost, direct labor cost, and factory overhead cost. Normal capacity for the plant is 15,000 direct labor hours.

(d) Compare the sum of the standard cost variances with the total of the work in process.

(a)

(1)		
(2)		
(3)		
(4)		
(5)		

(b)

Work in Process

(c)

Raw Materials Cost Variance

Quantity variance

Price variance

Total raw materials cost variance

Direct Labor Cost Variance

Time variance

Rate variance

Total direct labor cost variance

Factory Overhead Cost Variance

Volume variance

Controllable variance

Total factory overhead cost variance

(d)

SOLUTION

(a)

(1)	Raw Materials		33,000	
	Accounts Payable			33,000
(2)	Work in Process		29,250	
	Raw Materials			29,250
(3)	Work in Process		59,450	
	Cash			59,450
(4)	Work in Process		35,000	
	Cash			26,000
	Accumulated Depreciation			9,000
(5)	Finished Goods		113,400	
	Work in Process			113,400

(b)

Work in Process

(2)	29,250	113,400	(5)
(3)	59,450		
(4)	35,000		

(c)

Raw Materials Cost Variance

Quantity variance		
Actual quantity	15,000 lb	
Standard quantity	12,600 lb*	
Variance (unfavorable)	2,400 lb × standard price, $2	$4,800
Price variance		
Standard price	$2.00 per lb	
Actual price	1.95 per lb	
Variance (favorable)	$0.05 per lb × actual quantity, 15,000 lb	750
Total raw materials cost variance (unfavorable)		$4,050

*4,200 finished units × 3 lb per unit

Direct Labor Cost Variance

Time variance		
Actual time	14,500 hr	
Standard time	12,600 hr	
Variance (unfavorable)	1,900 hr × standard rate, $4/hr	$7,600
Rate variance		
Actual rate	$4.10	
Standard rate	4.00	
Variance (unfavorable)	$0.10 × actual time, 14,500 hr	1,450
Total direct labor cost variance (unfavorable)		$9,050

Factory Overhead Cost Variance		
Volume variance		
Normal productive capacity of 100%	15,000 hr	
Standard for product produced	12,600 hr	
Productive capacity not used	2,400 hr	
Standard fixed factory overhead rate	× 0.80*	
Variance (unfavorable)		$1,920
Controllable variance		
Budgeted factory overhead	$39,720†	
Actual factory overhead costs incurred	35,000	
Variance (favorable)		4,720
Total factory overhead cost variance (favorable)		$2,800

*Fixed factory overhead	$12,000
Normal production capacity in direct labor hours	÷15,000
Standard fixed factory overhead rate per direct labor hour	$0.80
†Variable factory overhead costs (12,600 standard hours × $2.20 standard variable rate)‡	$27,720
Fixed factory overhead costs	12,000
Budgeted factory overhead for standard product produced	$39,720
‡Standard factory overhead rate	$3.00
Less: Standard fixed factory overhead	0.80
Standard variable factory overhead rate	$2.20

(d)	Raw materials cost variance (unfavorable)	$ 4,050
	Direct labor cost variance (unfavorable)	9,050
	Factory overhead cost variance (favorable)	(2,800)
	Balance, work in process	$10,300

14.3 The following tentative trial balance was prepared by the Morton Manufacturing Company as of December 31, 19X1, the end of the current fiscal year.

Cash	$ 29,000	
Accounts Receivable	92,600	
Finished Goods	67,300	
Work in Process	31,500	
Materials	15,100	
Prepaid Expenses	3,500	
Plant and Equipment	549,200	
Accumulated Depreciation, Plant and Equipment		$193,000
Accounts Payable		53,700
Income Tax Payable		23,500
Common Stock, $11 par		308,000
Retained Earnings		210,000
	$788,200	$788,200

Factory output and sales for 19X2 are expected to be 95,000 units of product to be sold at $11 per unit. The quantity and cost of inventories (LIFO method) at December 31, 19X2, are expected to remain unchanged from the beginning of the year. Budget estimates of manufacturing costs and operating expenses for 19X2 are as follows:

	Fixed (total for year)	Variable (per unit sold)
Cost of Goods Manufactured and Sold		
Raw Materials	—	$1.60
Direct Labor	—	2.60
Factory Overhead		
Depreciation of Plant and Equipment	$38,000	—
Other Factory Overhead	94,000	0.80
Selling Expenses		
Sales Commissions	14,600	0.60
Advertising	21,000	—
Miscellaneous Selling Expenses	6,900	0.30
General Expenses		
Office and Officers' Salaries	74,900	0.15
Supplies	950	0.10
Miscellaneous General Expenses	7,950	0.15

Accounts Receivable, Prepaid Expenses, and Accounts Payable are expected to have balances close to those at the beginning of the year. Federal income taxes of $84,700 are expected for 19X2, of which $44,200 will be payable during the year. Dividends of $0.60 a share per quarter are expected to be declared and paid in March, June, September, and January. Plant and equipment purchases are expected to be $52,800 in December. (a) Prepare a budgeted income statement for 19X2. (b) Prepare a budgeted balance sheet as of December 31, 19X2.

(a)

Morton Manufacturing Company
Budgeted Income Statement
Year Ended December 31, 19X2

Sales

Cost of Goods Sold

Gross Profit on Sales

Operating Expenses

Total Operating Expenses

Income Before Income Tax	
Income Tax	
Net Income	

(b)

Morton Manufacturing Company
Budgeted Balance Sheet
December 31, 19X2

ASSETS

Current Assets

Total Current Assets

Plant Assets

Total Assets

LIABILITIES

Current Liabilities

Total Current Liabilities

STOCKHOLDERS' EQUITY

Common Stock

Retained Earnings

Total Stockholders' Equity

Total Liabilities and Stockholders' Equity

SOLUTION

(a)

Morton Manufacturing Company
Budgeted Income Statement
Year Ended December 31, 19X2

Sales			$1,045,000
Cost of Goods Sold			
Raw Materials		$152,000	
Direct Labor		247,000	
Factory Overhead		208,000	
Cost of Goods Sold			607,000
Gross Profit on Sales			$ 438,000
Operating Expenses			
Selling Expenses			
Sales Commissions	$71,600		
Advertising	21,000		
Miscellaneous Selling Expenses	35,400		
Total Selling Expenses		$128,000	

General Expenses			
Office and Officers' Salaries	$89,150		
Supplies Expense	10,450		
Miscellaneous General			
Expenses	22,200		
Total General Expenses		121,800	
Total Operating Expenses			249,800
Income Before Income Tax			$ 188,200
Income Tax			84,700
Net Income			$ 103,500

(b)

Morton Manufacturing Company
Budgeted Balance Sheet
December 31, 19X2

ASSETS

Current Assets			
Cash		$ 67,500*	
Accounts Receivable		92,600	
Inventories			
Finished Goods	$67,300		
Work in Process	31,500		
Materials	15,100	113,900	
Prepaid Expenses		3,500	
Total Current Assets			$277,500
Plant Assets			
Plant and Equipment		$602,000	
Less: Accumulated Depreciation		231,000	371,000
Total Assets			$648,500

*Cash balance, January 1, 19X2			$ 29,000
Plus: Cash from operations			
Net income		$103,500	
Plus: Depreciation, plant and equipment	$38,000		
Income tax payable, Dec. 31, 19X2	40,500	78,500	
		$182,000	
Less: Income tax payable, Jan. 1, 19X2		23,500	158,500
			$187,500
Less: Dividends paid in 19X2		$ 67,200	
Plant and equipment acquired in 19X2		52,800	120,000
Cash balance, Dec. 31, 19X2			$ 67,500

LIABILITIES

Current Liabilities			
Accounts Payable	$ 53,700		
Income Tax Payable	40,500		
Total Current Liabilities		$ 94,200	

STOCKHOLDERS' EQUITY

Common Stock	$308,000	
Retained Earnings	246,300†	
Total Stockholders' Equity		554,300
Total Liabilities and Stockholders' Equity		$648,500

†Retained earnings balance, Jan. 1, 19X2	$210,000
Plus: Net income for 19X2	103,500
	$313,500
Less: Dividends declared during 19X2	67,200
Retained earnings balance, Dec. 31, 19X2	$246,300

Examination II

Chapters 9–14

Part I. Circle T for true, F for false.

1. T F The three types of inventory in a manufacturing company are: direct materials, indirect materials, and factory overhead.

2. T F Direct labor includes the wages of factory employees who are associated with the product, such as supervisors and timekeepers.

3. T F Product costs are part of the inventory cost, while period costs are not.

4. T F Under the job-order cost system, the costs are accumulated by departments or cost centers.

5. T F Under the process cost system, the average unit cost is obtained by dividing the departmental cost by the number of units produced during the period.

6. T F "Equivalent units" means that the same number of units should be on hand at the end of the period as at the beginning of the period.

7. T F The direct labor budget represents the number of hours to complete the budgeted production times the direct labor rate.

8. T F Fixed costs include indirect labor and indirect materials.

9. T F Standard costs may be used with either the job order system or the process cost system.

10. T F When the budgeted cost exceeds the actual cost, the variance is unfavorable.

Part II. Circle the letter identifying the best answer.

1. Merchandising companies sell products:
   (a) they manufacture
   (b) in the same form as purchased
   (c) based on costs
   (d) in raw material form

2. Manufacturing companies sell products:
   (a) they produce
   (b) based on selling price
   (c) based on material cost
   (d) at a percentage over cost

3. An additional account required by a manufacturing company is:
   (a) Current Assets
   (b) Plant and Equipment
   (c) Accounts Payable
   (d) Finished Goods

4. Under a perpetual inventory system, it is:
   (a) necessary to take a physical inventory
   (b) best to use standard costs
   (c) hard to take a physical inventory
   (d) not necessary to take a physical inventory

5. Under the job-order cost system:
   (a) subsidiary ledgers are not maintained
   (b) the costs are applied to specific jobs
   (c) the costs are in good order
   (d) the jobs are costed at standard

6. Equivalent units are used with:
   (a) actual costs
   (b) standard costs
   (c) process costs
   (d) prime costs

7. Overhead costs are overapplied if:
   (a) standard overhead costs exceed actual costs
   (b) actual overhead costs exceed standard costs
   (c) controllable overhead costs exceed fixed costs
   (d) fixed overhead costs exceed actual costs

8. A budget performance report
   (a) reports the complete budget
   (b) compares actual costs to standard
   (c) compares fixed costs to controllable costs
   (d) is a continuous budget of costs

9. If the standard cost for a certain material used is 2,000 pounds at $10 and the actual cost is 2,100 pounds at $9, the quantity variance is:
   (a) $100
   (b) $90
   (c) $1,000
   (d) $900

10. The price variance for the data in Question 9 is:
    (a) $1,000
    (b) $2,100
    (c) $1,100
    (d) $3,200

Part III. Insert the answer in the amount column below.

Compute	Amount	Question Data
1. Purchases		Raw material used, $36,000; raw material inventory decreased by $8,500 during period.
2. Overhead rate		Three direct labor employees work 40 hours a week for 50 weeks a year. Factory overhead cost of $60,000 is distributed on the basis of direct labor hours.
3. Cost of goods manufactured		Raw materials: beginning inventory, $35,000; ending inventory, $30,000; purchases, $50,000. Direct labor, $40,000. Factory overhead, $32,000. Work in process: beginning, $95,000; ending, $90,000. Finished goods: beginning inventory, $18,000; ending inventory, $24,000.
4. Cost of goods sold		Same as in Question 3.

Compute	Amount	Question Data
5. (a) Work in process by jobs (b) Overapplied overhead in total		*Job* <table><tr><td></td><td>Total</td><td>#1</td><td>#2</td><td>#3</td><td>#4</td></tr><tr><td>Raw materials used</td><td>$6,500</td><td>$2,000</td><td>$2,500</td><td>$1,500</td><td>$500</td></tr><tr><td>Direct labor</td><td>10,000</td><td>3,000</td><td>4,000</td><td>2,000</td><td>1,000</td></tr><tr><td>Factory overhead incurred</td><td>7,500</td><td></td><td></td><td></td><td></td></tr></table> Factory overhead applied at 80% of direct labor Jobs #1 and #2 were completed.
6. Equivalent units of production		Opening inventory: 1,000 units, 2/5 completed. Completed during period: 5,000 units. Closing inventory: 1,200 units, 2/3 completed.
7. Processing cost per equivalent unit		The costs in the work in process account for the equivalent units in Question 6 were: Materials, $4,000; Direct Labor, $6,000; Factory Overhead, $4,800.
8. Production budget		Expected quantities for November were: opening inventory, 5,000; desired closing inventory, 6,000; expected sales volume (section 1), 6,000; expected sales volume (section 2), 4,000.
9. (a) Quantity variance (b) Price variance		The raw materials standard for the period was 15,000 pounds at $1.00; the actual was 15,500 pounds at $1.25.
10. (a) Time variance (b) Rate variance		The labor standard for the period was 10,000 hours at $3.00; the actual was 9,600 hours at $3.20.

Part IV

1. The W. F. Pierce Company expects that for Department 2, the total factory overhead cost for the coming year will be $75,000 and total direct labor cost will be $60,000. The actual costs for January were $7,000 and $5,000, respectively. (a) Compute the estimated factory overhead rate based on direct labor cost. (b) Show the entry applying factory overhead to January costs. (c) Find the balance of Factory Overhead, Department 2, at January 31. (d) Is the overhead overapplied or underapplied?

2. The Nostrand Company has the following entries on its books relating to material x for July 19X1.

    Balance:

    July 1   300 units at $8

    Received during July:

    July 3   300 units at $8

    July 15   500 units at $9

    July 24   400 units at $10

    Issued during July:

    July 7   200 units for Job #151

    July 17   300 units for Job #153

    July 28   450 units for Job #156

    Compute the cost of each of the issues using (a) FIFO; (b) LIFO.

3. The Hayden Manufacturing Company has the following entries for the month of May:

Work in Process

Bal., May 1	19,400
Raw Materials	37,300
Direct Labor	25,000
Factory Overhead	20,000

The following jobs were completed during May: Job #210, $15,600; Job #215, $28,300; Job #217, $27,400; Job #220, $13,800. (a) Show the general journal entry for the jobs completed. (b) Determine the amount applicable to uncompleted jobs at May 31.

4. The Payne Corporation records show the following data relating to raw materials cost for September:

Units of finished product manufactured, 8,700

Standard direct materials per unit of product, 5 pounds

Quantity of raw materials used, 45,000 pounds

Unit cost of raw materials, $4 per pound

Raw materials quantity variance (unfavorable), $2,400

Raw materials price variance (favorable), $5,000

There is no work in process at either the beginning or the end of the month. Determine the standard direct materials cost per unit of finished product.

5. Greentree Company manufactures a component for a chemical company. The component is mixed in two different departments. During March, $94,200 of direct material was put into production and $104,400 of direct labor was incurred in Department 1. The factory overhead rate is 62% of direct labor cost. Work in progress in Department 1 was $42,000 at the beginning of the month and $38,600 at the end of the month. Prepare journal entries to record (a) direct material; (b) direct labor; (c) factory overhead; and (d) cost of production transferred to Department 2.

6. Regal Tech manufactures special parts for a tractor company. Below is the data for Job #CM109.

Description, 100 turnbuckles #101

Date started, January 10

Date to be shipped, January 27

Material used, Department 1, $7,900

Direct labor rate, Department 1, $7.40 per hour

Labor hours used, Department 1, 1,150 hours

Direct labor rate, Department 2, $4.40 per hour

Labor hours used, Department 2, 510 hours

Machine hours, Department 2, 580 hours

Applied factory overhead, Department 1, $6.00 per labor hour

Applied factory overhead, Department 2, $2.90 per machine hour

Compute (a) cost for Job #CM109, and (b) cost per unit.

7. Babcock Manufacturing Company had the following balance in its pre-closing trial balance on October 31:

Raw Material Purchased	$154,600
Raw Material Inventory	52,900
Direct Labor	214,700
Factory Overhead (control)	153,200
Work in Process Inventory	71,440
Finished Goods Inventory	164,500
Sales	728,000
Selling Expense (control)	34,900
General Expense (control)	28,250

Inventories on October 31 were:

Raw Material	$ 64,900
Work in Process	59,400
Finished Goods	165,000

Prepare (*a*) a cost of goods manufactured statement, and (*b*) an income statement in good report form.

Answers to Examination II

Part I

1. F, **2.** F, **3.** T, **4.** F, **5.** T, **6.** F, **7.** T, **8.** F, **9.** T, **10.** F

Part II

1. *b;* **2.** *a;* **3.** *b;* **4.** *d;* **5.** *b;* **6.** *c;* **7.** *a;* **8.** *b*

9. *c:* $100 \times \$10 = \$1,000$ (unfavorable)

10. *b:* $2,100 \times \$1 = \underline{2,100}$ (favorable)
$\$1,100 (= 2,000 \times \$10 - 2,100 \times \$9)$

Part III

1. $\$36,000 - \$8,500 = \$27,500$

2. $\$60,000 \div 6,000 \text{ hours} = \$10 \text{ per hour}$

3. $\$95,000 + \$35,000 + \$50,000 + \$40,000 + \$32,000 - \$30,000 - \$90,000 = \$132,000$

4. $\$18,000 + \$132,000 - \$24,000 = \$126,000$

5. (a) Job #3: $1,500 + $2,000 + $1,600 = $5,100
Job #4: $500 + $1,000 + $800 = $2,300

(b) $8,000 − $7,500 = $500

6. $1,200 \times 2/3 − 1,000 \times 2/5 + 5,000 \times 1 = 5,400$

7. ($6,000 + $4,800) ÷ 5,400 = $2 per equivalent unit

8. $6,000 + $4,000 + $6,000 − $5,000 = $11,000

9. (a) (15,500 − 15,000) × $1.00 = $500 (unfavorable)

(b) ($1.25 − $1.00) × 15,500 = $3,875 (unfavorable)

10. (a) (10,000 − 9,600) × $3.00 = $1,200 (favorable)

(b) ($3.20 − $3.00) × 9,600 = $1,920 (unfavorable)

Part IV

1. (a) Estimated overhead rate: $75,000 ÷ $60,000 = 125% of direct labor cost.

(b)

Work in Process, Department 2	6,250	
Factory Overhead, Department 2		6,250*

---

*$5,000 × 125%.

(c) $7,000 (actual overhead) − $6,250 (estimated overhead) = $750 (debit balance).

(d) Underapplied, since the amount applied was less than the actual amount.

2. (a)

July 7	200 @ $8		$1,600
July 17	300 @ $8		$2,400
July 28	100 @ $8	$ 800	
	350 @ $9	3,150	$3,950

(b)

July 7	200 units @ $10		$2,000
July 17	200 units @ $10	$2,000	
	100 units @ $9	900	$2,900
July 28	400 units @ $9	$3,600	
	50 units @ $8	400	$4,000

3. (a)

Finished Goods	85,100	
Work in Process		85,100

(b)

Balance, May 1	$ 19,400
Add: Raw Materials	37,300
Direct labor	25,000
Factory overhead	20,000
	$101,700
Less: Jobs finished during May	85,100
Balance of Work in Process, May 31	$ 16,600

4.

Standard units for direct materials used (45,000 lb ÷ 5 lb per unit)	9,000 units
Actual units completed	8,700 units
Excess materials used	300 units
Quantity variance (unfavorable)	$2,400
Standard direct materials cost per unit	
Quantity variance divided by excess materials used ($2,400 ÷ 300 units)	$8

5. (*a*)

Work in Process, Department 1	94,200	
Materials		94,200

(*b*)

Work in Process, Department 1	104,400	
Wages Payable		104,400

(*c*)

Work in Process, Department 1	64,728	
Factory Overhead, Department 1		64,728

(*d*)

Work in Process, Department 2	267,128	
Work in Process, Department 1		267,128

6. (*a*)

	Dept. 1	Dept. 2	Total
Material	$ 7,900		$ 7,900
Direct Labor			
Department 1 ($7.40 × 1,150)	8,510		8,510
Department 2 ($4.40 × 510)		$2,244	2,244
Factory Overhead			
Department 1 ($6.00 × 1,150)	6,900		6,900
Department 2 ($2.90 × 580)		1,682	1,682
	$23,310	$3,926	$27,236

(*b*) Cost per unit = $27,236.00/100 = $272.36.

7. (*a*)

Statement of Cost of Goods Manufactured

Work in Process Inventory, Nov. 1		$ 71,440
Raw Materials		
Inventory, Nov. 1	$ 52,900	
Purchases	154,600	
Available for Use	$207,500	
Less: Inventory, Oct. 31	64,900	
Put in Production	$142,600	
Direct Labor	214,700	
Factory Overhead	153,200	
Total Manufacturing Costs		510,500
Total Work in Process During Period		$581,940
Less: Work in Process Inventory, Oct. 31		59,400
Cost of Goods Manufactured		$522,540

(b)   *Income Statement*

Sales		$728,000
Cost of Goods Sold		
Finished Goods Inventory, Nov. 1	$164,500	
Cost of Goods Manufactured	522,540	
Cost of Finished Goods Available for Sale	$678,040	
Less Finished Goods Inventory, Oct. 31	165,000	
Cost of Goods Sold		522,040
Gross Profit		$205,960
Less: Selling Expense (control)	$ 34,900	
General Expense (control)	28,250	
Total Expense		63,150
Net Income		$142,810

Chapter 15

Financial Statement Analysis: Horizontal and Vertical

15.1 INTRODUCTION

The periodic financial statements give owners, employees, creditors, investors, government agencies, and others a picture of management's performance. Thus, the solvency of the enterprise is presented in the balance sheet, and its profitability in the income statement.

Financial statement analysis is an evaluation of both a company's past financial performance and its potential for the future. The computation of various ratios is made to appraise financial status and operating performance of the firm for a given time period.

A company's ratios are compared with those of similar companies or with industry norms to determine how the company is performing relative to competition. Industry average ratios can be obtained from a number of financial advisory services including Dun & Bradstreet.

A firm's current-year ratio is compared with its previous and expected future ratios to determine if the entity's financial position is improving or worsening.

To obtain further details of the performance results, it is necessary to subject the published data to various analytical measurements. The measurements fall into three main types, which are presented in Sections 15.2, 15.3, and 16.1.

15.2 AMOUNT AND PERCENTAGE CHANGES (HORIZONTAL ANALYSIS)

In most cases published annual reports to stockholders show financial statements for prior years, sometimes extending back over a 10-year period. The year-to-year changes in each item can then be computed and intercompared. In such a *horizontal analysis*, the changes may be specified as absolute amounts or as percentages.

EXAMPLE 1

Ryefield Company
Comparative Balance Sheet
Years Ended December 31, 19X2, 19X1, and 19X0

	19X2	19X1	19X0	Increase or (Decrease) 19X2–X1	Increase or (Decrease) 19X1–X0	Percent of Increase or (Decrease) 19X2– X1	Percent of Increase or (Decrease) 19X1–X0
ASSETS							
Current Assets	$130,000	$120,000	$100,000	$ 10,000	$20,000	8.3%	20.0%
Plant Assets	69,000	60,000	65,000	9,000	(5,000)	15.0%	(13.0%)
Total Assets	$199,000	$180,000	$165,000	$ 19,000	$15,000	10.6%	9.1%
LIABILITIES							
Current Liabilities	$ 50,000	$ 60,000	$ 55,000	$(10,000)	$ 5,000	(16.7%)	9.1%
Long-Term Liabilities	85,000	70,000	70,000	15,000	—	21.4%	—
Total Liabilities	$135,000	$130,000	$125,000	$ 5,000	$ 5,000	3.8%	4.0%

	19X2	19X1	19X0	Increase or (Decrease) 19X2–X1	Increase or (Decrease) 19X1–X0	Percent of Increase or (Decrease) 19X2– X1	Percent of Increase or (Decrease) 19X1–X0
STOCKHOLDERS' EQUITY							
Preferred Stock, 5%, $100 par	$ 10,000	$ 10,000	$ 10,000	—	—	—	—
Common Stock, $5 par	30,000	30,000	30,000	—	—	—	—
Retained Earnings	24,000	10,000	—	14,000	10,000	140.0%	—
Total Stockholders' Equity	$ 64,000	$ 50,000	$ 40,000	$ 14,000	$10,000	28.0%	25.0%
Total Liabilities and Stockholders' Equity	$199,000	$180,000	$165,000	$ 19,000	$15,000	10.6%	9.1%

The above horizontal analysis of the balance sheets of Ryefield Company covers a 3-year period. The total assets increased from 9.1% to 10.6% while liabilities decreased from 4.0% to 3.8%, resulting in an increase in stockholders' equity from 25.0% to 28.0%.

EXAMPLE 2

The following horizontal analysis of Ryefield Company's income statements covers a 2-year period.

Ryefield Company
Comparative Income Statement
Years Ended December 31, 19X2 and 19X1

	19X2	19X1	Increase or (Decrease) Amount	Increase or (Decrease) Percent
Sales	$158,000	$100,000	$58,000	58.0%
Sales Returns and Allowances	8,000	10,000	(2,000)	(20.0%)
Net Sales	$150,000	$ 90,000	$60,000	66.7%
Cost of Goods Sold	96,000	49,000	47,000	95.9%
Gross Profit	$ 54,000	$ 41,000	$13,000	31.7%
Selling Expenses	$ 15,000	$ 10,000	$ 5,000	50.0%
General Expenses	10,000	8,000	2,000	25.0%
Total Operating Expenses	$ 25,000	$ 18,000	$ 7,000	38.9%
Net Operating Income	$ 29,000	$ 23,000	$ 6,000	26.0%
Other Expenses	5,000	7,000	(2,000)	28.6%
Income Before Income Tax	$ 24,000	$ 16,000	$ 8,000	50.0%
Income Tax	10,000	6,000	4,000	66.7%
Net Income	$ 14,000	$ 10,000	$ 4,000	40.0%

It is seen that while the net sales increased by a substantial amount, 66.7%, the cost of sales increased by even more, 95.9%. This would indicate a decrease in percentage of gross profit in relation to sales—a feature shown more clearly in the component analysis (vertical analysis) in Example 4.

Because horizontal analysis emphasizes the trends of the various accounts, it is relatively easy to identify areas of wide divergence that require further attention.

When an evaluation covers several years, comparative financial statements may become cumbersome. To avoid this, the results of horizontal analysis may be presented by showing trends compared to a base year. In this instance, a typical year is chosen as the base. Each account of the base year is assigned an index of 100. The index for each respective account in subsequent years is found by dividing the account's amount by the base-year amount and multiplying by 100. For instance, if 19X1 is the base year, cash of $20,000 is assigned an index of 100. If cash is $25,000 in 19X4, the index is 1.25.

15.3   COMPONENT PERCENTAGES (VERTICAL ANALYSIS)

In vertical analysis, each item is expressed as a percentage of a significant total (e.g., an asset item would be expressed as a percentage of total assets). Percentages for various years can then be compared, as in horizontal analysis.

EXAMPLE 3

For the balance sheets of Ryefield Company (see Example 1), we have the following vertical analysis:

Ryefield Company
Comparative Balance Sheet
Years Ended December 31, 19X2, 19X1, and 19X0

	Amount			Percent of Group Total		
	19X2	**19X1**	**19X0**	**19X2**	**19X1**	**19X0**
ASSETS						
Current Assets	$130,000	$120,000	$100,000	65.3%	66.7%	60.6%
Plant Assets	69,000	60,000	65,000	34.7%	33.3%	39.4%
Total Assets	$199,000	$180,000	$165,000	100.0%	100.0%	100.0%
LIABILITIES						
Current Liabilities	$ 50,000	$ 60,000	$ 55,000	25.1%	33.3%	33.3%
Long-Term Liabilities	85,000	70,000	70,000	42.7%	38.9%	42.5%
Total Liabilities	$135,000	$130,000	$125,000	67.8%	72.2%	75.8%
STOCKHOLDERS' EQUITY						
Preferred Stock	$ 10,000	$ 10,000	$ 10,000	5.0%	5.6%	6.0%
Common Stock	30,000	30,000	30,000	15.1%	16.6%	18.2%
Retained Earnings	24,000	10,000	—	12.1%	5.6%	—
Total Stockholders' Equity	$ 64,000	$ 50,000	$ 40,000	32.2%	27.8%	24.2%
Total Liabilities and Stockholders' Equity	$199,000	$180,000	$165,000	100.0%	100.0%	100.0%

The current assets showed an improvement from 60.6% in 19X0 to 65.3% in 19X2, indicating an improvement in working capital. Current liabilities showed a decrease from 33.3% in 19X0 to 25.1% in 19X2, which further helped working capital. The specific improvement in working capital will be discussed and shown in Chapter 16, Example 1.

EXAMPLE 4

For the income statements of Example 2, we have the following vertical analysis:

Ryefield Company
Comparative Income Statement
Years Ended December 31, 19X2 and 19X1

	Amount		Percent	
	19X2	**19X1**	**19X2**	**19X1**
Sales	$158,000	$100,000	105.3%	111.1%
Sales Returns and Allowances	8,000	10,000	5.3%	11.1%
Net Sales	$150,000	$ 90,000	100.0%	100.0%
Cost of Goods Sold	96,000	49,000	64.0%	54.4%
Gross Profit	$ 54,000	$ 41,000	36.0%	45.6%
Selling Expenses	$ 15,000	$ 10,000	10.0%	11.1%
General Expenses	10,000	8,000	6.7%	8.9%
Total Operating Expenses	$ 25,000	$ 18,000	16.7%	20.0%
Net Operating Income	$ 29,000	$ 23,000	19.3%	25.6%
Other Expenses	5,000	7,000	3.3%	7.8%
Income Before Income Tax	$ 24,000	$ 16,000	16.0%	17.8%
Income Tax	10,000	6,000	6.7%	6.7%
Net Income	$ 14,000	$ 10,000	9.3%	11.1%

As pointed out in Example 2, there was a substantial increase in sales, which was favorable, but there was an even greater increase in cost of goods sold, which would indicate a decrease in gross profit. This is clearly borne out in the above vertical analysis. A serious problem is indicated for Ryefield Company, since there is normally a tendency for the cost of goods sold percentage to *decrease* when there is a very large increase in sales. Further investigation would be required to pinpoint the cause. There may have been an increase in purchase prices that was not yet reflected in sales prices. If manufacturing was involved, the increase may be due to increases in labor rates or labor use, materials cost, etc.

The percentages developed for one company by vertical analysis can be compared to those of another company or to the industry percentages that are published by trade associations and financial services. The comparison is displayed on a *common-size statement*, so called because all dollar amounts are omitted.

Solved Problems

15.1 Epp Company had the following income and expense data:

	Year 2	Year 1
Net sales	$350,000	$200,000
Cost of goods sold	245,000	130,000
Expenses	70,000	40,000

(*a*) Prepare a comparative income statement for Year 2 and Year 1 showing each item in relation to sales. (*b*) Comment on the significant changes shown by the statement.

(*a*)

Epp Company
Comparative Income Statement
Years Ended December 31, Year 2 and Year 1

	Dollars		Percentages	
	Year 2	**Year 1**	**Year 2**	**Year 1**

SOLUTION

(*a*)

Epp Company
Comparative Income Statement
Years Ended December 31, Year 2 and Year 1

	Dollars		Percentages	
	Year 2	**Year 1**	**Year 2**	**Year 1**
Net Sales	$350,000	$200,000	100%	100%
Cost of Goods Sold	245,000	130,000	70	65
Gross Profit	$105,000	$ 70,000	30%	35%
Expenses	70,000	40,000	20	20
Net Income	$ 35,000	$ 30,000	10%	15%

(*b*) The cost of goods sold showed a substantial increase, from 65% to 70%, giving an increase of cost of $17,500 (5% × $350,000). The percentage of expenses to sales remained the same. Net income was $5,000 more in Year 2, but the percentage to sales decreased from 15% to 10%. If the percentage of net income for Year 2 had been the same as for Year 1, the amount of net income would have been $52,500 instead of $35,000.

15.2 Revenue and expense data for the current calendar year for Timpano Toy Company and for the toy manufacturing industry are presented below.

	Timpano Toy Company	Toy Industry Averages
Sales	$4,590,000	101.5%
Sales returns and allowances	90,000	1.5%
Cost of goods sold	2,655,000	61.2%
Selling expenses	450,000	9.5%
General expenses	427,500	8.8%
Other income	49,500	.5%
Other expenses	54,000	1.0%
Income tax	495,000	10.5%

(*a*) Prepare a common-size income statement comparing operations for Timpano Toy Company with the toy industry. (*b*) Comment on the relationships revealed in the common-size income statement.

(a)

Timpano Toy Company and Industry Averages
Common-Size Income Statement
Year Ended December 31, 19X1

	Timpano	Industry

SOLUTION

(a)

Timpano Toy Company and Industry Averages
Common-Size Income Statement
Year Ended December 31, 19X1

	Timpano	Industry
Sales	102.0%	101.5%
Sales Returns and Allowances	2.0	1.5
Net Sales	100.0%	100.0%
Cost of Goods Sold	59.0	61.2
Gross Profit	41.0%	38.8%
Selling Expenses	10.0%	9.5%
General Expenses	9.5	8.8
Total Operating Expenses	19.5%	18.3%
Net Operating Income	21.5%	20.5%
Other Income	1.1	0.5
	22.6%	21.0%
Other Expenses	1.2	1.0
Income Before Income Tax	21.4%	20.0%
Income Tax	11.0	10.5
Net Income	10.4%	9.5%

(b)   The net income of Timpano Toy Company is 0.9% over the industry average, mainly because Timpano's cost of goods sold is 2.2% below the industry average. This condition is the result of efficiency in the purchasing department and minimal amounts of lost and spoiled goods. The total operating expense percentage of Timpano Toy Company is 1.2% above the industry average. This warrants a close look at general and selling expenses to determine where expenses can be cut. The percentage of sales returns and allowances for Timpano Toy Company is .5% higher than the industry average—a situation that also warrants attention.

15.3   Catanese Company is in the midst of a promotional campaign to boost sales. In Year 2 an additional $70,000 was spent for advertising. Presented below are revenue and expense data for the company.

	Year 2	Year 1
Sales	$816,000	$656,500
Sales returns and allowances	16,000	6,500
Cost of goods sold	400,000	312,000
Selling expenses	200,000	130,000
General expenses	120,000	78,000
Other income	6,400	6,500
Income tax	32,000	67,600

(a) Prepare a comparative income statement for Year 2 and Year 1 for Catanese Company.
(b) Comment on the relationships revealed in the comparative income statement.

(a)

	Dollars		Percentages	
	Year 2	Year 1	Year 2	Year 1

SOLUTION

(a)

	Dollars		Percentages	
	Year 2	Year 1	Year 2	Year 1
Sales	$816,000	$656,500	102.0%	101.0%
Sales Returns and				
Allowances	16,000	6,500	2.0	1.0
Net Sales	$800,000	$650,000	100.0%	100.0%
Cost of Goods Sold	400,000	312,000	50.0%	48.0
Gross Profit	$400,000	$338,000	50.0%	52.0%
Selling Expenses	$200,000	$130,000	25.0%	20.0%
General Expenses	120,000	78,000	15.0	12.0
Total Operating				
Expenses	$320,000	$208,000	40.0%	32.0%
Net Operating				
Income	$ 80,000	$130,000	10.0%	20.0%
Other Income	6,400	6,500	0.8	1.0
Income Before Tax	$ 86,400	$136,500	10.8%	21.0%
Income Tax	32,000	67,600	4.0	10.4
Net Income	$ 54,400	$ 68,900	6.8%	10.6%

(b)   Among the significant relationships revealed by the comparative income statement are:

     (1)   The ratio of cost of goods sold increased and thus the gross profit ratio decreased from 52% to 50%; the Catanese Company suffered a $16,000 (2% × $800,000) decrease in potential gross profit.

     (2)   The ratio of selling expenses rose from 20% to 25%. This can be explained by the increase in advertising expense.

     (3)   The 3% general expense increase may be explained by a strike in the Hicksville plant.

     (4)   The sales returns and allowances doubled. This may be a result of poorer product quality or a too-aggressive sales policy.

15.4   Hebbco and Davco are considering a merger and have prepared the following financial data:

	Hebbco	Davco
Sales, all on account	$2,000,000	$1,500,000
Total assets	1,000,000	500,000
Total liabilities	200,000	100,000
Gross profit, based on sales	40%	33%
Operating expenses, based on sales	30%	20%
Net income, based on sales	8%	9%

Compute for each company: (a) net income as a percentage of sales, (b) net income as a percentage of total assets, (c) net income as a percentage of stockholders' equity.

(a)   Hebbco   Davco

(b)   **Hebbco:**

        Davco:

(c)   Hebbco   Davco

Hebbco:

Davco:

SOLUTION

(a)

		Hebbco		Davco
Sales		$2,000,000		$1,500,000
Cost of goods sold		1,200,000		1,000,000
Gross profit	(40%)	$ 800,000	(33%)	$ 500,000
Operating expenses	(30%)	600,000	(20%)	300,000
Operating income		$ 200,000		$ 200,000
Income tax		40,000		65,000
Net income	(8%)	$ 160,000	(9%)	$ 135,000

(b)   **Hebbco:** $160,000 ÷ $1,000,000 = 16%

Davco: $135,000 ÷ $500,000 = 27%

(c)

	Hebbco	Davco
Total assets	$1,000,000	$500,000
Less: Total liabilities	200,000	100,000
Stockholders' equity	$ 800,000	$400,000

Hebbco: $160,000 ÷ $800,000 = 20%

Davco: $135,000 ÷ $400,000 = 34%

Chapter 16

Financial Statement Analysis: Ratios

16.1 ANALYSIS BY RATIOS. ASSET MANAGEMENT

In both horizontal and vertical analysis, we compare one figure to another figure of the same category. In many cases it is more revealing to compare two figures belonging to different categories.

Ratios for Working Capital

A company's *working capital* is the excess of its current assets over its current liabilities.

Current ratio. The current ratio is the ratio of current assets to current liabilities. Since it shows *how many times over* the company could pay its current debts, it is a better index of liquidity than the dollar amount of working capital.

EXAMPLE 1

Ryefield Company
Current Ratio
19X2 and 19X1

	19X2	19X1
Current Assets	$130,000	$120,000
Less: Current Liabilities	50,000	60,000
Working Capital	$ 80,000	$ 60,000
Current Ratio	2.6	2.0

The improvement in the current ratio from 2.0 to 2.6 might influence a banker to make a short-term loan to the company. The current ratio is sometimes called the *banker's ratio*.

Quick or acid test ratio. When inventories and prepaid expenses are excluded from current assets, the current ratio becomes the *quick ratio*, a measure of the company's ability to pay its debts quickly. Inventories are left out because they are subject to decline in market value and because much time may be needed to convert them into cash. Prepaid expenses are not counted, since they are not convertible into cash.

EXAMPLE 2

Ryefield Company (Example 1) had inventories of $75,000 in 19X2 and $60,000 in 19X1.

Ryefield Company
Quick Assets
19X2 and 19X1

	19X2	19X1
Quick Assets	$55,000	$60,000
Current Liabilities	50,000	60,000
Quick Ratio	1.1	1.0

Ratios for Accounts Receivable

The control of the amount of accounts receivable at any given moment is an important part of the overall control of working capital. Through effective control of accounts receivable, inventories, and other components of working capital many companies today have been able to finance a volume of sales two or three times that of a decade ago without a comparable increase in working capital.

Turnover of accounts receivable. The turnover of accounts receivable ratio is formed by dividing the net sales for the year by the average balance of accounts receivable for the year. Thus, the ratio reflects the number of times the accounts receivable amount has *turned over* during the year. To compute the average balance of accounts receivable, one can take half the sum of the beginning and year-end balances. (A better average can be obtained from the monthly balances, but usually these are known only to management.) If a breakdown between charge and cash sales is available, only the charge sales should be included in net sales.

EXAMPLE 3

Cornfeld Company
Turnover of Accounts Receivable
19X2 and 19X1

	19X2	19X1
Net Sales for the Year	$1,250,000	$1,000,000
Accounts Receivable (net)		
Beginning of the Year	$ 72,000	$ 88,000
End of the Year	93,600	72,000
Total	$ 165,600	$ 160,000
Average	$ 82,800	$ 80,000
Turnover of Accounts Receivable	15.1	12.5

The larger the turnover the better; therefore, the trend from 19X1 to 19X2 was favorable.

Number of days' sales in receivables. Another measure of accounts receivable activities is computed by dividing the accounts receivable at the end of the year by the average daily sales on account. The latter figure is obtained by dividing net sales on account by 365. For this ratio, small values are desirable, as they indicate small amounts of working capital tied up in receivables.

EXAMPLE 4

From Example 3, the average daily sales on account are $1,000,000/365 = $2,740 for 19X1 and $1,250,000/365 = $3,425 for 19X2.

Cornfeld Company
Number of Days' Sales in Receivables
19X2 and 19X1

	19X2	19X1
Accounts Receivable at End of Year	$93,600	$72,000
Average Daily Sales on Account	$ 3,425	$ 2,740
Number of Days' Sales in Receivables	27.3	26.3

Here the trend is unfavorable, since the number of days' sales in receivables *increased* from 26.3 to 27.3.

Ratios for Inventory

The firm's investment in inventory also has a direct effect on its working capital. If there is excess inventory, it means that funds are tied up in inventory that could be used more profitably elsewhere. Also, additional costs are being incurred for storage, insurance, and property taxes, not to mention the danger of a price decline and obsolescence of goods. But if the inventory level is too low, the company may be out of stock, resulting in bad customer's relations. The two principal ratios for inventory are analogous to those for accounts receivable.

Turnover of inventory. The inventory turnover ratio is the ratio of the cost of goods sold to the average inventory. The average inventory in most published statements is obtained by taking half the sum of the beginning and ending inventories.

EXAMPLE 5

Oates Company
Turnover of Inventory
19X2 and 19X1

	19X2	19X1
Cost of Goods Sold	$750,000	$550,000
Merchandise Inventory		
Beginning of the Year	84,200	53,300
End of the Year	130,100	84,200
Total	$214,300	$137,500
Average	10,750	68,750
Turnover of Inventory	7.0	8.0

In this case there was an unfavorable trend in inventory turnover from 8.0 in 19X1 to 7.0 in 19X2. While cost of goods sold increased by 36.4%, average inventory increased by 55.9%. The various classifications of inventory should be compared for the two years to find the classification in which the large change occurred. A new product requiring the carrying of additional items in inventory often accounts for part of an increase.

Number of days' sales in inventory. The relationship between inventory and cost of goods sold can also be expressed as the number of days' sales in inventory. In this ratio the inventory at the end of the year is divided by the average daily cost of goods sold. The latter figure is determined by dividing the cost of goods sold by 365. The number of days' sales in inventory provides a rough measure of the length of time required to buy, sell, and then replace the inventory.

EXAMPLE 6

For Oates Company (Example 5), the average daily cost of goods sold is $550,000/365 = $1,507 for 19X1 and $750,000/365 = $2,055 for 19X2.

Oates Company
Number of Days' Sales in Inventory
19X2 and 19X1

	19X2	19X1
Inventory at End of Year	$130,100	$84,200
Average Daily Cost of Goods Sold	$ 2,055	$ 1,507
Number of Days' Sales in Inventory	63.3	55.9

This ratio would, of course, reflect the same unfavorable trend as in Example 5. Here the number of days' sales in inventory increased from 55.9 days to 63.3 days.

Operating Cycle

The *operating cycle* of a business is the number of days required to convert inventory and receivables to cash. Hence, a short operating cycle is desirable.

$$\text{Operating cycle} = \text{average collection period} + \text{average age of inventory}$$

For Oates Company, the operating cycle in 19X2 is:

$$27.3 + 63.3 = 90.6 \text{ days}$$

$$\text{Working capital} = \text{current assets} - \text{current liabilities}$$

$$\text{Current ratio} = \frac{\text{current assets}}{\text{current liabilities}}$$

$$\text{Acid test (quick)} = \frac{\text{current assets exclusive of inventory and prepaid expenses}}{\text{current liabilities}}$$

$$\text{Accounts receivable turnover} = \frac{\text{net sales (on account)}}{\text{average accounts receivable}}$$

$$\frac{\text{Number of days' sales}}{\text{tied up in accounts receivable}} = \frac{\text{accounts receivable (ending)}}{\text{average sales made on account per day}}$$

$$\text{Merchandise turnover} = \frac{\text{cost of goods (merchandise) sold}}{\text{average inventory}}$$

$$\text{Number of days of inventory} = \frac{\text{inventory (end)}}{\text{average cost of goods sold per day}}$$

16.2 ANALYSIS BY RATIOS. LIABILITIES AND CAPITAL

Ratio of Stockholders' Equity to Liabilities

It is important to know the sources of funds for an enterprise. If funds obtained from creditors are large in proportion to stockholders' equity, there will likely be a substantial fixed obligation each period in the form of interest. The equity-to-liabilities ratio indicates the margin of safety for creditors and the ability of the enterprise to weather business hardship.

EXAMPLE 7

From the data in Example 3 in Chapter 15:

Ryefield Company
Ratio of Stockholders' Equity to Liabilities
19X2 and 19X1

	19X2	19X1
Total Stockholders' Equity	$ 64,000	$ 50,000
Total Liabilities	135,000	130,000
Ratio of Stockholders' Equity to Liabilities	0.47	0.38

The slight improvement in the ratio is due primarily to the increase in owners' equity.

Ratio of Plant Assets to Long-Term Liabilities

The ratio of plant assets to long-term liabilities gauges the safety of those holding notes or bonds of the firm. Further, it gives an indication of the extent of possible additional long-term borrowings.

EXAMPLE 8

From the data in Example 3 of Chapter 15:

Ryefield Company
Ratio of Plant Assets to Long-Term Liabilities
19X2 and 19X1

	19X2	19X1
Plant Assets (net)	$69,000	$60,000
Long-Term Liabilities	85,000	70,000
Ratio of Plant Assets to Long-Term Liabilities	0.81	0.86

Ratio of Net Sales to Assets

The ratio of net sales to assets is a good means of comparing companies in regard to their utilization of assets. For example, two companies may have approximately the same amount of assets, but the sales of one may be two or three times those of the other. Long-term investments are excluded from total assets, as they are unrelated to sales. As the denominator of the ratio, one uses an average of the total assets based on as much data as possible. Thus, one may take the average of the beginning and year-end amounts, which are usually shown in published reports. For internal company purposes, the average may be based on monthly totals.

EXAMPLE 9

From the data in Examples 3 and 4 of Chapter 15:

Ryefield Company
Ratio of Net Sales to Assets
19X2 and 19X1

	19X2	19X1
Net Sales	$150,000	$ 90,000
Total Assets		
Beginning of Year	$180,000	$165,000
End of Year	199,000	180,000
Total	$379,000	$345,000
Average	$189,500	$172,500
Ratio of Net Sales to Assets	0.79	0.52

Rate Earned on Total Assets

The rate earned on total assets is the ratio of net income (suitably defined) to average total assets. It indicates the productivity of the total assets without distinguishing between stockholders' equity and liabilities. Therefore the rate is independent of whether the company uses equity funding, debt funding, or a combination of the two. (See Section 7.4.) Since interest expense is related to a particular method of financing, the amount in the current year is added back to true net income to give the "net income" that is divided by total assets.

EXAMPLE 10

Ryefield Company
Rate Earned on Total Assets
19X2 and 19X1

	19X2	19X1
Net Income	$ 14,000	$ 10,000
Add: Interest Expense	4,200	4,200
Total	$ 18,200	$ 14,200
Total Assets		
Beginning of Year	$180,000	$165,000
End of Year	199,000	180,000
Total	$379,000	$345,000
Average	$189,500	$172,500
Rate Earned on Total Assets	9.6%	8.2%

Earnings per Share on Common Stock

Earnings per share on common stock is the financial ratio that is quoted most often. Where there are both preferred stock and common stock, the net income must be reduced by preferred stock dividends to arrive at the amount applicable to common stock. Where there is only one class of stock, the full net income is divided by the number of shares outstanding to give the earnings per share on common stock. Any changes in outstanding shares, such as those from stock dividends or stock splits, should be disclosed when reporting earnings per share on common stock. If extraordinary items are included in net income, the per share earnings should be shown in three amounts: (1) net income per share before extraordinary items, (2) extraordinary gain (or loss) per share, and (3) net income per share. The earnings per share is used by the investor to evaluate the performance of a company and to estimate its future possibilities. Also, the dividends that might be expected by the investor are generally tied to earnings.

EXAMPLE 11

Ryefield Company
Earnings per Share
19X2 and 19X1

	19X2	**19X1**
Net Income	$14,000	$10,000
Less: Preferred Dividends	500	500
Available for Common Stock	$13,500	$ 9,500
Shares of Common Stock Outstanding	6,000	6,000
Earnings per Share on Common Stock	$2.25	$1.58

Summary: Chapters 15 and 16

1. The analysis of changes in each item in comparative financial statements is called _____ analysis.

2. The analysis of changes of each item expressed as a percentage of a significant total is called _____ analysis.

3. The vertical analysis of the percentages of one company compared with percentages published by trade associations is presented in _____ .

4. The excess of current assets over current liabilities is referred to as _____ .

5. The ratio obtained by dividing current assets by current liabilities is called the _____ ratio.

6. The _____ ratio indicates the ability of a company to pay its debts quickly.

7. Accounts receivable turnover is computed by dividing _____ by the average balance of _____ .

8. Merchandise inventory turnover is computed by dividing the _____ by the _____ .

9. The rate earned on stockholders' equity is computed by dividing _____ by _____ .

10. The earnings per common share, where there is only one class of stock, is computed by dividing _____ by the _____ .

Answers: (1) horizontal; (2) vertical; (3) common-size statements; (4) working capital; (5) current; (6) acid test; (7) net sales on account, accounts receivable; (8) cost of goods sold, average inventory; (9) net income, total stockholders' equity; (10) net income, number of shares outstanding

Solved Problems

16.1 Reilly Company had the following financial position data:

	Year 2	Year 1
Cash	$ 95,000	$50,000
Marketable securities	50,000	35,000
Receivables (net)	90,000	60,000
Inventories	100,000	85,000
Prepaid expenses	15,000	20,000
Notes payable	55,000	30,000
Accounts payable	70,000	40,000
Accrued liabilities	50,000	30,000

Compute (*a*) working capital, (*b*) current ratio, (*c*) acid test ratio.

SOLUTION

(*a*)		Year 2	Year 1
	Current assets	$350,000	$250,000
	Less: Current liabilities	175,000	100,000
	Working capital	$175,000	$150,000
(*b*)	Current assets ÷ current liabilities	$\dfrac{\$350,000}{\$175,000}$	$\dfrac{\$250,000}{\$100,000}$
		= 2.0 to 1	= 2.5 to 1
(*c*)	Quick assets ÷ current liabilities	$\dfrac{\$235,000}{\$175,000}$	$\dfrac{\$145,000}{\$100,000}$
		= 1.3 to 1	= 1.5 to 1

16.2 Giordano Company has the following data:

	Year 2	Year 1
Accounts receivable, end of year	$ 380,000	$ 370,000
Monthly average of accounts receivable (net)	410,000	390,000
Net sales on account	3,000,000	2,500,000
Terms of sale: 1/10, n/60		

(*a*) Compute for each year: (1) the number of days' sales in receivables, and (2) the accounts receivable turnover.

(*b*) Analyze the results obtained in (*a*).

SOLUTION

(a)

	Year 2	**Year 1**

(1)
$$\frac{\$3,000,000}{365} = \$8,219 \qquad \frac{\$2,500,000}{365} = \$6,849$$

$$\frac{\$380,000}{\$8,219} = 46 \text{ days} \qquad \frac{\$370,000}{\$6,849} = 54 \text{ days}$$

(2)
$$\frac{\$3,000,000}{\$410,000} = 7.3 \text{ times} \qquad \frac{\$2,500,000}{\$390,000} = 6.4 \text{ times}$$

(b) The number of days' sales in receivables dropped from 54 to 46. However, this is still not satisfactory in view of the credit terms, since many customers pay their bills during the discount period. The accounts receivable turnover increased from 6.4 to 7.3, a substantial favorable change. Even with the above improvements the credit and collection policies should be reviewed for possible further improvements.

16.3 The following information is received from Knox Company:

	Year 2	**Year 1**
Accounts receivable, end of year	$ 365,000	$ 355,000
Monthly average of accounts receivable (net)	390,000	380,000
Net sales on account	3,150,000	2,750,000
Terms of sale: 1/10, n/60		

Compute for each year: (a) the number of days sales in receivables, and (b) the accounts receivable turnover.

SOLUTION

	Year 2	**Year 1**

(a)
$$\frac{\$3,150,000}{365} = \$8,630 \qquad \frac{\$2,750,000}{365} = \$7,534$$

$$\frac{\$365,000}{\$8,630} = 42 \text{ days} \qquad \frac{\$355,000}{\$7,534} = 47 \text{ days}$$

(b)
$$\frac{\$3,150,000}{\$390,000} = 8 \text{ times} \qquad \frac{\$2,750,000}{\$380,000} = 7.2 \text{ times}$$

16.4 Whyte Company's income statements show the following data:

	Year 2	**Year 1**
Sales	$1,500,000	$1,200,000
Beginning inventory	175,000	225,000
Purchases	750,000	550,000
Ending inventory	200,000	175,000

(a) Compute for each year: (1) the inventory turnover, and (2) the number of days' sales in inventory.

(b) Analyze the results obtained in (a).

(a)

	Year 2	**Year 1**
(1)		
(2)		

SOLUTION

(a)

	Year 2	Year 1
(1)	$725,000* ÷ $187,500 = 3.9	$600,000* ÷ $200,000 = 3.0
(2)	$725,000 ÷ 365 = $1,986	$600,000 ÷ 365 = $1,644
	$200,000 ÷ $1,986 = 100.7 days	$175,000 ÷ $1,644 = 106.4 days

*$175,000	Inventory (beg.)	$225,000
750,000	Purchases	550,000
$925,000		$775,000
200,000	Inventory (end)	175,000
$725,000	Cost of goods sold	$600,000

(b)   The inventory turnover and the number of days' sales in inventory showed favorable trends for the current year. Further comparisons should be made with the data of other firms in the same industry.

16.5   Income statements of Kraft Company show the following information:

	Year 2	Year 1
Sales	$1,650,000	$1,250,000
Beginning inventory	180,000	200,000
Purchases	900,000	600,000
Ending inventory	225,000	180,000

Compute for each year: (a) the inventory turnover, and (b) the number of days' sales in inventory.

	Year 2	Year 1
(a)		
(b)		

SOLUTION

	Year 2	Year 1
(a)	$855,000 ÷ $202,500 = 4.2	$620,000 ÷ $190,000 = 3.3
(b)	$855,000 ÷ 365 = $2,342	$620,000 ÷ 365 = $1,699
	$225,000 ÷ $2,342 = 96.1 days	$180,000 ÷ $1,699 = 105.9 days

16.6   Folk Company balance sheet showed the following data:

Total current liabilities	$275,000
Bonds payable, 7% (issued in 1975, due in 1995)	300,000
Preferred stock, 7%, $100 par	200,000
Common stock, $20 par	400,000
Premium on common stock	250,000
Retained earnings	175,000

Income before income tax was $150,000, and income taxes were $60,000 for the current year. Compute: (a) rate earned on total assets; (b) rate earned on common stock; (c) number of times bond interest charges were earned; and (d) earnings per share on common stock.

(a) _____

(b) _____

(c) _____

(d) _____

SOLUTION

(a) Net income, $90,000 ($150,000 − $60,000) + interest expense, $21,000 =

    $111,000 ÷ total assets, $1,600,000 (equal to liabilities and capital) = 7.0%

(b) Net income, $90,000 − preferred dividends, $14,000 = $76,000 ÷

    common stockholders' equity, $825,000 = 9.2%

(c) Income before income tax, $150,000 + interest expense, $21,000 =

    $171,000 ÷ interest charges, $21,000 = 8.1 times

(d) Net income, $90,000 − preferred dividends, $14,000 = $76,000 ÷

    number of shares of common stock, 20,000 = $3.80

16.7 The following data have been taken from the current balance sheet of Rolston Manufacturing Company:

Cash	$ 83,000	Accounts payable	$80,000
Marketable securities (at cost)	40,000	Notes payable (short-term)	16,000
Accounts receivable	95,000	Income taxes payable	11,000
Allowance for uncollectible		Accrued liabilities	18,000
accounts	3,000	Current portion of long-term debt	10,000
Inventories	199,000		
Prepaid expenses	16,000		

(a) Compute the working capital, current ratio, and acid test ratio.

(b) State the *immediate* effect (increase, decrease, no change) that each of the following transactions has on the working capital, the current ratio, and the acid test ratio. Use the letters, I, D, and N to indicate your answers. Consider each transaction separately, but indicate a transaction's *simultaneous* effect on all three of the above.

  (1) Wrote off an account receivable against the allowance for uncollectible accounts, $10,000.

  (2) Purchased raw materials on account, $50,000.

  (3) Collected cash in payment of an account receivable, $15,000.

  (4) Paid for fire insurance in advance, $12,000.

  (5) Paid a short-term note payable, $30,000.

  (6) Declared and distributed a 10% stock dividend, $40,000.

  (7) Sold marketable securities costing $20,000 for $15,000.

  (8) Borrowed $10,000 from the bank on a short-term note.

  (9) Disposed of equipment with a book value of $12,000 for $5,000 cash.

 (10) Declared and paid a cash dividend, $6,000.

 (11) Issued additional common stock for $20,000.

 (12) Purchased raw materials for cash, $15,000.

(a)

_____
_____
_____
_____
_____
_____
_____
_____
_____
_____
_____
_____
_____
_____

(b)

	Effect on			Stated in M Dollars				Ratios	
	Work. Cap.	Curr. Ratio	Acid Test Ratio	Quick Assets	Curr. Assets −	Curr. Liabil. =	Work. Cap.	Curr. Ratio	Acid Test Ratio
Bal.									
(1) Bal.									
(2) Bal.									
(3) Bal.									
(4) Bal.									
(5) Bal.									
(6) Bal.									
(7) Bal.									
(8) Bal.									
(9) Bal.									
(10) Bal.									
(11) Bal.									
(12) Bal.									

SOLUTION

(a)

Current assets	$430,000
Less: Current liabilities	135,000
Working capital	$295,000

Current ratio = current assets ÷ current liabilities

  = $430,000   ÷ $135,000

  = 3.2 : 1

Acid test ratio =   quick assets ÷ current liabilities

  = $215,000   ÷ $135,000

  = 1.6 : 1

(b)

	Effect on			Stated in M Dollars				Ratios	
	Work. Cap.	Curr. Ratio	Acid Test Ratio	Quick Assets	Curr. Assets −	Curr. Liabil. =	Work. Cap.	Curr. Ratio	Acid Test Ratio
Bal.				215	430	135	295	3.2	1.6
(1)	N	N	N	−10 +10	−10 +10		0		
Bal.				215	430	135	295	3.2	1.6
(2)	N	D	D		+50	+50	0		
Bal.				215	480	185	295	2.6	1.2
(3)	N	N	N	+15 −15	+15 −15				
Bal.				215	430	135	295	3.2	1.6
(4)	N	N	D	−12	−3 +3				
Bal.				203	430	135	295	3.2	1.5
(5)	N	I	I	−30	−30	−30			
Bal.				185	400	105	295	3.8	1.8
(6)	N	N	N	0	0	0			
Bal.				215	430	135	295	3.2	1.6
(7)	D	D	D	+15 −20	+15 −20		−5		
Bal.				210	425	135	290	3.15	1.56
(8)	N	D	D	+10	+10	+10			
Bal.				225	440	145	295	3.0	1.55
(9)	I	I	I	+5	+5		+5		
Bal.				220	435	135	300	3.22	1.63
(10)	D	D	D	−6	−6		−6		
Bal.				209	424	135	289	3.1	1.55
(11)	I	I	I	+20	+20		+20		
Bal.				235	450	135	315	3.3	1.7
(12)	N	N	D	−15	+15 −15				
Bal.				200	430	135	295	3.2	1.5

16.8   The financial statements of B. R. Blaine & Co. are presented below.

B. R. Blaine & Co.
Income Statement
Year Ended December 31, 19X1

Sales	$2,935,500	
Less: Sales Returns and Allowances	85,500	
Net Sales		$2,850,000
Cost of Merchandise Sold		
Merchandise Inventory, Jan. 1, 19X1	$ 360,000	
Purchases (net)	2,111,000	
Merchandise Available for Sale	$2,471,000	
Merchandise Inventory, Dec. 31, 19X1	476,000	
Cost of Merchandise Sold		1,995,000
Gross Profit on Sales		$ 855,000
Operating Expenses		
Selling Expenses	$ 427,500	
General Expenses	133,000	
Total Operating Expenses		560,500
Net Operating Income		$ 294,500
Other Income		8,550
		$ 303,050
Other Expense (Interest)		38,000
Income Before Income Tax		$ 265,050
Income Tax		126,350
Net Income		$ 138,700

B. R. Blaine & Co.
Balance Sheet
December 31, 19X1

ASSETS

Current Assets		
Cash	$ 102,600	
Marketable Securities	57,000	
Accounts Receivable (net)	303,000	
Merchandise Inventory	476,000	
Prepaid Expenses	11,400	
Total Current Assets		$ 950,000
Long-Term Investments		
Investment in Affiliated Company		190,000
Plant Assets		
Equipment (net)	$ 617,500	
Buildings (net)	1,163,750	
Land	118,750	
Total Plant Assets		1,900,000
Total Assets		$3,040,000

LIABILITIES

Current Liabilities		
Accounts Payable		$ 469,000
Long-Term Liabilities		
Mortgage Note Payable, due 1995	$ 170,000	
Bonds Payable, 5%, due 1998	570,000	
Total Long-Term Liabilities		740,000
Total Liabilities		$1,209,000

STOCKHOLDERS' EQUITY

Preferred Stock, 6%, Cumulative,		
Nonparticipating, $100 Par	$ 475,000	
Common Stock, $25 Par	475,000	
Retained Earnings	881,000	
Total Stockholders' Equity		1,831,000
Total Liabilities and Stockholders'		
Equity		$3,040,000

B. R. Blaine & Co.
Retained Earnings Statement
Year Ended December 31, 19X1

Retained Earnings, Jan. 1, 19X1		$805,000
Add: Net Income for Year		138,700
Total		$943,700
Deduct: Dividends		
On Preferred Stock	$28,500	
On Common Stock	34,200	62,700
Retained Earnings, Dec. 31, 19X1		$881,000

The following data is from the balance sheet at December 31 of the preceding year:

Accounts Receivable (net)	$ 211,000
Long-Term Investments	166,250
Total Assets	2,940,000
Total Stockholders' Equity	1,755,000

The number of preferred and common shares and their dollar value are the same for both years. Determine for 19X1: (*a*) working capital, (*b*) current ratio, (*c*) acid test ratio, (*d*) accounts receivable turnover, (*e*) number of days' sales in receivables, (*f*) merchandise inventory turnover, (*g*) number of days' sales in merchandise inventory, (*h*) ratio of plant assets to long-term liabilities, (*i*) ratio of stockholders' equity to liabilities, (*j*) rate earned on total assets, (*k*) rate earned on stockholders' equity, (*l*) earnings per share on common stock.

(*a*) _____

(*b*) _____

(*c*) _____

(*d*) _____

(*e*) _____

(*f*) _____

(*g*) _____

(h) _____

(i) _____

(j) _____

(k) _____

(l) _____

SOLUTION

(a) $950,000 − $469,000 = $481,000

(b) $950,000 ÷ $469,000 = 2.02

(c) $462,600 ÷ $469,000 = 0.99

(d) $2,850,000 ÷ $\frac{1}{2}$($303,000 + $211,000) = 11.1

(e) $2,850,000 ÷ 365 = $7,808; $303,000 ÷ $7,808 = 38.9 days

(f) $1,995,000 ÷ $\frac{1}{2}$($476,000 + $360,000) = 4.8

(g) $1,995,000 ÷ 365 = $5,466; $476,000 ÷ $5,466 = 87.1 days

(h) $1,900,000 ÷ $740,000 = 2.6

(i) $1,831,000 ÷ $1,209,000 = 1.5

(j) $176,700 ÷ $\frac{1}{2}$($3,040,000 + $2,940,000) = 5.9%

(k) $138,700 ÷ $\frac{1}{2}$($1,831,000 + $1,755,000) = 7.7%

(l)   ($138,700 − $28,500) ÷ 19,000 = $5.80 per share

Examination III

Chapters 15–16

1. The Nell Corporation had the following financial position data:

	Year 2	Year 1
Cash	$105,000	$145,000
Accounts Receivable (net)	65,000	35,000
Inventories	90,000	35,000
Prepaid Expenses	40,000	10,000
Accounts Payable	100,000	150,000
Notes Payable	40,000	25,000

Compute: (a) working capital, (b) current ratio, and (c) acid test ratio.

2. Borak Company had the following income and expense data:

	Year 2	Year 1
Net Sales	$420,000	$340,000
Cost of Goods Sold	280,000	240,000
Expenses	95,000	25,000

Prepare a comparative income statement for Year 2 and Year 1, showing each item in relation to sales.

3. The Sunshine Company's income statements show the following data:

	Year 2	Year 1
Sales	$1,400,000	$1,000,000
Inventories (beginning)	140,000	250,000
Purchases	750,000	700,000
Inventories (ending)	150,000	140,000

Compute for each year: (a) the inventory turnover, and (b) the number of days' sales in inventory.

4. The Caren Corporation had the following data for each December 31:

	Year 2	Year 1
Cash	$ 45,000	$ 41,200
Accounts Receivable (net)	36,200	35,000
Inventories	180,000	181,000
Prepaid Expenses	72,000	68,000
Equipment	94,000	80,000
Accumulated Depreciation, Equip.	12,000	7,000
Accounts Payable	47,000	45,400
Notes Payable	21,600	21,600
Dividends Payable	5,000	7,000
Common Stock	122,000	122,000
Retained Earnings	51,500	42,400

Prepare a schedule of changes in components of working capital.

5. Indicate the effect of the following transactions on working capital by placing a check mark if there is no effect, or by indicating the amount of increase or decrease.

Transaction	No Effect	Increase	Decrease
(a) Bought merchandise, $3,000, on account			
(b) Sold $2,000 of merchandise for $2,800			
(c) Paid $4,200 for operating expenses			
(d) Purchased equipment, $6,900, on account			
(e) Paid $3,200 on notes payable			
(f) Received $1,000 on account from customers			
(g) Borrowed $1,500 on a 30-day note			
(h) Declared and paid a cash dividend of $2,500			

Answers to Examination III

1.

		Year 2	Year 1
(a)	Current assets	$300,000	$225,000
	Less: Current liabilities	140,000	175,000
	Working capital	$160,000	$ 50,000
(b)	Current assets ÷ current liabilities	$300,000 / $140,000	$225,000 / $175,000
		= 2.1 to 1	= 1.3 to 1
(c)	Quick assets ÷ current liabilities	$170,000 / $140,000	$180,000 / $175,000
		= 1.2 to 1	= 1.0 to 1

2.

	Dollars		Percentages	
	Year 2	Year 1	Year 2	Year 1
Net Sales	$420,000	$340,000	100%	100%
Cost of Goods Sold	280,000	240,000	67%	71%
Gross Profit	$140,000	$100,000	33%	29%
Expenses	95,000	75,000	22%	22%
Net Income	$ 45,000	$ 25,000	11%	7%

3.

	Year 2	Year 1
(a)	$740,000 ÷ $145,000 = 5.1	$810,000 ÷ $195,000 = 4.2
(b)	$740,000 ÷ 365 = $2,027	$810,000 ÷ 365 = $2,219
	$150,000 ÷ $2,027 = 74 days	$140,000 ÷ $2,219 = 63 days

4.

Increase (Decrease) in Current Assets:

Cash	$ 3,800	
Accounts Receivable (net)	1,200	
Inventories	(1,000)	
Prepaid Expenses	4,000	$8,000

Increase (Decrease) in Current Liabilities:

Accounts Payable	$ 1,600	
Notes Payable	—	
Dividends Payable	(2,000)	(400)
Increase in Working Capital		$8,400

5.

	No Effect	Increase	Decrease
(a)	✓		
(b)		$800	
(c)			$4,200
(d)			$6,900
(e)	✓		
(f)	✓		
(g)	✓		
(h)			$2,500

Statement of Cash Flows

A.1 INTRODUCTION

In the previous pages of this accounting text and also in *Schaum's Outline of Accounting I*, the three basic financial statements presented were the balance sheet, the income statement, and the statement of owners' equity (known as the retained earnings statement). Because of the need for full and adequate disclosure, a fourth basic financial statement has been introduced.

At the close of 1987, the Financial Accounting Standards Board (FASB) issued *Statement of Financial Accounting Standards No. 95*. It stated that the inclusion of a "statement of cash flows" in the annual report for fiscal years ending after July 15, 1988, was mandatory. Therefore, it has now become very important to be able to analyze and interpret this new financial statement.

The purpose of the statement of cash flows is to give readers essential information about an entity's cash receipts and cash disbursements for a period as they apply to operating, investing, and financing activities. The net effect of the flows on cash and cash equivalents for the period must be reported so that the beginning and ending balances of cash and cash equivalents may be reconciled. Separate reporting is also needed for some types of data related to noncash financing and investment transactions. A reconciliation has to be made tracing net income to net cash flow from operating activities.

The emphasis is placed on explaining the change in cash and cash equivalents for the year. What is a cash-equivalent as defined by the pronouncement? It is a short-term, very liquid investment that may quickly be sold for cash and that has a very near maturity date so that it is extremely unlikely that market value will be affected by changes in money market rates. In general, the initial maturity date must be 3 months or less. Commercial paper and Treasury bills are examples. The entity's policy in deciding what constitutes a cash equivalent must be disclosed. If the classification policy changes, there is a change in accounting principle requiring the restatement of previous years' financial statements. This requirement is to aid in comparability.

A.2 TYPES OF CASH FLOWS

In the statement of cash flows there is a segregation between cash receipts and cash payments due to investing, financing, or operating activities.

Cash flows from operating activities make up the first section in the statement. These apply to the production and sale of merchandise. The rendering of professional services is also included. In general, cash flow from operating activities usually relates to transactions affecting net income. Examples of cash inflows are cash sales, customer collections on account, interest income, dividend income, insurance recovery, and an award from a court arising from winning a lawsuit. Examples of cash outflows for operating activities include the purchase of inventory, paying suppliers of merchandise, paying suppliers of operating expense items (e.g., office supplies), employee wages, charitable contributions, interest expense, taxes, governmental penalties and fees, payment to a plaintiff in a lawsuit, and cash refunds to customers for deficient goods.

Investing activities relate to the purchase and subsequent sale of equity and debt securities of other entities, acquisition and sale of property, plant and equipment, and making and collecting on loans. There is a section in the statement of cash flows that shows cash flows from investing activities. Included in this section are the cash inflows and cash outflows of investing. Examples of cash inflows are amounts received upon sale of bonds or stocks in other companies as well as the proceeds from disposal of equipment. Examples of cash outflows to be presented are payments for investments in stock or bonds in other companies as well as the acquisition of machinery.

Another section in the statement presents cash flows from financing activities. This section appears last in the statement. Financing activities relate to obtaining equity capital, dividend payments to stockholders, debt issuance, repayment of bonds, and paying for other resources derived from creditors on a noncurrent basis. Examples of cash inflows are amounts obtained from floating a new stock or zero-coupon bond. Examples of cash outflows are payments for the early extinguishment of debt, purchase of treasury stock, and other principal payments to long-term creditors.

In the case that a cash receipt or cash payment is for more than one classification (investing, financing, operating), classification is based on the activity that is the prime reason for that cash flow. For instance, the purchase and sale of equipment to be used by the company is often deemed as an investing purpose.

A.3 FOREIGN TRANSACTIONS

With foreign currency cash flows, use the exchange rate at the time of the cash flow in reporting the currency equivalent of foreign currency cash flows. The impact of changes in the exchange rate on cash balances held in foreign currencies is shown as a separate element of the reconciliation of the change in cash and cash equivalents for the period.

A.4 DIRECT AND INDIRECT METHODS

While the direct and indirect methods are permitted, the former is preferred. Under the direct method, the company should report cash flows from operating activities by major classes of gross cash receipts and gross cash payments and the resulting net amount. Separate presentation should be given of the following types of operating cash receipts and cash payments: (1) cash received from customers, licensees, and lessees; (2) receipts from dividends and interest; (3) other operating cash receipts; (4) tax payments; (5) cash paid to employees and suppliers for goods or services; (6) payment of interest; (7) cash paid to advertising agencies and insurance companies; and (8) other operating cash payments.

Additional breakdowns of operating cash receipts and disbursements may be made to enhance financial reporting. For example, a manufacturer may segregate cash paid to suppliers into payments for inventory and payments for administrative expenses.

If the indirect method is followed, the company will report net cash flow from operating activities indirectly by adjusting profit to reconcile it to net cash from operating activities. The adjustment to reported earnings involves:

1. Effects of deferrals of past operating cash receipts and cash payments (e.g., changes in inventory and deferred revenue), and accumulations of anticipated future operating cash receipts and cash payments (e.g., changes in receivables and payables).

2. Effects of items whose cash impact relates to investing or financing cash flows (e.g., depreciation expense, amortization expense, gain or loss on the retirement of debt, and gain or loss on the sale of fixed assets). Under the indirect method, there should be disclosure of interest and income taxes paid.

Regardless of whether the direct or the indirect method is employed, a reconciliation is needed of net income to net cash flow from operating activities. The reconciliation should identify the principal types of reconciling items. For example, major classes of deferrals and accruals affecting cash flows should be reported including changes in accounts receivable, inventory, and accounts payable that apply to operating activities.

When the direct method of reporting cash flows from operating activities is used, the reconciliation of profit to cash flow from operations should be disclosed in a separate schedule. When the indirect method is followed, the reconciliation may appear within the body of the statement of cash flows or may be shown in an accompanying schedule.

A.5 OTHER CONSIDERATIONS

There should be separate presentation within the statement of cash flows of cash inflows and cash outflows from investing and financing activities. For example, the purchase of fixed assets is an application of cash, while the sale of fixed assets is a source of cash. Both are shown separately to aid analysis by readers of the financial statements. Debt incurrence would be a source of cash, while debt payment would be an application of cash. Thus, cash received of $800,000 from debt incurrence would be shown as a source, while the payment of debt of $250,000 would be presented as an application. The net effect is, of course, $550,000.

Separate disclosure should be made of investing and financing activities affecting assets or liabilities that do *not* affect cash flow. This disclosure may be narrative in form or shown in a schedule. Further, a transaction having cash and noncash elements should be discussed, but only the cash aspect should be shown in the statement of cash flows. Examples of noncash activities of an investing and financing nature are bond conversion, purchase of a fixed asset by the incurrence of a mortgage payable, capital lease, and nonmonetary exchange of assets.

Cash flow per share should *not* be shown in the financial statements, since it will detract from the importance of the earnings-per-share statistic.

A.6   FINANCIAL ANALYSIS

Analysis of the statement of cash flows will provide financial managers with vital information regarding a company's cash receipts and cash payments for a period as they relate to operating, investing, and financing activities. The statement assists in the evaluation of the impact on the firm's financial position of cash and noncash investing and financing transactions.

Comparative statements of cash flows must be thoroughly appraised, because they hold clues to a company's earnings quality, risk, and liquidity. They show the degree of repeatability of the company's sources of funds, their costs, and whether such sources may be relied on in the future. Uses of funds for growth as well as for maintaining competitive share are revealed. Analysis of comparative statements of cash flows holds the key to a complete and reliable analysis of corporate financial health in the present and future. It aids in planning future ventures and financing needs. Comparative data help financial analysts identify abnormal or cyclical factors as well as changes in the relationship among each flow component.

The statement serves as a basis to forecast earnings based on plant, property, and equipment posture. It assists in evaluating growth potential and incorporates cash flow requirements, highlighting specific fund sources and future means of payment.

The financial analyst should calculate cash flow per share equal to net cash flow divided by the number of shares. A high ratio is desirable because it indicates the company is in a very liquid position.

We now discuss the analysis of the operating, investing, and financing sections of the statement of cash flows.

Operating Section

Analysis of the operating section of the statement of cash flows enables the financial manager to determine the adequacy of cash flow from operating activities to satisfy company requirements. Can the firm obtain positive future net cash flows? The reconciliation tracing net income to net cash flow from operating activities should be examined to see the effect of noncash revenue and noncash expense items.

An award under a lawsuit is a cash inflow from operating activities that results in a nonrecurring source of revenue.

An operating cash outlay for refunds given to customers for deficient goods indicates a quality problem with the firm's merchandise.

Payments of penalties, fines, and lawsuit damages are operating cash outflows that show poor management in that a problem arose requiring a nonbeneficial expenditure to the organization.

Investing Section

Analysis of the investing section of the statement of cash flows allows identification of an investment in another company that may presage an eventual attempt to control for diversification purposes. It may also indicate a change in future direction or a change in business philosophy.

An increase in fixed assets indicates capital expansion and future growth. An analysis should be made as to which assets have been purchased. Are they assets for risky (specialized) ventures, or are they stable (multipurpose) ones? An indication exists as to risk potential and expected returns. The nature of the assets provides signs as to future direction and earning potential with regard to the introduction or reinforcement of product lines, business segments, etc. Are these directions sound and viable?

The financial executive should ascertain if there is a contraction in the business arising from the sale of fixed assets without adequate replacement. Is the problem corporate (e.g., the product line is weakening) or industry wide (e.g., the industry is on the downturn)? If corporate, management is not optimistic regarding the future. Nonrecurring gains may occur because of the sale of low-cost-basis fixed assets (e.g., land). Such gains cause temporary increases in profits above normal levels and represent low quality of earnings sources. They should be discounted by the analyst.

Financing Section

An evaluation of the financing section will provide the financial manager with an opinion regarding the company's capability to obtain financing in the money and capital markets as well as its ability to meet its obligations. The financial mixture comprising bonds, long-term loans from banks, and equity instruments affects the cost of financing. One major advantage of debt is the tax deductibility of interest while dividends are not deductible. Further, during inflation, paying debt back will result in purchasing power gains, since the payback is made in cheaper dollars. However, there is a greater risk associated with debt financing in that the company must have adequate funds to pay interest and retire the obligation at maturity. If funds are insufficient, higher-interest sources may have to be used (e.g., factors). The stability of the fund source must be appraised to determine if it may be relied on continuously, even during tight money markets. Otherwise, potential difficulties of maintaining corporate operations during recessionary periods exist. The question is: Where can the company go for funds during times of cash squeeze?

By evaluating the financing sources, the financing preferences of management are revealed. Is there an inclination toward risk or safety? Creditors would prefer to see equity issuances as protection of their loans. Excessive debt may be a problem during economic downturn.

The ability of a company to finance with the issuance of common stock on attractive terms (high stock price) indicates that the investing public is optimistic about the financial well-being of the entity.

The issuance of preferred stock may be a negative sign, since it may mean that the company has difficulty issuing common stock.

An appraisal should be made of the company's ability to satisfy debt. If debt is excessive, it points to greater corporate risk. The problem is acute if earnings are unstable or declining. On the other hand, the reduction in long-term debt is favorable because it points to less risk associated with the firm.

A financing cash outflow for the early extinguishment of debt will result in an extraordinary gain or loss, resulting in a one-time effect on earnings.

A bond conversion is a positive sign about the entity's financial health, since it indicates that bondholders are optimistic about the company's financial health or that the market price of the common stock has risen. A conversion of preferred stock to common stock is also favorable, because it shows that preferred stockholders are positive on the company's future and are willing to accept a lower priority in the event of corporate liquidation.

Note that bond and preferred stock conversions affect the existing position of long-term creditors and stockholders. For example, a reduction in debt by conversion to stock protects to a greater degree the loans of the remaining bond holders and banks.

The financial analyst should evaluate the firm's dividend-paying ability. Stockholders favor a company that has a high dividend payout.

Index